THE THIN BLUE LINE

A humanitarian aid worker, Conor Foley has worked for a variety of human rights and humanitarian aid organizations, including Liberty, Amnesty International and the UNHCR, in Kosovo, Afghanistan, Colombia, Sri Lanka, Indonesia and Bosnia-Herzegovina. His books include *Combating Torture: A Manual for Judges and Prosecutors* (2003).

THE THIN BLUE LINE

How Humanitarianism Went to War

Conor Foley

VERSO
London • New York

First published by Verso 2008
© Conor Foley 2008
This edition published by Verso 2010
All rights reserved

1 3 5 7 9 10 8 6 4 2

Verso
UK: 6 Meard Street, London W1F 0EG
US: 20 Jay Street, Brooklyn, NY 11201
www.versobooks.com

Verso is the imprint of New Left Books

ISBN-13: 978-1-84467-628-6

British Library Cataloguing in Publication Data
A catalogue record for this book is available from the British Library

Library of Congress Cataloging-in-Publication Data
A catalog record for this book is available from the Library of Congress

Typeset in Bembo by Hewer Text UK Ltd, Edinburgh
Printed in Sweden by Scandbook AB

Contents

Glaucia
Minha Flor do Cerrado

Introduction

I WATCHED THE television screen with horrified amaze-
ment, seeing familiar faces stumble out of the rubble of the
United Nations headquarters in Baghdad. A friend from Kosovo
guided one group of colleagues through the smoke to safety.
Another woman returned to the wreckage as if looking for
someone. American soldiers tried to lead her away, but she shook
them off and ran back again. Cameras focused in on her
intrusively and I ended up shouting at the television, venting
my rage and anguish on those who were bringing me the images.
I later discovered the woman was Carolina Larriera desperately
trying to save the life of her fiancé, Sergio Vieira de Mello, the
Brazilian UN official who lay dying under the wreckage nearby.[1]

It was 19 August 2003 and I was in the Afghanistan capital of
Kabul, having turned down a job with the UN mission to Iraq a
few months earlier. I knew that had I accepted the post I would
have been in that building, working for the UN Office of the High
Commissioner for Human Rights (OHCHR). I also knew that, as
the number of casualties kept rising, I would no doubt have friends
and colleagues among the dead and injured. The final death toll
was twenty-one, four of whom – Fiona Watson, Jean Selim
Kanaan, Christopher Klein-Beekman and Nadia Younes – had
worked in Kosovo at the same time as me. Vieira de Mello, who
combined his job in Iraq with heading OHCHR, had previously
led the UN missions in Kosovo and East Timor. As the UN

Secretary-General Kofi Annan was to say: 'We grieve for the friends and colleagues we lost, for the loved ones they left behind, for the talent and potential the world lost on that terrible day.'[2]

Although humanitarian aid workers were soon to experience similar attacks in Afghanistan, in summer 2003 it was still considered a safer place than Iraq and some organizations began to redeploy their staff from Iraq to Afghanistan. A new house-mate arrived straight from Baghdad, and I heard the anguish in his long distance satellite phone calls to his wife, still working there, as he begged her to get out. Other friends in Iraq were injured in roadside bombs and rocket attacks. One was hit by flying glass when a bomb killed twenty people only yards from where she had been standing. Gruesome videos began to circulate of kidnapped aid workers being executed by insurgents or pleading for their lives.

The initial invasion of Iraq had been controversial, and western public opinion swung firmly against it as the country descended into chaos. Iraq has become as emblematic a political issue for my generation as Vietnam was for a previous one. It has already had a huge impact on domestic politics and civil society in Britain and the United States, one that will probably last for decades to come. As western public opinion continues to pick over the rubble, two broad schools of thought contend with its legacy.

For 'anti-imperialists' the invasion was the culmination of a period of misguided western intervention that has seen the weakening of both national sovereignty and international law. Iraq exposed the folly of the belief that human rights and democracy can ever be imposed on other countries by force of arms. Such rhetoric, they argue, masks a more traditional concern with securing western strategic, economic and political interests. The doctrine of 'humanitarian intervention', they maintain, is just a new name for old-fashioned imperialism.

For 'liberal interventionists', by contrast, Iraq was primarily a contest between good and evil. Saddam Hussein was a vile dictator with an appalling human rights record that included using chemical weapons against his own people. While the post-invasion administration of Iraq may have been mishandled, even a flawed democracy must be supported against the motley group of Islamists and former Ba'athists who comprise the Iraqi 're-sistance'. In the eyes of this group, those who opposed the invasion and occupation, whatever their actual intentions, were objectively supporting fascism.

A significant segment of the liberal-left, particularly in Europe and North America, accepted the arguments put forward by the liberal interventionists, most notably the then British Prime Minister Tony Blair. Drawing on themes he had first articulated during the Kosovo conflict of the late 1990s, he repeatedly argued that the awfulness of Saddam Hussein's regime justified the actions taken to overthrow it. As he stated in one speech, 'we surely have a responsibility to act when a nation's people are subjected to a regime such as Saddam's.'[3]

The notion of a 'responsibility to act' lies at the heart of the humanitarian impulse. It motivates those who care about human rights in far-off places – and it was what had taken me from Kosovo to Kabul. Whether it is writing a letter for Amnesty International or dropping a coin into an Oxfam collecting tin, the idea that we should 'do something' to help alleviate human suffering underpins our basic concept of global solidarity.

Despite what they have in common, human rights and humanitarian non-governmental organizations (NGOs) ap-proach the issue of international interventions from quite different standpoints. Human rights organizations seek to pro-mote universal observance of and respect for human rights, defined as the set of entitlements each individual should possess by virtue of their humanity. The enjoyment of these rights is an indispensable aspect of being human, and thus considered indivisible, inalienable and universal. Through their political advocacy, human rights activists are interventionists in support of these objectives.

Humanitarian organizations also base themselves on universal standards, primarily those contained within the Geneva Conventions, sometimes referred to as the 'rules of war'. They are interventionist in that their activists are directly involved in providing relief assistance during conflicts and natural disasters. However, they have traditionally relied on neutrality to gain access to these places. They do not have an overarching vision for how societies should be ordered, and consciously restrict themselves to helping certain categories of people on a temporary basis.

These two movements have drawn increasingly close together, giving rise to what could be called 'political humanitarianism'. Until recently, this phrase would have been considered a contradiction in terms since one of humanitarianism's defining features was its reluctance to comment on political issues. During the 1990s, however, a number of humanitarian organizations, particularly in Britain and North America, began to advocate for international military interventions during grave humanitarian crises. Drawing on the language of universal human rights, they stated that the international community has a 'right', or even a 'duty', to intervene in certain circumstances, to protect people and uphold basic moral standards. This book discusses how that argument has developed in more detail and the consequences it has had both for the human rights movement and for traditional humanitarianism.

There is no explicit recognition of the doctrine of humanitarian intervention in international law, and even the UN is prohibited from interfering in matters 'which are essentially within the domestic jurisdiction' of its members.[4] The UN Charter prohibits the use of force, save for in the two narrowly defined circumstances of self-defence and where the UN Security Council has authorized such action in response to a threat to peace. However, some legal scholars describe humanitarian intervention as 'an emerging norm' within international law and argue that states should be held accountable for the way they treat their own populations, by military force if necessary.[5] The 'responsibility to protect' doctrine has been unanimously endorsed by the UN's highest decision-making bodies and much discussion now focusses on whether they are really competent to fulfil the tasks it sets. The failure of the UN in Rwanda and Bosnia-Herzegovina, discussed later in this book, led many to conclude that the UN-based system of collective security has become an excuse for indifference to, and inertia in the face of, global suffering and crimes against humanity.

NATO's intervention in Kosovo in 1999 was the high watermark of political humanitarianism, and came at the end of a decade in which the principle of state sovereignty had been increasingly challenged by advocates of international human rights law. This included both humanitarian and human rights NGOs, and led to a convergence between the two groups. Organizations such as Amnesty International and Human Rights Watch moved beyond documenting violations against individual 'prisoners of conscience' to campaigning against mass human rights violations during conflicts. Aid workers also felt increasingly compelled to speak out about the atrocities they witnessed, moving away from their traditional neutral 'Red Cross' stance and drawing on international human rights norms to guide their work. A group of prominent international NGOs has published a Humanitarian Charter which asserts that people have a 'right to assistance and protection' during conflicts and natural disasters.

The UN Security Council did not authorize NATO's use of force in Kosovo, a precedent subsequently cited during the debates that led to the invasion of Iraq. Blair's biographer, John Rentoul, has written that he was 'led on to Iraq by the unexpected and – he was told – impossible success of his campaign of high moral statesmanship to defend the Muslims of Kosovo'.[6] Clare Short, a former British government minister, notes that it was in Kosovo where Blair first acquired the image of a 'humanitarian war leader', but her memoir also gives a revealing insight into a much wider public sentiment about such interventions.[7]

Short describes how, in the spring of 1999 at the start of the crisis, she was on a train on her way to spend the Easter holidays with her family when she received a call from Blair asking her to go to Macedonia to see what could be done to help the Kosovan refugees who were being driven out of their homes by Serbian forces as a consequence of the ongoing civil war in the province. The Macedonian Government had closed its borders, leaving the refugees stuck in no-man's land, and she had to 'cajole and threaten' the authorities to let them in. While in Macedonia she visited NATO's headquarters, meeting with its commander, General Sir Mike Jackson. She recalls that 'there was speculation over the likelihood of a [NATO] bombing campaign [against the Serbs]' and that the NATO soldiers had expressed concern about the ineffectual response of the international community given its failure to stand up to previous ethnic cleansing in Bosnia-Herzegovina. On her return to Britain, Short says that she 'stressed to Blair that such widespread expectations that NATO would compromise over Kosovo would only strengthen Milosevic's intransigence'.

The problem with this anecdote is that its central point cannot be true. In 1999, Easter fell on 4 April – but NATO's military action in Kosovo started on 24 March. By her own account Short could not have arrived in Macedonia until at least a week after the bombing campaign began, and so cannot have had a conversation with NATO's overall commander based on speculation about whether or not it was going to happen. NATO in fact suffered its first military loss on 28 March when the Yugoslav army shot down a US F-117 stealth bomber; four days later three US soldiers were captured by Serb forces near the border with Macedonia. The impression she gives of a military leader asking for stronger political support is, therefore, highly implausible. Jackson's memory of the encounter, which he also places on Easter Sunday, eleven days after the start of the bombing, is of being hectored by Short as 'weak-willed' for not wanting to march straight into Kosovo to liberate its people.[8]

Short switches the order of events around so it appears that her visit took place before the talks at Rambouillet in February 1999, aimed at resolving the crisis through diplomatic means. She then goes on to describe a 'terrible outbreak of ethnic violence and destruction of Serb churches [in Kosovo] during 2004', but fails to mention that the much more serious violence occurred immediately after NATO troops entered the province in the summer of 1999, when up to quarter of a million of Kosovo's Serb and Roma ethnic minorities fled their homes fearing revenge attacks by Albanian extremists.

I have a personal reason to remember this set of events. My girlfriend at the time had worked as Short's special adviser, and I travelled to Macedonia myself a few weeks after her visit. I was then working at Amnesty International and was asked by the Council of Europe to help run training courses in the refugee camps of Albania and Macedonia. I went to Kosovo for the first time in August 1999, returning the following year to work for the UN High Commissioner for Refugees (UNHCR). Most of our work focussed on helping the displaced Serb and Roma ethnic minorities. It might seem morbid to dwell on the details of how many were killed and when, but Short's anecdote is important for a number of reasons. Part of the legal debate regarding intervention rests on the question of 'proportionality' and whether there constitutes a threshold of atrocities which could affect the legitimacy of an external intervention to protect people's basic rights. By reversing the order of events Short's book provided a *post facto* rationale for NATO's decision to attack. At a more basic level, those advocating interventions need to be reasonably confident that they are not going to make a bad situation worse.

Kosovo set a precedent for Iraq, in this context, because the short-term consequence of the military intervention was to turn a simmering crisis into a full-scale humanitarian disaster. The

invading forces then created an international administration to
govern the territory that was to prove hopelessly inept and under
which hundreds of thousands of people were driven from their
homes. Kosovo also set a precedent of western politicians lying to
the public in order to justify the war and then lying about its
causes and consequences. Most people who know Short would
describe her as a conviction politician who is often too honest for
her own good, but she has constructed an account about this
particular intervention which is transparently untrue.

Several years after Kosovo a new humanitarian crisis grabbed the
world's attention. In 2003 an uprising began in the Darfur region
of Sudan and the Sudanese government launched a counter-
insurgency campaign. This involved arming a militia (the
janjaweed), burning villages and terrorizing people suspected of
supporting the rebels. In response to these atrocities a Save Darfur
Coalition began to mobilize, particularly in the US, urging
international intervention and creating a network stretching from
schools, colleges and churches to high-profile movie celebrities.

This campaign, backed by the main human rights and humanitarian NGOs, aimed to shame western governments into
action. Its supporters also carried out interview-based research on
the Darfur–Chad border, which led US Secretary of State Colin
Powell to declare in September 2004 that an act of genocide was
taking place. That same month, the UN responded by setting up
its own Commission of Inquiry, which reported its findings in
January 2005,[9] stating that almost two million people had been
terrorized out of their homes and that a large-scale destruction
of villages in the region had taken place. It also noted that
'the Commission found that Government forces and militias
conducted indiscriminate attacks, including killing of civilians,
torture, enforced disappearances, destruction of villages, rape and
other forms of sexual violence, pillaging and forced displacement, throughout Darfur.'

The Commission did not attempt to estimate the number of
violent deaths, but noted rebel claims that more than 70,000

people had been killed, as well as the government's insistence that the number of dead was fewer than 10,000. For lack of evidence, the commission rejected claims that the killings amounted to a policy of genocide, instead recommending that the UN Security Council refer Sudan to the newly created International Criminal Court (ICC) for investigation. In April 2005, the Save Darfur Coalition responded that it believed the death toll from the crisis was 400,000, a claim based on its previous research and an analysis of other data. It reiterated its view that the killings amounted to a deliberate policy of genocide and concluded that: 'Despite the death toll so far, not enough is being done to save the thousands who will inevitably die unless the world community supports the type of intervention needed to stop the killing.'[10]

In 2006, the coalition ran adverts in the US and Britain claiming that '400,000 innocent men, women and children have been killed' in Darfur, and urging western intervention. Both Bush and Blair made a series of bellicose statements hinting that they might take unilateral military action if the UN Security Council failed to impose tough measures on Sudan. According to Samantha Power, a Harvard professor and author of a best-selling book on genocide, 'the fact that Darfur merits an 8a.m. statement by the president [of the United States] is testament to one thing and one thing alone, and that is this movement.'[11]

However, by the summer of 2007, a number of humanitarian agencies had publicly distanced themselves from the Coalition, which they accused of 'confusing the public and damaging the relief effort'.[12] The Coalition's US executive director, David Rubenstein, was forced to resign and the British Advertising Standards Authority (ASA) ruled that its adverts were misleading.[13] 'We do try to be more sensitive when it comes to charities but there are limits', said an ASA spokesperson. 'We would encourage them to make sure that any figures or facts they use in adverts are accurate.'[14]

The Darfur crisis began while I was working in Afghanistan and several of my friends and colleagues were deployed to Sudan as their next posting. We kept in touch by email and swapped stories from our respective locations. I spent a few months in northern Uganda in 2006–7 and many of the aid workers there had recently been redeployed from across the border in Sudan. All had fairly similar tales to tell about the problems of working in the region, but their analysis of events was starkly different to the message put out by the Save Darfur Coalition.

There was unanimous agreement that Darfur was a humanitarian crisis, though most dismissed the Coalition's estimate of the death toll, which was twice as high as the figure used by the aid agencies. The majority of these deaths was not a result of physical violence but of malnutrition or disease, while attacks on aid workers were being carried out by all sides, not only by the government and its militias. Rebel groups were terrorizing people in the areas under their control, and the Coalition's failure to draw attention to this damaged its credibility. The Sudanese Government was harassing aid workers and some of my friends were arrested or deported, but this was partly a consequence of its increasing paranoia due to the threats of western military intervention.

More fundamentally, some people asked, what was the point in calling for such intervention while western forces were becoming increasingly bogged down in Afghanistan and Iraq? The idea that foreign troops could fight their way into Darfur and disarm the various militias by force was a fantasy, but as long as the rebel groups thought there was a chance of western military intervention – as happened in Kosovo – they had every incentive to keep fighting. The threats also played into the hands of hardliners in the Sudanese Government who were able to dismiss all criticism as propaganda and portray themselves as the latest country in a line of targets for western aggression.

This viewpoint was diametrically opposed to the one put forward by the Save Darfur Coalition, with which the humanitarian organizations were publicly identified. The Coalition continued to issue statements saying that 'the time for negotiating with the Sudanese government has ended', and calling for military action to enforce a no-fly zone. Eventually, in May 2007, one aid agency issued a public response:

> Action Against Hunger is among the few non-governmental humanitarian organizations still operating in Darfur, Sudan, and its teams witness the atrocities committed against local populations on a daily basis. The organization's teams have concluded that because the conflict is spreading and the number of instigators of violence is increasing, an armed and non-negotiated intervention would be dangerous. An intervention would most likely make an already bad situation even worse by triggering yet more violence. Somalia and Iraq have demonstrated this.[15]

The Coalition responded that its critics were 'missing the point' and that its statistics of dead and wounded could only be estimates 'because the Government of Sudan actively denies the international community – including diplomats, humanitarian workers and epidemiology experts – real access to the Darfur region'.[16] However, it was clear that a rift had opened up between the organizations working in the region and those lobbying for it from outside. One British journalist, Nick Cohen, reported that the humanitarian agencies on the ground were 'contributing to the crisis' by their refusal to speak out against the violations. He argued that it has been rare to find condemnations of the Sudanese Government on agency websites, because 'the worse a regime was the less the NGOs say about it.'[17]

This claim was complete nonsense since the NGO he singled out for criticism, CAFOD, included a very full account of the Darfur crisis on its website. However, it is true that humanitarian NGOs sometimes have to consider the potential trade-offs between access and advocacy and, in a situation where the vast majority of deaths were due to malnutrition and disease, access meant the difference between life and death on a massive scale.

As a series of UN reports noted, the influx of humanitarian aid organizations into Darfur from 2004 onwards did much to improve conditions for suffering civilians and had 'averted a humanitarian catastrophe, with no major outbreaks of disease or famine'.[18] Campaigners for western military intervention completely ignored this sharp fall in the death toll and continued to write as though the violence was continuing at its worst intensity. This abstracted the crisis from any time or context, which meant that their proposed solution became not just unrealistic but counter-productive.

Negotiations between the warring parties in Darfur, carried out under international auspices, broke down in May 2006, when only one rebel group signed up to the terms on offer. Another attempt failed in November 2007 when most of the rebel groups did not even turn up for the talks. The month before, rebels attacked peacekeeping soldiers from the African Union's small mission in the country, killing ten of them. One British government minister, the former deputy head of the UN, Mark Malloch Brown, subsequently admitted what had been fairly obvious for several years to most people on the ground: 'No one is up for deploying a military force in the heart of Africa. People do not want to do it and it has never been a realistic option, so there has always been an element of empty threat there.'[19]

The failure by western governments and aid agencies to spell this out much earlier undoubtedly contributed to the suffering in the region. Prime Minister Blair even threatened to bomb the Sudanese air force while his own Ministry of Defence and Foreign Office were insisting that: 'There are absolutely no plans for any UK military action at all in Sudan or the Darfur region of Sudan.'[20] A joint UN–African Union (AU) peacekeeping force was eventually deployed in the region in January 2008, but its effectiveness was greatly hindered both by the reluctance of the Sudanese Government to accept its deployment and by a failure of western countries to provide it with sufficient logistical equipment, such as air support. In December 2007, a coalition of humanitarian aid organizations warned that the mission was being 'set up to fail' by the international community. Fighting resumed in 2008 and has periodically spread to neighbouring countries. In May 2008, a rebel column attacked Sudan's capital, Khartoum.

Western public opinion has a short attention span and humanitarian organizations involved in advocacy will always face problems trying to maintain public interest in particular crises. The probable solution to the Darfur crisis will be either a decisive military victory by one side over the other or a negotiated settlement involving mutual compromise. Exaggerating the scale of the atrocities committed or portraying the conflict as a Manichean struggle between good and evil will clearly do more harm than good, but downgrading it to just another horrible, messy African civil war lessens the moral pressure on the general public to care about such situations, or to make donations to aid agencies trying to relieve the suffering. For humanitarian organizations that rely on fundraising appeals to carry out their work, this dilemma has some obvious practical consequences.

In April 2003, shortly before I went to Afghanistan, I attended a meeting in London involving most of the major international humanitarian NGOs with British offices. The war in Iraq was ending and attention turning towards the post-war reconstruction effort. A high-ranking official from the UK Department for International Development (DFID) gave an off-the-record briefing about what this would entail. He announced that the British government had earmarked £210 million for the reconstruction of the country and that it would be encouraging bids from humanitarian agencies. A shocked silence ensued as it dawned on everyone that this amount was double DFID's entire humanitarian relief budget of two years previously. The silence was followed by embarrassed shuffling as people started to speak. The world's second-largest potential producer of oil is not a natural candidate for humanitarian assistance and everyone knew there were far greater areas of need elsewhere. We also knew that this assistance was being given for political reasons: to shore up support for a controversial invasion. Nevertheless, virtually no agency wished to rule itself out of receiving project funding, as they began to make clear in their presentations.

Most aid to poor countries comes from western government donors who either provide it directly through bilateral assistance or through international institutions such as the World Bank and UN agencies. An increasing amount is now also delivered by NGOs, who raise some of their money from public appeals and receive the rest in grants from governments and multilateral donors. Most NGOs receive well over half their money in such grants. There is a simple correlation between the profile of a particular humanitarian crisis and the amount of money available to fund organizations that credibly claim to be working on it. Agencies consequently seek to position themselves so they can take advantage of these funds when they become available. This makes sense as a business strategy and is not incompatible with a traditional Red Cross view of humanitarian relief. Aid organizations establish a presence where a humanitarian crisis is likely to happen, publicize it – if and when it occurs – and then highlight the work they are doing and the need to continue it. The calculation is that subsequent donations will pay for this ongoing work and the initial investment and overhead costs.

Humanitarianism has grown into a multibillion dollar industry. Its agencies, both UN and NGO, are at the forefront of delivering assistance in what have become known as 'complex emergencies' and are often the first on the scene, with distinctive logos emblazoned on T-shirts and vehicles. The headquarters costs of the major humanitarian agencies are considerable and require a constant fund-raising effort. Fund-raising appeals need to be dramatic and often perform better in financial terms if they are accompanied by a call for action aimed at the national or international authorities. Most British and American aid agencies now have sizeable media and advocacy departments whose work

is based on, and essentially funded by, their operational programmes. Press offices and lobbyists are employed to highlight
particular crises and make the public care about them. Their job
is to stir people's consciences to 'do something to help'. This has
institutionalized political humanitarianism in the work of most
relief agencies.

Both human rights and humanitarian NGOs recognize that
they operate in a political environment and that their reports can
be used for purposes they may not agree with. In December
2002, when the British Government released a dossier of human
rights violations in Iraq largely culled from Amnesty International reports, the organization accused it of being 'opportunistic
and selective' in its use of the material.[21] Saddam Hussein was a
brutal dictator, but there was no evidence that repression was
increasing in Iraq at the time or that the country was experien-
cing the kind of ongoing humanitarian crisis that might provide
legal justification for an invasion. The invasion itself was publicly
opposed by most human rights and humanitarian NGOs who
argued that it would bring increased suffering to the people of
the region. Many also described it as a violation of international
law, and this brought the discussion of dry legal theory to a much
wider audience.

One advantage of international human rights and humanitarian law is that it provides an objective framework within which
humanitarians can locate their activities. Much of the discussion
about both political advocacy and 'rights-based' programming
has involved drawing up codes of conduct and statements of
principle based on international legal instruments. Starting with
the Geneva Conventions of 1949 and the Universal Declaration
of Human Rights of 1948, many argue that the growing body of
international human rights law also provides an important
normative structure for their work. However, there is still
considerable disagreement about what international law actually
means on certain subjects. Once they move away from the
principles of neutrality and impartiality, it is also difficult to see

how humanitarian agencies can ever be regarded as anything but political organizations.

One of Nick Cohen's accusations, that the UN's initial failure to label the killings in Darfur as genocide made it 'close to being an accessory to mass murder',[22] echoed a denunciation of the International Committee of the Red Cross (ICRC) in Biafra made by Bernard Kouchner almost forty years earlier. Kouchner, who was appointed France's foreign minister in 2007, is perhaps the most articulate champion of the political humanitarian creed. In 1967, he was one of a number of French doctors who split from the ICRC during the Biafran war over the Committee's reluctance to publicly denounce the Nigerian Government. Kouchner argued that this made the Red Cross 'accomplices in the systematic massacre of a population' and that aid workers had a duty to 'bear witness' to the violations they encountered. He helped found the humanitarian aid charity *Médecins Sans Frontières* (MSF) in 1971, which combined relief activities with high-profile political advocacy.

The Biafran war, which began in 1967, lasted two and a half years and cost over a million lives. As Alex de Waal noted in *Famine Crimes*, 'an entire generation of NGO relief workers was moulded by Biafra and several agencies were either born from the relief operation or forever changed by it.'[23] From early on it became apparent that the Igbo nationalists who had tried to secede from Nigeria were hopelessly outgunned and had no chance of military success. Within a year they had lost all their major towns and strategic facilities to the much larger Nigerian army. All that was left was a small heartland 'crowded with refugees, short on food, running out of ammunition, its funds all but finished'.[24] At this stage, the decision of its leaders to reject all attempts at international mediation and fight on showed a combination of raw courage and obstinacy that greatly exacerbated the suffering of their own people.

What enabled this act of wilful defiance was an extraordinary outpouring of international sympathy as Biafra became the *cause célèbre* of western Europe. A massive private relief operation began, the logistics of which were comparable to the Berlin airlift. Aid workers took enormous personal risks to bring in food and medical supplies, making up to forty flights a night to Biafra's one make-shift runway. However, the Biafra intervention is also now widely recognized, in humanitarian circles at least, as a huge political error. The Igbo leadership used it to raise money to keep the war going by effectively taxing the NGOs who were delivering supplies. They turned down the offer of a supervised 'land corridor', realizing how dramatic the night flights had become. The flights were also used as cover for bringing in weapons along the same route, in clear violation of international humanitarian law.

Britain attracted international condemnation for continuing to supply Nigeria with weapons during the conflict. France and Portugal, which still held African colonial interests, supplied the Biafrans with weapons for quite cynical reasons of their own. Church agencies also mobilized their supporters in solidarity with the 'Christian Igbo', who were said to be facing genocide from the Muslims of northern Nigeria. Oxfam ran advertisements warning that 'the price for a united Nigeria is likely to be millions of lives.' Such fears had a rational basis since the Igbo had been the victims of sectarian riots the year before their secession. But when Biafra finally surrendered in January 1970, the central government was noticeably conciliatory to its defeated foes. Civil servants and soldiers were reabsorbed into the Nigerian federal state and many of those who lost property had it restored. Nigeria's president quoted Abraham Lincoln's words about 'binding up the nation's wounds' after the American civil war. The predictions of the political humanitarians, in other words, turned out to be spectacularly wrong.

Of course it is easy to be wise in hindsight, though from as early as September 1968 it was clear that Nigerian forces were not carrying out genocide in the areas they had overrun. The conflict was also marked by a willingness of aid agencies and the international media to collude in a skilful campaign by the Biafran political leaders who hired a PR company to promote their cause. The image of starving children would become an iconic symbol of the intervention. As Frederick Forsyth, then working as a journalist, explained: 'Quite suddenly we'd touched a nerve. Nobody in this country at that time had seen children looking like that. The last time the Brits had seen anything like that must have been the Belsen pictures . . . The war itself would have never set the Thames on fire, but the pictures of starving children put Biafra on the front page of every British newspaper.'[25]

In fact, as Oxfam was to admit subsequently, the stories of suffering were exaggerated. Tony Vaux, a senior Oxfam official, notes that the Biafra war 'was the first humanitarian disaster to be seen [on television] by millions of people and also the first to be the subject of systematic distortion'.[26] In its official history Oxfam admits to having fallen 'hook, line and sinker' for the propaganda.[27] Yet, as David Rieff writes in *A Bed for the Night*, there was a profitable paradox in this gullibility. Oxfam first rose to national prominence as a result of Biafra. It also gave a huge boost to other humanitarian aid organizations and led to the formation of the Irish group, Concern, and the split in the ICRC which gave birth to MSF.

Most aid organizations now admit that the main effect of their efforts was to prolong the conflict by a further eighteen months and that they needed to 'learn the lessons' from their mistakes. If the business of humanitarian aid is to reduce human suffering, then actions that increase it should presumably be subject to some sort of sanction. Yet it is doubtful if any aid worker suffered disciplinary action for violating humanitarian principles over Biafra. On the contrary, it proved of enormous benefit to the careers of a number of individuals and the creed of political humanitarianism. In other words, Biafra became a prototype for future interventions.

Ironically, the only organization whose reputation suffered from the debacle was the ICRC, which had provided one of the most effective relief efforts for most of the conflict. It spent $1.4 million a month on its Biafra operation, almost triple its previous worldwide annual budget, but it did so without publicity and sought agreement, wherever possible, from both parties to the conflict. The willingness of other relief organizations to abandon the principle of neutrality made this increasingly difficult, and in June 1969 a Swedish Red Cross plane was shot down by Nigerian forces. Nigeria then imposed a ban on further aid flights, which the ICRC complied with but other agencies did not. It privately protested to the Nigerian Government but did not speak out publicly, and it was this decision that prompted Kouchner to denounce his former employers. By this stage, however, the course of the war was clear and Biafra surrendered six months later. Placed in this context, it is difficult to read Kouchner's statement as anything other than hyperbole. Perhaps it is no coincidence that he has become a standard bearer for the political humanitarian creed.

In recent years political humanitarianism has had a significant influence on international relations and the domestic politics of Europe and North America. It has quite literally pushed humanitarianism into the firing line in a number of conflicts. There are now more UN-mandated peacekeeping missions in the world than ever before. Western soldiers are engaged in large-scale confrontations with anti-government insurgents in Afghanistan and Iraq and humanitarians have frequently been targeted in both countries. A number of former heads of state have been indicted and imprisoned by international criminal tribunals and the work of these bodies is impacting on humanitarian relief efforts in some countries. The UN has formed quasi-protectorates, assuming executive powers over territories in which local politicians are reduced to observer status. There is also an increasingly contentious argument over the way humanitarian assistance is distributed during conflicts and how to hold humanitarian organizations to account for their actions.

This book discusses these events and challenges some of the underlying assumptions of political humanitarianism. The first two chapters describe the growing significance of human rights during the 1990s and how this influenced the humanitarian intervention debate. Chapters three and four are based on my own experiences of working in Kosovo and Afghanistan, while chapter five is mainly based on my experiences in post-tsunami Sri Lanka and Aceh. The remaining chapters take a broader look at three thematic issues that have caused particular dilemmas for humanitarians working in conflict zones: assistance and protection, justice and peace, and humanitarian accountability.

Humanitarianism is a new and comparatively under-studied area of work. It raises issues of profound moral and ethical importance and concerns subjects that are complex and controversial. Yet, although its influence on international relations is clearly growing, it has been subject to very little academic scrutiny and remains surrounded by many myths and misconceptions. This book is written from the perspective of a subjective partisan within the debates that have shaped my views and opinions. I got as much wrong as everyone else around me at the time, but I hope I learned a few lessons in the process.

Chapter One

Human Rights and Humanitarians

'Y Viva Espanha, Pinochet, Pinochet Dictador
Y Viva Espanha, Espanha por favor'

WE WERE standing on Parliament Green in Westminster on 24 March 1999, when the news came through. The British House of Lords had ruled that the extradition of Chile's former dictator could go ahead. I was with a group of human rights activists and Chilean exiles and someone had a transistor radio to keep up with the lengthy judgment as it was being read out. This was how we found out that NATO would begin its military operations over Kosovo that night. Having repeatedly warned the government of Slobodan Milošević that another genocide in Europe would not be tolerated, western governments authorized a bombing campaign against Serbian forces that was to last for seventy-eight days and eventually resulted in the withdrawal of Yugoslav forces from Serbia's historical province of Kosovo. Human rights, long considered something of a fringe issue in British politics, suddenly emerged centre stage.

Torture and genocide are among the two most serious crimes under international law. Both have universal jurisdiction, that is, states are required to prosecute them irrespective of where they have been committed or the nationality of the perpetrators or victims. Pinochet had awarded himself an amnesty for his crimes in Chile and assumed that, as a former head of state and senator for life, he would enjoy diplomatic and state immunity when travelling abroad. However, Britain, Chile and Spain were all signatories of the UN Convention against Torture, and the British Law Lords ruled that, since it defined torture as something that could only be carried out by a public official, it would be absurd to provide former public officials with state immunity for the crime. The principle of state immunity is that public officials cannot be held personally responsible for acts carried out in their official capacities, but, as the Law Lords noted, torture can never be regarded as a legitimate official activity.

The Genocide Convention goes one step further in challenging state sovereignty and sovereign immunity, stating, 'Any Contracting Party may call upon the competent organs of the United Nations to take such action under the Charter of the United Nations as they consider appropriate' to prevent or suppress acts of genocide.[1] This implies that the UN could not only arrest the perpetrators of such acts but could also authorize military intervention in a state's national territory to prevent their occurrence.

Both Conventions form part of a body of international human rights law that can theoretically be used to trump state sovereignty when, in the words of the Universal Declaration of Human Rights, events occur that 'outrage the conscience of mankind'.[2] But the circumstances in which the principle of 'non-interference in another state's internal affairs', which is itself enshrined in Article 2 of the UN Charter, can ever be put to one side are hotly disputed. Who should decide when such interference is legitimate, what form it should take and how those who intervene can be held to account themselves?

I was working for Amnesty International UK at the time of the Pinochet case and had responsibility for our work within the UK section on 'combating impunity'. Impunity, in this context, refers to how powerful people who violate human rights do so because they think they can get away with it. Creating mechanisms to bring them to justice therefore provides a disincentive for others to commit similar violations in the future. Combating impunity has a simple and compelling logic, but it is also a process whose emergence involved a significant mind-shift regarding human rights. Amnesty, as its name suggests, was formed to help get people out of prison, not to put them in. In his now celebrated letter to the *Observer* of 28 May 1961, Peter Benenson, a British barrister, suggested a letter-writing campaign to free a group of Portuguese students imprisoned for raising a toast to liberty. Two months later Benenson co-founded Amnesty International to co-ordinate future letter-writing activity and other campaigns. Benenson became Amnesty's first secretary-general, while another barrister, Sean MacBride, was made chairperson of its international executive.

MacBride, who became secretary-general of the International Commission of Jurists two years later, was a former Minister for External Affairs in the Irish Government that had declared a Republic in 1948. His father, Major John MacBride, was executed by the British for his part in the 1916 Rising, and MacBride himself was briefly chief of staff of the Irish Republican Army (IRA) during the 1930s. He took part in hunger strikes and prison break-outs and once woke up to find his cellmate about to be taken out and shot at dawn. MacBride also served as president of the Council of Europe and assistant secretary-general of the United Nations. He is the only person ever to have received the Nobel Peace Prize, the American Medal of Justice and the Lenin Peace Prize. The significance of the latter achievement at the height of the cold war should not be underestimated.

The key to the success of the advocacy organization created by Benenson and MacBride was political neutrality. Amnesty would adopt 'prisoners of conscience' and encourage its members to write polite letters to the government concerned requesting their release. A prisoner of conscience was defined as someone imprisoned solely for expressing his or her peaceful political views. The legal background of both Benenson and MacBride was much in evidence in the construction of this formulation, which became known as the organization's mandate.

The formulation excluded the imprisoned Nelson Mandela and those leaders of anti-colonial movements who advocated or involved themselves in violent resistance. It would also have excluded MacBride himself in his revolutionary days. Indeed, it was probably because he knew how his Irish republican background was viewed in some quarters that MacBride was so aware of the need to ensure that Amnesty positioned itself as politically neutral. The organization tried to adopt equal numbers of dissidents in the Soviet bloc and those facing persecution by Spain and Portugal's right-wing dictatorships. Its national sections were forbidden from campaigning in their own countries, and when the organization hired specialist researchers it stipulated that they could not come from the country they were investigating. It also refused to accept government funding and held itself consciously aloof not only from political parties but from other pressure groups as well. The organization still prides itself on how scrupulously it cross-checks its facts – though some new staff members are told the perhaps apocryphal story of the time it 'adopted' a former railway station in Cambodia because someone confused the Khmer word for 'detained' with the one for 'closed down'.

Amnesty's mandate gradually expanded, adding campaigns against torture and the death penalty. If it is wrong to imprison someone solely for their political views then it must, by logical extension, be wrong to imprison them for their race, gender or sexual orientation. Thus Amnesty also embraced the cause of those persecuted for these reasons. It also spoke out on behalf of refugees fleeing such persecution and, by the time I joined its staff, against the sale of weapons to countries where they might be used to carry out human rights violations. In 2004, it expanded its mandate to campaigning on economic, social and cultural rights alongside the more traditional civil and political ones. As it moved further and further from its original focus, Amnesty increasingly began to look to international human rights and humanitarian law to provide a framework for its campaigns.

The origins of Amnesty's campaign against impunity emerged from its work against torture, which was itself largely motivated by the overthrow of Chile's democratic government in 1973. Augusto Pinochet, the new dictator, instituted torture as a means of terrorizing his political opponents, and Amnesty launched its first international anti-torture campaign the following year. Its efforts resulted in the UN adopting a declaration against torture in 1975, which eventually became a convention in 1984. Amnesty then instructed its sections in different countries to encourage their members to write letters calling on their own governments to ratify the new convention. Treaty-ratification became, in Amnesty-speak, an 'exception to the Work-on-own-Country rule (WooC)', and similar exceptional practices have been used in its death penalty campaign.

This type of lobbying at an international level has become an important part of Amnesty's work, and its interaction with parts of the UN contributed to a political cross-fertilization. Geoffrey Robertson QC (a noted human rights lawyer who went on to become president of the Special Court that the UN established for Sierra Leone), remembers how Amnesty introduced him to human rights as a student, inspiring him to write polite letters to Idi Amin. Nigel Rodley, the longest-serving head of its legal department, went on to become UN Special Rapporteur on Torture and later a member of the UN Human Rights Committee. Numerous other staff subsequently joined UN field missions, and Ian Martin, a former secretary-general, led the first UN mission to East Timor in 1999. Amnesty's first field-based researcher in Kosovo, Liz Griffin, later joined the UN mission as a human rights adviser to the new Kosovan police force. Others, such as Irene Khan, who became Amnesty's secretary-general in 2001, had previously worked for the UN High Commissioner for Refugees (UNHCR).

Like many Amnesty staff, I joined the organization because I was impressed by its campaigning, but I was also drawn to it by other issues. I learned my most important human rights lesson when I was arrested in London under the Prevention of Terrorism Act in 1985. I was twenty at the time, and was staying at a friend's flat when I was picked up in an early-morning raid. I remember waking to the sound of a sledgehammer crashing through the door and reaching for my clothes as gunmen burst in. We were spreadeagled against a wall, still half-dressed, on a bitterly cold winter morning, while the police ransacked the flat with hammers and crowbars. They took us to a maximum security police station where we were held for two days. I was swabbed for explosives, strip-searched, deprived of sleep and interrogated in the absence of a lawyer. Then they let us go and that was it. No explanation or apology.

I was not particularly surprised. Only a tiny proportion of the people detained under this Act were ever charged with terrorist offences, and the Act itself is widely believed to have been used by the police for harassment and intimidation. I was born in England of Irish parents and the Troubles were part of the political background I grew up in. I am also distantly related to the Irish guerrilla leader Michael Collins. Ken Loach's award-winning film, *The Wind that Shakes the Barley* (2006), could almost tell my family's history: like my grandfather, its central character was a medical student in Cork when he joined the IRA. Another relative was second-in-command of the West Cork Flying Column whose ambush at Kilmichael the film so vividly portrays.

A brush with more contemporary events came in 1970 when my father's brother-in-law, Captain James Kelly, was arrested and charged with attempting to send guns to Northern Ireland. Kelly was a career soldier in the Irish army, attached to its intelligence division, and had served in one of the UN's first peacekeeping missions in Syria's Golan Heights. He went to Northern Ireland in 1969 and witnessed how peaceful demonstrations demanding civil rights for the Catholic minority provoked a backlash from extremists within the Protestant loyalist population. After reporting back to his superiors, he was instructed to make contact with the Defence Committees that were emerging in many Catholic areas and would go on to become the nucleus of the Provisional IRA.

In August 1969, British troops were deployed on the streets when thousands of Catholic homes were burned down as the police looked on. Riots broke out in Derry's Bogside where the residents defended their area against a police incursion. The Irish army moved to the border and politicians in Dublin drew up contingency plans to arm republicans in the north. Charles Haughey, the finance minister, chaired a committee that oversaw these covert preparations and Kelly reported directly to the minister for defence, James Gibbon. At one meeting Gibbon jokingly dubbed Kelly 'Ho Chi Minh', in reference to the trail named after the North Vietnamese president whose government was equipping the communist rebels in the south at the time.

When the operation became public in April 1970, however, Ireland's politicians quickly moved to distance themselves from it. Haughey and Kelly were among those put on trial for gunrunning, but were acquitted by a sympathetic jury. Haughey was sacked, but staged a comeback and served as Ireland's prime minister for much of the 1980s. When Kelly died, in 2003, Ireland's prime minister, Bertie Ahern, was among those who paid tribute to him for doing what he considered to be his duty.

As Northern Ireland descended into chaos, most Irish nationalists viewed the emergence of the Provisional IRA with growing horror. I remember my family's reaction to the Birmingham pub bombings and how my mother was sometimes embarrassed to speak in public in case people heard her accent. Nevertheless, our views of the root causes of political violence were always different from those of our English neighbours. The hunger strike of 1981, in which ten prisoners died protesting against their being treated as common criminals, made a lasting impression, and my own personal experiences drew me into the campaigns to free the Guildford Four and Birmingham Six. Later, as I became involved in human rights work and then humanitarian aid, words such as conflict, torture, terrorism and famine always held particular meanings for me, rooted as they were in my Fenian heritage.

It is probably no coincidence that the human rights movement attained its respectability in Britain just as the Northern Ireland conflict was coming to a close and before the start of George Bush's war on terror. It is always easier to condemn human rights violations in far-off places than those committed nearer home by your own government or its closest allies. The end of the cold war and the collapse of the Soviet Union also convinced many on the left that human rights could, in the words of Professor Boaventura de Sousa Santos, 'fill the void left by socialist politics'.[3]

The metamorphosis of many anti-colonial freedom fighters into corrupt autocrats, such as Robert Mugabe, discredited the notion that groups mouthing radical slogans can be trusted to help the people they claim to represent. There now exists a burgeoning literature dedicated to documenting the almost complete failure of international aid to have any impact on poverty reduction in Africa over the last few decades.[4] Aid agencies such as Oxfam, Save the Children and CARE explicitly adopted a 'rights-based' approach to their programming during the mid-1990s.[5] This replaced what David Reiff calls 'third worldism', which often manifested itself in romanticism about the revolutionary liberation movements of Africa and Latin America.[6] Collective ownership and state-led economic development went out of fashion. By focussing on the essentially liberal notion of individual rights, they repositioned themselves in response to the wider political changes taking place in the world.

For many involved in international development work, human rights and political humanitarianism seemed to provide the basis for a new movement for social justice. According to one estimate, humanitarian expenditure witnessed a six-fold increase during the 1980s and 1990s.[7] This came while most western governments were cutting back on their long-term development assistance budgets. Development purists have traditionally dismissed humanitarian assistance as 'ambulance chasing', but, after the billions spent trying to support economic and social development in some of the poorest countries in the world, its supporters could retort that at least they were saving lives. Political humanitarianism conveys a sense of urgency and righteousness that attracts the same kind of idealistic partisan for development. For many former leftists growing to middle age, it also provides a comforting connection between the youthful idealistic dreams that 'another world is possible' and the increasing material possessions that make their previous socialist certainties seem less plausible. A liberal-leftist in the early 1980s might have gone to pick Nicaraguan coffee with the Sandinistas, but was more likely ten years later to be campaigning to lift the siege of Sarajevo or protesting the genocide in Rwanda.

Political humanitarianism was also partly a response to the declining participation in mainstream politics in Europe and North America. Amnesty International UK now has over a quarter of a million members, overtaking that of the British Labour Party. Oxfam Great Britain has over 100,000 active supporters and the combined supporter bases of the main aid charities in Britain easily exceeds those of the three major main political parties. These organizations are also highly effective at using the media and have gained real influence with opinion-formers and decision-makers. Through their advocacy efforts they play a leading role in defining what constitutes a humanitarian crisis, and have become an important factor in shaping the foreign policy of western governments.

These types of pressure groups exerted a particular influence over the Labour Party during its long years in opposition in the 1980s and 1990s. Labour moved from a leftist unilateralism during the 1980s towards a full embrace of multilateral institutions such as the European Union (EU) and NATO by the 1990s. Its 1997 manifesto included a proposal to incorporate the European Convention on Human Rights into domestic law, upgrade its commitment to international development and 'put human rights at the heart of its foreign policy'.

Human rights also became a recognized force in international relations during the 1990s. The EU made ratification of the European Convention a precondition for states applying for membership, and this process helped the former communist countries of Eastern Europe in their transition to democracy. Turkey's human rights record significantly improved as a result of the European Court's judgments and diplomats often spoke of the growing importance of the Court's 'soft power' in world affairs. President Bill Clinton also increasingly allied the US Government's rhetorical support for the promotion of democracy and human rights to the more specific standards contained within international human rights treaties. The 1993 World Conference on Human Rights led to the creation of a new UN Office of the High Commissioner for Human Rights (OHCHR) the following year. The genocides in Rwanda and Bosnia-Herzegovina gave a new sense of urgency to the debates on human rights violations and bridged the gap between human rights and humanitarian organizations. At the same time, in the aftermath of the cold war, some argued that human rights transcended, or even counter-posed, traditional politics. For example, in *Values for a Godless Age* Francesca Klug contrasted the 'ethical values' of human rights with the 'failed ideologies' of the mainstream left and right.[8]

International human rights law establishes standards by which governments can be held accountable for the way they treat their own citizens. It also states that there are certain fundamental rights that can never be set to one side, even during an emergency which 'threatens the life of a nation'. One of the first and most controversial cases to reach the European Court was 'Ireland v UK', brought during the 1970s by the Irish Government against Britain over the 'in-depth interrogation' of a select group of internees in Northern Ireland. They were subjected to a variety of techniques including deprivation of food and sleep, being held in stress-positions for long periods of time, as well as threats of and subjections to painful abuse and severe disorientation, all of which were specifically intended to cause psychological damage without leaving physical marks. The Court ruled that while it was permissible to detain people without trial on the grounds of a State of Emergency, this treatment violated the Convention's prohibition of torture and ill-treatment. It distinguished, in this case, between torture on the one hand and cruel, inhuman and degrading treatment on the other, although subsequent rulings have confirmed that the difference between the two is not so easy to draw.[9]

More cases followed over the next two decades and owed much to the efforts of two Belfast-based solicitors, Peter Madden and Pat Finucane. These cases challenged extended detentions, shoot-to-kill operations and mistreatment of prisoners, which gave concrete expression to the Conventions' protections of life, liberty and freedom from torture. At the same time another group of lawyers, based at the University of Essex, adopted a similar strategy towards violations committed by Turkey in its counter-insurgency campaign against the Kurds from the mid-1980s onwards. The Essex lawyers included Kevin Boyle, a former leader of the Northern Ireland civil rights movement, and Nigel Rodley, the former head of Amnesty's legal department.

Between them these cases helped establish how long people can be legitimately held in custody before they are charged; what safeguards must be put in place to protect them from mistreatment; what type of investigations must be mounted when it is alleged that this has occurred; in what circumstances lethal force can be used against terrorist suspects; and what type of investigations are necessary when actions by the security forces result in a death. By establishing a considerable caseload of legal precedence they helped put flesh on the human rights skeleton.

Nigel Rodley received a knighthood in 1998 for his work against torture. In 2001, Kevin Boyle was appointed as a special adviser to Mary Robinson, who headed OHCHR. Francesca Klug received an Order of the British Empire in 2002. Pat Finucane, who can also legitimately claim to have played a part in this particular human rights story, received a more traditional recognition a few years earlier when he was murdered in front of his family by British agents working inside a loyalist paramilitary gang.[10] In 2003, the European Court ruled that the British Government had violated his right to life by failing to provide a prompt and effective investigation into the allegations of collusion by security force personnel in his killing.[11]

These contrasting fates sum up the human rights paradox. Governments of the world routinely pledge their commitment to the ideals of human rights. The Universal Declaration was first proclaimed at the United Nations in 1948. Since then governments have drawn up and ratified a variety of human rights treaties. The UN has also established various treaty-monitoring mechanisms which report on how governments are complying with them in practice. Yet torture, arbitrary arrests, extra-judicial executions and other violations continue. If anything, the gap between standard-setting and standard-enforcement became wider during the 1990s. This led to a growing sense of frustration and impotence on the part of many human rights activists. By the end of the 1990s there was little to choose between a report documenting violations produced by Amnesty or one produced by a UN monitoring body. In fact it was fairly likely that their authors would have had some experience of working for both organizations. We could persuade the UN to adopt a new set of human rights principles, or endorse our findings about a particular atrocity, but our common culture meant that we were mainly influencing people like us, rather than those who were responsible for the abuses. The bigger question was what to do about the situation on the ground. Here both Amnesty and the traditional humanitarian NGOs found themselves hampered by their mandates.

During the war in Kosovo, for example, MSF called a press conference to highlight the point that while most of the international media's attention was on the suffering of Kosovan refugees in neighbouring countries, it was those trapped inside the province who were in most immediate danger. James Orbinski, MSF's international president, demanded action to protect them. Pressed on what such action might entail, he responded 'that is not our responsibility as humanitarians to determine. We are not going to say if the bombing should go on or stop, if there should be a land war or a truce. That is up to governments. We are simply calling on them to live up to their obligations.'[12] Given the circumstances, most observers could be forgiven for wondering: what exactly was the point of such advice?

I often encountered similar frustrations at Amnesty. Pierre Sané, its former secretary-general, concedes that 'When AI [Amnesty] calls on governments to protect people from human rights violations and to bring perpetrators to justice, we understand that this may require the use of force, even lethal force.'[13] However, in practice, the organization was extremely reluctant to spell it out when this is what it was calling for. During the late 1990s we ran 'arrest now' campaigns calling for action against the indicted war criminals in the Balkans. At the end of 1999 we also called for the deployment of 'an effective UN force' in East Timor. Neither could have been achieved without the threat or use of force and, it seemed to me at the time, that our standard formulation, 'Amnesty neither supports nor opposes' military action, damaged our credibility.

Although Sané refused to accept that 'the only choices in a humanitarian crisis are inaction or invasion', we often failed to outline the alternatives to these courses of action we might have had in mind. His condemnation of the 'hypocrisy, double-standards and selectivity' of the governments involved in such interventions only made sense if Amnesty was prepared to take a clear position itself. We were demanding that governments show the courage to take action to achieve certain human rights goals without being brave enough ourselves to say what this action should be.

Here, again, it seemed that international law might come to the rescue. In response to the crises in Rwanda and the Balkans, the UN established two international criminal tribunals to prosecute those committing war crimes and crimes against humanity. The main purpose of these tribunals was to ward off pressure for direct military intervention. Nevertheless, the idea that international law might be able to respond proactively to human rights violations was a powerful one. Amnesty was among the groups to participate actively in the discussions that led to the drawing up of the Statute for the International Criminal Court (ICC) in Rome in 1998, and it subsequently ran a treaty-ratification campaign to persuade the sixty states needed to back it for it to come into effect.

The arrest of Augusto Pinochet in London in October 1998 also demonstrated the growing importance of international law for the human rights movement. Pinochet gave himself an amnesty – in the other sense of the word – when he agreed to step down from power in Chile, and as a senator for life he was also immune from prosecution in his own country. Home Secretary Jack Straw's decision to allow the law to take its course showed that the new Labour Government intended to take a rather different approach to its Conservative predecessor on such issues. Former Prime Minister Margaret Thatcher defended her old friend Pinochet at the Conservative Party conference the following year. Likening the human rights conventions to 'international lynch law', she claimed that he faced 'lingering death in a foreign land' after his 'judicial kidnap' in Britain.[14] By contrast, New Labour's Peter Mandelson said that it would be 'gut-wrenching' for people of his generation to see the man who toppled Salvador Allende escape prosecution under the cloak of diplomatic immunity.[15]

Pinochet's arrest coincided with an event Amnesty organized where Foreign Secretary Robin Cook outlined how he intended to 'put human rights at the heart of UK foreign policy'. Pinochet first appeared in court on 11 December 1998, almost fifty years to the day after the Universal Declaration was proclaimed. Although Straw was eventually to return him to Chile on medical grounds, the symbolism of his arrest was powerful and the judgment of the House of Lords made legal history. The Law Lords quoted with approval the judgment of the Nuremburg tribunal that convicted a group of Nazis of war crimes and crimes against humanity after the Second World War:

> He who violates the rules of war cannot obtain immunity while acting in pursuance of the authority of the State, if the State in authorising action moves outside its competence in international law . . . the principle of international law, which under certain circumstances protects the representatives of a State, cannot be applied to acts which are condemned as criminal by international law.[16]

The 'Pinochet precedent' was soon used to prosecute other former dictators, while the arrest rate of war crimes suspects for the International Criminal Tribunal for Yugoslavia (ICTY) finally started to increase. NATO's intervention in Kosovo, the UN intervention in East Timor at the end of 1999 and a British military intervention in Sierra Leone the following year seemed to reinforce the same message: perpetrators of grave human rights violations could no longer act with impunity. The international community appeared increasingly prepared to use both 'hard' and 'soft' power to override national sovereignty where it was deemed necessary to protect basic rights.

The reality was far more complicated, but it is easy to see how political humanitarianism constructed such a powerful narrative. By the end of the 1990s the limitations of traditional 'neutral' humanitarianism and human rights were very clear to those involved in both movements. While I was desperate for lobbying instructions from my immediate superiors at Amnesty, humanitarians in the field were facing similar frustrations. John Fawcett, a senior official in the International Rescue Committee (IRC) – a US aid organization I would subsequently work for in Afghanistan and Aceh – summed up the feelings of many about the weakness of the international community's response to the Balkan wars of the mid-1990s. 'You cannot defeat fascism with humanitarian aid,' he said. 'Fascism has to be hit with military force. When it goes violent, you have to use violence.'[17]

During the conflict in Bosnia-Herzegovina, it seemed that western governments were using the delivery of humanitarian aid as an excuse for not adopting more forceful measures of military intervention. At the start of the Kosovo war, in the spring of 1999, NATO soldiers also became involved in distributing aid and building refugee camps, partly to cover up for the lack of any other visible signs of progress in its bombing campaign. One journalist noted that subsequent adverts portrayed the British army as 'a bit like Oxfam's military wing'.[18] Others, however, contrasted the supposed efficiency of the military with the humanitarians in delivering aid.

UNHCR was particularly criticized for its slowness in responding to the Kosovo crisis. Some argued it would be better to rely on commercial contractors to take over the service delivery tasks from humanitarian agencies, as would later happen in Afghanistan and Iraq. UNHCR became the *de facto* lead humanitarian agency in the Balkans during the 1990s. It carried out a massive humanitarian operation, airlifting supplies into besieged areas and organizing land convoys between the conflict's front lines. It was estimated to be giving aid to 2.7 million people out of Bosnia's pre-war total of 4.5 million, and spending around $1 million a day at the height of the conflict.[19] Much of the actual delivery of aid was subcontracted to humanitarian NGOs, who became increasingly dependent on UNHCR to maintain their field operations. Although this assistance was vital, it meant that UNHCR often had to either arrange the evacuation of civilians from areas where their lives were threatened – which made it an agent of ethnic cleansing – or sustain populations in places such as Srebrenica, where they were subsequently massacred. An agency set up to protect refugees was, in other words, doing precisely the opposite of what its mandate demanded.

The philanthropist billionaire George Soros made a substantial donation through UNHCR to the Bosnian relief effort, with the explicit goal of 'helping Sarajevo survive' against what he saw as the besieging forces of 'Serbian fascism'. His explicitly political approach to humanitarianism jarred with UNHCR's traditional neutrality, but linking the delivery of aid to standards rooted in international human rights law helped reassure many agencies that they were not straying too far from their mandates. Humanitarians have long argued against a 'truck and chuck' approach to aid delivery and sensibly point out the importance of comprehensive assessments and evaluation on the wider impact of their programmes. Some, like Fawcett, argued that this is what gave the humanitarians a competitive edge over the private sector who, however efficient they might be at service delivery, 'can't deal with human rights'.[20] Many humanitarians embraced the idea that aid should be delivered to people not only on the basis of their needs, but as part of a process that recognized their rights.

The 1995 Dayton Peace Accords, which ended the conflict in Bosnia-Herzegovina, contained an explicit guarantee that everyone displaced by the conflict had a 'right to return to their homes'. Similar language was adopted by the UN Security Council after the Kosovo conflict. Western government donors were prepared to fund substantial programmes in order to 'reverse the effects of ethnic cleansing' and support the return of people to areas where particular ethnic groups had been driven out. As well as constructing houses, this involved creating jobs and ensuring the provision of basic social services in areas of return. It also required initiatives to foster reconciliation between different communities so that minorities were not coerced again. 'Rights-based programming', up until then a rather theoretical concept, was now seized upon as something that could 'create the conditions for sustainable return'.

In several locations one early obstacle to return was the presence of known war criminals, thus humanitarians added their voices to the human rights NGOs running the 'arrest now' campaigns. Another was that the national and local authorities in the new states emerging from the former Yugoslavia were often extremely hostile to minority return, applying their laws in a blatantly discriminatory manner in order to prevent it. Those who fled the conflict were regarded as having made themselves 'intentionally homeless', and their houses were given to other people. Many of the displaced also lost all their personal documents, including property deeds and identification papers, which made it very difficult for them to prove what they owned, or even their entitlement to welfare benefits. UNHCR supported legal aid projects for people with such problems, and some of these projects helped prepare cases for the European Court of Human Rights.

Since the new Balkan states were keen on EU membership, winning cases at the European Court might help force them to improve their human rights records. Human Rights Watch went even further and called on the EU and World Bank to make the provision of aid conditional on compliance with international standards:

> First a mechanism should be established whereby human rights organizations . . . can report to and work with international financial institutions (IFIs) on the question of whether local authorities are truly complying with the Dayton Peace

Accords – including the surrender of indictees – and are otherwise not violating basic international standards. This would allow IFIs to receive accurate, timely and specific information on which entities should receive assistance and which should not, and would enable IFIs to outline specific steps that jurisdictions must undertake to receive assistance, as well as to specify the conduct that would trigger the reduction or termination of that assistance.[21]

The implications of this proposal – which could place human rights NGOs in a far more powerful position than the elected representatives of a state – are considerable. A report published in 2001 by the International Commission on Intervention and State Sovereignty (ICISS) went even further in suggesting that NGOs should be formally incorporated into discussions of when military interventions on human rights grounds are justified. It argued that: 'Ideally there would be a report as to the gravity of the situation, and the inability or unwillingness of the state in question to manage it satisfactorily, from a universally respected and impartial non-government source.'[22] In other words, bodies that were established to alleviate human suffering could, on occasion, be given the task of making the case for war.

The vast expansion of humanitarian activities during the 1990s and the role as semi-official distributors of relief that humanitarian agencies have often been called upon to play has massively increased the potential influence they exercise, not only over when humanitarian interventions are justified but as operational actors when interventions occur. In some conflict and post-conflict countries aid agencies have taken on state-like functions, such as running health, education and welfare systems. A number of western donors, including the British Government's DFID, have drawn up 'conflict assessment guidance notes' so that agencies can 'assess how they interact with the dynamics of conflict and the potential for more effective, coherent or co-ordinated responses'. The aim is to encourage 'joined-up-analysis' and 'opportunities for programmes/policies to better contribute to peace-building'.[23] One suggested policy recommendation is that donors should 'increasingly rely on NGOs rather than government implementing partners'.[24] Many donors now also have specific 'protection' or 'human rights' budget lines that are often used to support 'peace-building' and 'reconciliation' programmes.

Professor Mary Anderson, a noted theorist on humanitarian aid, argues that: 'Although [humanitarian] aid agencies often seek to be neutral or non-partisan towards the winners and losers of a war, the impact of their aid is not neutral regarding whether conflict worsens or abates.'[25] She says that it is naive to deny that these agencies impact on the politics of the society in which they are working and so they should ensure that their assistance is provided in ways that actively contribute to 'justice, peace and reconciliation'. Anderson ran a training session for a group of agencies when I was working for UNHCR in Kosovo, and I could see that her basic argument has some merits. However, it also involves tying aid to explicitly political objectives, such as undermining support for insurgents or political extremists and the promotion of philosophical convictions associated with western liberal values. Clearly this will have an impact on the way the distribution of such aid is perceived. When such activities can be carried out only with the support of western military forces, it is not difficult to imagine how those who do not share the philosophies that humanitarians are trying to promote are likely to react.

Western perceptions of how the human rights of one group of people need to be balanced with that of society as a whole differ sharply from those in other parts of the world, particularly on issues such as freedom of expression and attitudes towards religion, gender and sexual relations. The 'right to private property' is also basically a western concept, one which may be politically sensitive in societies where it is associated with capitalism or colonialism. In many parts of the world land is held under customary tenure and is sometimes deemed to be 'held in stewardship' for the whole community. Women and children often do not have an individual right to own property, but have access to land through their relationship to male heads of household. In situations of mass displacement, where whole families may have left their land for several years and where many households are now headed by widows and orphans, attempting to implement a 'rights-based approach' to property restitution can frequently do more harm than good by subverting the traditional protections for vulnerable groups.[26]

Aid agencies have also become increasingly involved in human rights because of the impact of their own programmes. For most humanitarians the traditional distinction between civil and political rights, and social, economic and cultural rights makes very little sense. Basic rights, including the right to life, dignity and freedom from discrimination, obviously fit into both categories, while other rights, such as education, also bridge the divide. Civil and political rights are sometimes described as 'negative', meaning that it only requires the state to refrain from interfering in people's lives, while social and economic rights are 'positive' and require active intervention by governments to provide people with education and employment, among other things. However, rights such as 'a fair trial or hearing', which have become of vital importance in post-conflict situations, can only be realized through an effective system of justice, and this is often far more expensive than providing people with basic healthcare or welfare. Similarly, freedom of movement, the 'right to return home' or restitution of personal property could also require extensive security provisions in a post-conflict environment.

Monitoring social and economic rights, however, is obviously much more difficult than gathering evidence for a case of torture, censorship or arbitrary execution. Violations of economic, social and cultural rights affect groups as well as individuals in direct and indirect ways. Individuals are sometimes denied the rights to education, housing, healthcare, work or employment because of their membership of a particular national, ethnic or religious group, hence the monitoring requires analyzing wider-ranging information: why was a school built here rather than there, or why did a local authority allocate a certain percentage of its expenditure to one thing rather than another? Social and economic rights are supposed to be implemented 'progressively and to the maximum of its available resources', but when a government of a poor country says it has no money, whose obligation is it to ensure that the benchmarks for implementation are met? International aid makes up a significant proportion of the budgets of most of the poorest countries in the world and these are the places where humanitarian crises most frequently occur. To what extent can donors and international agencies impose their own 'rights-based' views on such societies without destroying local accountability?

Recent years have seen the UN create an increasing number of international human rights mechanisms whose reports and recommendations help guide its work. It has also adopted a number of new declarations, resolutions or bodies of principles on human rights issues. These are often referred to as 'soft law' in that they are not directly legally binding on states but are considered to have 'the persuasive power' of having been negotiated by governments or adopted by political bodies such as the UN General Assembly. Sometimes these 'soft laws' affirm principles that are already considered legally binding as principles of general or customary international law. They often also fill in the gaps or spell out in more detail the necessary steps to safeguard the broadly defined rights contained in international treaties.

The problem with this approach is that in adopting extremely high normative standards to guide their work, humanitarian organizations create a huge gap between their theoretical principles and the reality in the country in question. The poorer the country the larger this gap is likely to be. In such circumstances, lectures on human rights can resemble missionary activity; the comparison comes even closer when this is linked to military interventions on human rights grounds.

I received my first lesson in this shortly after arriving in Kosovo, when I attended a seminar for a group of Kosovan social workers on the theme of children's rights. A young Scandinavian lawyer working for UNICEF gave one of the speeches, during which she went through the Convention on the Rights of the Child that came into force in 1989, and is one of the most extensive of the human rights conventions. It contains both civil and political and social and economic rights, and its provisions go far beyond those even the most liberal European societies have ever granted to their children. I noticed that everyone took copious notes while she was speaking but no one challenged any of her assertions, though they must have jarred with the cultural ethos of the society in which they were raised. Walking back to the office with one of my national colleagues, I asked her about this. She replied that in order to be appointed to any professional position in the former Yugoslavia it was necessary to pass an exam in Marxist-Leninism. 'Everyone knew it was nonsense, but we just learned it off by heart and repeated what the examiner wanted us to say. Then we forgot about it and just got on with our jobs. The communists ruled us then and now you do. It is basically the same thing though,' she concluded.

Chapter Two

Humanitarian Interventions

'HE IS just repeating the same kind of stuff,' our translator told us, 'but keep nodding while you are listening so that he thinks I am translating what he said. Then let's get out of here before we get killed. Those missiles are coming closer.'

It was May 1994 and I was in northern Iraq, crouched on the bare ridge of a mountainside taking incoming Turkish shellfire. We bumped into a group of guerrillas from the Kurdish Workers' Party (PKK) who offered us their customary sweet tea and responded to our questions about current political events with interminable speeches about socialism and revolutionary warfare. The thuds of Turkish artillery were indeed getting louder, and while it did not seem to bother the PKK guerrillas it was making the rest of us very nervous.

I went to the Kurdish region of south-east Turkey to write an article about the conflict between the Turkish security forces and the PKK. The war was at its most intense and around 3,000 Kurdish villages had been burned over the previous decade as part of a 'scorched earth' policy by the security forces. The conflict had caused an estimated 30,000 deaths and displaced hundreds of thousands. It was difficult to get people to talk to us in Turkey because of the ubiquitous presence of plain-clothes security forces, who even followed us into our hotel rooms. Eventually we decided to cross into northern Iraq, where many refugees had fled, to ask what had driven them out of their homes.

The first Gulf war had ended three years earlier and a safe haven created to protect the Kurds, after their abortive rising against Saddam Hussein collapsed when the western backing they expected failed to materialize. Fearing another chemical weapons attack, like the one at Halabja in 1988, two million people fled towards the Turkish border, but found it sealed off by the Turkish government. A journalist I was travelling with had been in the region at the time and recalled seeing bodies hanging from every lamp post in the towns that Saddam Hussein's Republican Guard had retaken. Soon, up to a thousand people a day were dying from hunger and cold up in the Kurdish mountains. The world had just witnessed US air power anni-hilate the Iraqi armed forces, and western public opinion refused to accept that nothing could be done to save the Kurds from another act of genocide. When the UN passed Security Council Resolution 688 on 5 April 1991 calling for action, Britain, France and the United States deployed ground troops to turn back the Iraqi army and persuade the refugees that it was safe to come down from the mountains.[1]

Western troops were withdrawn after a few months and replaced by a handful of lightly armed UN guards. Western coalition forces enforced a no-fly zone in the region using planes operating out of Turkish airbases to discourage the Iraqi army from venturing too far north. Turkey's support was vital for the no-fly zone policy, but this meant that the coalition had to ignore Turkish cross-border raids against Kurdish rebels based inside Iraq. In response to one Turkish ground and air attack, in which napalm bombs were reportedly dropped on a village in October 1991, a US military spokesman said that the allies were there to protect the Kurds from Iraq, but not from Turkey.

For most of the 1990s northern Iraq was a hellhole. In the first refugee camp we visited five people died from disease the previous week, and one man told me that his brother was killed by a landmine the day before. Another refugee said it was like living in the world's biggest concentration camp. The Turkish government pressurized the largest Iraqi Kurdish faction, the Kurdish Democratic Party (KDP), to take action against the PKK, and both Turkey and Iraq helped manipulate the factional struggles between other rival Kurdish groups. When I was there the region was engulfed in constant clashes and skirmishes between the KDP and its main rival, the Patriotic Union of Kurdistan (PUK), while the battle we witnessed on the mountainside was the result of a series of cross-border incursions by the Turkish army designed to crush the PKK. Given that people considered themselves safer here than in south-east Turkey, we could only guess what they must have fled from.

Back in south-east Turkey we finally found a taxi driver in Diyarbakir, the regional capital, willing to take me and a photographer into the countryside where the fighting was taking place. We slipped out past a US Air Force base onto an unapproved road. Our driver grew increasingly nervous the further we travelled into no-man's land. He had been tortured by the Turkish security forces and the experience had left him with a facial twitch that became more pronounced the deeper into the countryside we went. In the first village, we were met by worried-looking people who thought we were plain-clothes security men. They had been told to leave their village the previous week and they tried to assure us that they were about to go. Their fear spoke volumes.

The only people who had stayed in this area had agreed to become 'village guards' and collaborate with the authorities. They operated a shoot-to-kill policy against suspected guerrillas; the Turkish air force also patrolled the skies on the lookout for PKK columns. The PKK regarded village guards as legitimate targets and sometimes mined roads in these areas. Our car slowed to a crawl as we scanned the dirt in front of us for metallic objects. Finally we reached Sihocoban, a village where 800 people had been driven out a few weeks before. The village had been stripped, looted and burned. We took a few photographs and got back into the taxi to return to

Diyarbakir, feeling wretched for what we had put our driver through.

Back in Britain, I had a story that no one was interested in. The Kurds were old news by then and, besides, I had the plot wrong. The west had saved the Kurds from Saddam Hussein, so how could it be colluding in their repression by Turkey? Messy, confusing conflicts in far-off places do not make compelling news stories. One of the lessons the political humanitarians have learned is that you need to keep it simple to grab the public's attention.

Of course, real life is not usually like that, but the mid-1990s at least provided plausible examples with which to make the case. While I was on a mountain in northern Iraq, the conflict in Bosnia-Herzegovina was heading towards its brutal climax. Meanwhile, another genocide was underway in Rwanda and a peacekeeping mission in Somalia ending in ignominy. The combined effects of these three conflicts had a profound effect on the way the UN responded to subsequent humanitarian crises. It also did enormous damage to its reputation for dealing with future crises.

The establishment of the Kurdish safe haven is often portrayed as the prototype for other humanitarian interventions in the 1990s. In his final report to the UN General Assembly, its former secretary-general Javier Perez de Cuellar cited it as an example of 'the collective obligation of States to bring relief and redress in human rights emergencies'.[2] The term 'humanitarian intervention' covers a variety of acts – ranging from the provision of assistance to the use of force – by which a state, a group of states or some other organization interferes in another state's internal affairs in order to aid people who have been identified as being either in acute distress or facing imminent danger. Some scholars restrict the use of the term humanitarian intervention to political and military operations that infringe on the territory or sovereignty of another state.[3] Conversely, many humanitarian workers dislike the use of the term to cover anything other than the impartial distribution of relief assistance.[4] These are, obviously, different phenomena, though operational issues in the field can sometimes blur the distinctions.

Attempts to replace the use of force with a system of collective security can be traced back to the Peace of Westphalia in 1648, by which states agreed to end the European 'wars of religion' and respect the principle of non-intervention in one another's internal affairs. The principle also underpins the system of international relations envisaged by the UN Charter, Article 1 of which states the UN's primary purpose is to be the maintenance of international peace and security. Article 2 of the Charter was clearly intended to make the prohibition on the use of force by individual states comprehensive and watertight:[5]

> All Members shall refrain in their international relations from the threat or use of force against the territorial integrity or political independence of any State, or in any other manner inconsistent with the purposes of the United Nations.
>
> Nothing contained in the present Charter shall authorise the United Nations to intervene in matters which are essentially within the domestic jurisdiction of any State or shall require the members to submit such matters to settlement.[6]

The non-interference rule cannot, however, be absolute. By virtue of their membership of the UN, states must accept certain restrictions on their actions. Membership is open to all 'peace-loving nations' irrespective of the nature of their government, providing that they accept the obligations of the Charter. The promotion of respect for human rights is listed in Article 1, though the wording indicates that it is a more aspirational goal. Articles 55 and 56 also state that the UN shall promote 'universal respect for, and observance of, human rights' – which are deemed to contribute to conditions of peace and stability – and that all members of the UN 'pledge themselves to take joint and separate action' to achieve these purposes.

These rights have been spelled out in more detail in the 1948 Universal Declaration of Human Rights (UNDHR), the conventions against genocide and torture, and a number of other human rights treaties. These recognize some rights as being non-derogable, that is, they cannot be set aside in any circumstances, even in an emergency threatening the life of the nation. The International Court of Justice (ICJ) has ruled that the prohibition of genocide and assaults on the 'basic rights of the human person' are part of customary international law, which means they are binding on all states, even if they have not signed treaties to this effect.[7] When the totality of the UN Charter is read together with these instruments, it can therefore be argued that states are restricted from inflicting harm on people within their own territorial borders by virtue of the UN Charter.[8]

Some proponents of humanitarian intervention also argue that the wording of Article 2 may not preclude the use of force so long as it is not directed 'against the territorial integrity or political independence' of a state. Powerful states that believe a weak state is violating international law may be tempted to rely on this formulation if they decide to take matters into their own hands. This point was made in 1949 by the United Kingdom in the 'Corfu Channel' case, in which the British Navy sent minesweepers into Albanian territorial waters following damage to its ships. The ICJ criticized Albania for neglecting to warn shipping that its waters were mined. However, it also stated that:

> The Court can only regard the alleged right of intervention as a policy of force . . . and as such cannot, whatever be the present defects in international organisation, find a place in international law. Intervention is perhaps less admissible in the particular form it would take here, for, from the nature of things, it would be reserved to the most powerful states.[9]

In the 1986 case of 'Nicaragua v the United States', the ICJ referred to its decision in the 'Corfu Channel' case, and held that the principle of non-intervention between independent states has customary international law character.[10] 'Nicaragua v the United States' concerned a complaint by Nicaragua, which accused the US of laying mines in its ports and giving assistance to right-wing contra guerrillas seeking to overthrow its left-wing government. The ICJ rejected the US justification of collective self-defence on the grounds that Nicaragua had allegedly helped rebels in neighbouring El Salvador. It also rejected the US argument that its intervention was justified by the human rights situation in Nicaragua:

> A strictly humanitarian objective cannot be compatible with the mining of ports, the destruction of oil installations, or again with the training, arming and equipping of the *contras* . . . the argument derived from the preservation of human rights in Nicaragua cannot afford a legal justification for the conduct of the United States.[11]

The only explicit exception to the prohibition of the threat or use of force by states is the 'inherent right of self-defence' recognized by Article 51.[12] States have the right to defend themselves if they come under attack and may also come to the aid of their allies. States may also have the right to take 'anticipatory measures' to defend themselves if they are threatened with attack, although the scope of this remains controversial.[13] In addition to this, the UN Security Council may authorize the use of force under Chapter VII of the Charter in discharging its responsibility for upholding international peace and security.[14] However, force should only be used if the pacific methods envisaged in Chapter VI of the Charter are deemed insufficient. There is no reference to human rights in Article 2 of the UN Charter and so, according to the Charter at least, the principle of non-intervention cannot be set aside solely on this basis. However, since the ICJ cannot actually review the legality of the UN Security Council's actions,[15] there is nothing to prevent the Council referring to human rights when it invokes its

Chapter VII powers. As one commenter put it, 'A threat to peace . . . seems to be whatever the Security Council says is a threat to peace.'[16] This argument is discussed further in chapter six.

The biggest obstacle to a Chapter VII-authorized humanitarian intervention is that its five permanent members all have the individual power to veto such actions. As former UN secretary-general Boutros Boutros-Ghali commented in 1992, 'Since the creation of the United Nations in 1945, over 100 major conflicts around the world have left some 20 million dead. The United Nations was rendered powerless to deal with many of these crises because of the vetoes – 279 of them – cast in the Security Council, which were a vivid expression of the divisions of that period.'[17] Between 1946 and 1986 the Security Council recognized the existence of a threat to international peace and security seven times,[18] resorted to military force on three occasions[19] and twice imposed binding non-military sanctions.[20]

This changed with the end of the cold war as the Security Council began to take a more expansive view of what constituted a threat to international peace and security.[21] Between 1988 and 1994 it mounted almost twice as many peacekeeping or peace enforcement operations as it had done over the previous forty years.[22]

As described above, the end of the first gulf war led to the establishment of the Kurdish safe haven. Operation Provide Comfort was principally undertaken by troops from the United States, Britain and France in April 1991. Up to 7,000 ground troops were deployed and a no-fly zone declared over northern Iraq. Apart from the military forces, thirty other countries contributed relief supplies and some fifty international NGOs either offered assistance or participated in this operation.[23] NGO staff attended regular briefings held by military commanders and also had access to military telecommunications and transportation. In *Humanitarian Challenges and Intervention*, Thomas Weiss and Cindy Collins observe, 'The NGOs perceived the military as an ally in their efforts to assist a persecuted minority group.'[24]

This involved a considerable mind-shift by soldiers and aid workers who had previously had little contact with each other, but such co-operation was to become increasingly frequent in future interventions.

UN Security Council Resolution 688 was not in fact adopted under Chapter VII of the Charter, nor did it explicitly authorize military intervention. However, it used similar language, describing the refugee crisis that was threatening to overwhelm neighbouring states as constituting a 'threat to international peace and security in the region'. It also demanded 'humanitarian access' to the affected Kurdish population, while reaffirming support for Iraq's territorial integrity. It was adopted by ten votes to three, with Cuba, Yemen and Zimbabwe voting against and India and China abstaining. The Iraqi government vigorously protested that the resolution constituted interference in the country's internal affairs, but subsequently signed a Memorandum of Understanding with the UN which 'welcomed humanitarian measures to avert new flows of refugees and displaced persons from Iraq'.[25]

The apparent success of this initiative coincided with the wave of optimism that swept the world at the end of the cold war. In December 1991, the UN General Assembly adopted a resolution aimed at strengthening the co-ordination of UN humanitarian assistance during emergencies, which also stressed the obligation of governments to permit the distribution of relief to people in need.[26] Although some concern was expressed during this debate about respect for state sovereignty, most speakers stressed that the issue of international human rights was a legitimate concern for the whole international community under the UN Charter. British Prime Minister John Major commented during discussions at the UN that 'the opening line of our Charter . . . doesn't talk about states or governments, it talks about people.'[27]

In January 1992, a Heads of State summit discussed the institutionalization of a new conflict-management role for the

UN. In his *Agenda for Peace* report, Boutros Boutros-Ghali urged the re-establishment of its Military Staff Committee, the creation of 'peace enforcement' units and an increased role for the ICJ.[28] These proposals were not accepted, but the following month the Security Council decided to establish a mission to help oversee elections in Cambodia, which was to be the UN's biggest single field operation to date.[29] Then, in December 1992, the Security Council explicitly sanctioned a military humanitarian intervention in Somalia, invoking its Chapter VII powers for the first time ever with respect to a purely internal conflict.[30]

Operation Restore Hope was authorized in December 1992 by Resolution 794, which was supported by all the permanent members of the Security Council. It described the situation in Somalia as 'unique' and stated that 'the magnitude of the human tragedy . . . constituted a threat to international peace and security.'[31] Member states were permitted to 'use all necessary means to establish as soon as possible a secure environment for humanitarian relief operations'. It also stated that 'impediments to humanitarian relief violated international humanitarian law', and that anyone interfering with distribution of relief assistance 'will be held individually responsible in respect of such acts'.[32] Subsequent resolutions expanded the mandate to include disarming the main militias and pledging to bring to justice the perpetrators of acts of violence that were hampering the relief effort.[33]

Somalia has been the subject of numerous memoirs written by those involved, most of which focus on the period after the UN's military intervention. The crisis which prompted it began in early 1991 with the toppling of the country's dictator Mohammed Siad Barre and the fracturing of the country into civil war and lawlessness. During the 1980s, when Somalia was backed by the west as a counterweight to Soviet support for Ethiopia, it is estimated to have received more aid per person than any other country in Africa.[34] This aid was mainly used to sustain Siad Barre's regime and reward his supporters, and was seen by Somalis as a source of political patronage. A major cause of the civil war following his downfall was the attempts by the militias that ousted him to gain control over its distribution.

Many aid organizations periodically scaled their operations in Somalia up and down and Mohamed Sahnoun, the UN's special representative to Somalia, noted that this led to considerable mistrust and cynicism towards the international relief effort on the part of ordinary Somalis.[35] The UN itself had withdrawn all its staff in 1990 and then made sporadic attempts to return during the course of 1991. The only organization to maintain a consistent presence in the country was the Somali Red Cross (SRC), which became the main focus of the relief effort during most of 1991 and 1992. Somalia became the Red Cross movement's largest ever operation, surpassing the previous record set in Biafra in 1967. It has been widely praised and Alex de Waal argues that it was the only kind of operation that could have been mounted in such circumstances. The ICRC supported it strongly and flexibly, empowering its Somali delegation to make all major decisions. It used considerable ingenuity to deliver food supplies and its 24,000 staff took significant risks in doing so. Thirteen staff members of the SRC were killed during the operation, including two internationals. However, as in Biafra, it contrasted greatly with the political humanitarian approach that ultimately ensured its demise.

In Somalia the ICRC broke with a major tradition in hiring armed guards, and Oxfam's Tony Vaux remembers his surprise at seeing Red Cross vehicles mounted with heavy machine guns.[36] It also tolerated the large-scale diversion of its supplies. According to the ICRC around 15–20 per cent of its deliveries did not reach their intended beneficiaries, though others put the estimate much higher. One of the main arguments from those who supported the UN's military intervention in 1992 was that the aid effort was sustaining a war economy. Weiss and Collins claim that up to 80 per cent of the food being sent to Somalia was looted and that the militias used the proceeds of 'humanitarian taxes' to try and ship weapons in from Serbia.[37] Others believe that this figure is grossly exaggerated, but the impression that the aid community was effectively subsidizing the militias was certainly widespread. The open-backed land cruisers mounted with heavy weapons that the militias relied on were commonly known as 'technicals', in reference to the budget line 'technical assistance' by which the aid agencies accounted for some of their extraordinary items of expenditure.

The ICRC maintained a relatively low profile for its Somalia operation, partly because this was its normal practice and partly because drawing attention to its delivery of aid increased the prospects of that aid being looted. It helped shame the UN into a proper deployment of its agencies in January 1992 but, as other humanitarians began to mount their own operations, they also started to shape the political agenda towards the crisis. One of the first NGOs to arrive was CARE, which had a warehouse full of food looted in January 1992. In November of that year CARE tried, unsuccessfully, to deliver a large convoy of aid without paying off the various militias along the way. Five people were killed in the resulting shoot-out, which became the subject of sensationalist media reports. CARE, which was criticized for failing to listen to its local staff regarding strategy, began to lobby hard for military intervention by the UN. Its president, Philip Johnstone, was seconded into a senior position with the UN's emergency programme at around the same time. His widely quoted comment that, in order to deliver aid, 'we have to fight the Somalis themselves', was subsequently to earn the mission its soubriquet of 'Operation Shoot-to-Feed'.

A number of US-based NGOs, including the International Rescue Committee and Oxfam America, also publicly called for military intervention. Save the Children UK opposed the move, while others remained silent. The UN's representative, Mohamed Sahnoun, also opposed it, preferring to negotiate with militia leaders and any representatives of Somali civil society he could find. Most informed commentators agree that this policy of trying to re-empower traditional community leaders through dialogue offered by far the most realistic chance of building a peace process in Somalia from the 'bottom up'.[38] However, Sahnoun was increasingly marginalized within the UN, and was forced out of office in October 1992. He subsequently argued that 'integrating security with assistance and rehabilitation programmes is intensely challenging in the best situations, but I believe that specific decisions were taken that were wrong in this case and that, from a moral perspective, were likely to undermine the UN and its partners'.[39]

The UN scaled up its operation from fifty observers in April 1992 to 500 peacekeeping soldiers in September. Finally, in December, it authorized the deployment of 35,000 soldiers in a phenomenally expensive US-led mission. Marines swarmed onto the beaches at Mogadishu harbour to be greeted by the world's news corps. The famine was already abating by the time the soldiers arrived, but troops were initially deployed to guard deliveries. The militias kept a low profile at first but gradually began to reassert themselves, leading to clashes with the US troops in February 1993. That May, the UN assumed control of the operation from the US, but there was no marked change of tactics and the UN appointed a senior US official, a former aide to President Bush, as its special envoy to ensure continuity.

The basic strategy remained to try and uphold basic law and order while persuading Somalia's feuding warlords to participate in some form of national reconciliation. While this made sense, the UN occupation was soon beginning to experience the same kind of organizational problems that have characterized all other interventions since. Sahnoun's 'bottom up' strategy was abandoned by his successors in the search for quick-fix deals with the warlords in an attempt to cobble together a coalition government. A succession of international administrators soon alienated most of Somali civil society through their arrogance and ignorance of the country's political culture. The key turning point came in June 1993 when a group of eighty Pakistani soldiers in the UN mission were killed or injured in a clash with a militia group led by the prominent warlord Mohamed Farah Aidid. Some troops were literally ripped limb from limb while escorting a food convoy. The UN pledged to bring the perpetrators to justice and the operation moved into a more aggressive phase.

Over the next few months several thousand people were killed or injured as the UN forces tried to hunt down Aidid. In one incident, in July 1993, US helicopters attacked a house in which a group of Somali elders had gathered, killing seventy-three people. In September, a US helicopter fired on a crowd and killed sixty. MSF published a detailed communiqué on violations of humanitarian law by UN troops that summer.[40] Photographs also began to emerge of US, Canadian, Belgian, Pakistani, Tunisian and Italian UN soldiers torturing people. One series showed two soldiers dangling a child over an open fire, urinating on a dead body, forcing a child to drink vomit and kicking and stabbing a person on the ground. Another showed soldiers posing beside the battered and bloody corpse of a boy with his hands tied behind his back. Human rights groups documented accounts of children placed in metal containers and left in the boiling sun for days without food or water. Others said they were forced to dig their own graves. Women were reportedly subject to sexual violence and tortured with electric shocks.[41]

In October 1993, two US Black Hawk helicopters were shot down by Aidid's militia and eighteen American soldiers killed, an incident later portrayed in the film *Black Hawk Down*. Over a thousand Somalis are thought to have died during the battle to rescue the surviving US troops. This was effectively the end of the mission, though the formal withdrawal did not take place until the following March.

A few days after the Black Hawk incident another UN force, consisting of US and Canadian soldiers, was prevented from landing in Haiti by a mob of supporters of the military dictatorship chanting Aidid's name. The force was sent to help restore the country's democratically elected president, Jean-Bertrand Aristide, but events in Somalia caused the US government to lose its nerve.

The incident came at almost exactly the same time as the Security Council was discussing the size of the UN force to despatch to Rwanda. In October 1993, the UN agreed to establish a mission in Rwanda (UNAMIR) using its Chapter VI powers, which permit international intervention but not the use of force. Its commanding officer, Roméo Dallaire, had asked for 4,500 troops but this number was scaled back following US objections resulting from its experiences in Somalia. By the end of that year Dallaire had only managed to assemble 1,300 soldiers. Further troops were approved in January 1994, bringing the force up to a strength of 2,500, but the UN's cumbersome budgetary procedures meant that the money to pay for the mission did not arrive for several more months. Dallaire's requests for sufficient supplies to make this force operational were also subject to repeated obstacles and delays, and he never received vital equipment such as functioning armoured personnel carriers to transport his own troops. He has written that 70 per cent of his time was devoted to administrative battles with the UN.[42]

UNAMIR was originally deployed to monitor a ceasefire agreed between Rwanda's army and the Rwandan Patriotic Front (RPF), a Tutsi-based force headed by Paul Kagame, which had invaded from neighbouring Uganda. The RPF was mainly composed of Tutsi exiles who had fled Rwanda to escape a previous genocide thirty years earlier. By 1990, almost a million Tutsis were living in neighbouring countries, making them one of the largest refugee communities in Africa. Many had spent their whole lives in refugee camps, while others settled into a sometimes uneasy existence with their host communities in Uganda, Zaire, Burundi and Tanzania.

Tutsis in Uganda faced persecution from President Milton Obote's government, which was mainly backed by groups from the north of the country. Many joined Yoweri Museveni's southern-based National Resistance Army in a rebellion which eventually brought him to power in 1986. Tutsis comprised around a quarter of Museveni's armed forces, which then became the Ugandan army, and he relied heavily on them to help him suppress a rebellion in the north. These forces formed the RPF in 1987 and three years later, 4,000 of its members deserted from the Ugandan army overnight to invade Rwanda, taking their weapons, uniforms and equipment with them.

The 1990 invasion prompted France to intervene militarily in support of the Rwandan president Juvénal Habyarimana. Rwanda's armed forces rapidly expanded and its government unleashed a wave of repression against its internal opponents. The RPF was initially beaten back, but under Kagame's leadership transformed itself into an effective guerrilla force using hit-and-run tactics. Although its base of support was small it benefited from growing discontent with President Habyarimana's rule and opened talks with the government's opponents. Reports of human rights violations by international monitors led to growing pressure for reform from western governments and donors. In 1991, Habyarimana agreed to a constitutional amendment to end his one-party dominance and a new coalition government signed a ceasefire with the RPF in July 1992, which led to an agreement signed in Arusha in August the following year.

UNAMIR was deployed to monitor this ceasefire. It was mandated to use force only in self-defence, and was prohibited from acting in 'deterrence or retaliation'. Western diplomats, wary of getting sucked into another African civil war, preferred to ignore the increasingly ominous warnings they were receiving about the Hutu political extremists. The CIA conducted a desk study of potential scenarios based on its own intelligence reports, which included a worst-case scenario of 500,000 killed in a genocide, but it failed to share this with the UN mission.[43]

The killings began on 6 April 1994, after a plane carrying the presidents of Rwanda and Burundi was shot down over Kigali airport. Responsibility for the attack is disputed, but it served to destroy the nascent Rwandan peace process. Hutu extremists used it as a signal to launch a ferocious campaign of murder against ethnic Tutsis and moderate Hutu sympathizers. The Rwandan genocide claimed up to 800,000 lives, and UN peacekeeping soldiers were accused of remaining passive instead of intervening to save lives. According to one of the earliest reports by the *Guardian*, on 12 April 1994:

> A few yards from the French troops, a Rwandan woman was being hauled along the road by a young man with a machete. He pulled at her clothes as she looked at the foreign soldiers in the desperate, terrified hope that they could save her from her death. But none of the troops moved. 'It's not our mandate,' said one, leaning against his jeep as he watched the condemned woman, the driving rain splashing at his blue United Nations badge. The 3,000 foreign troops now in Rwanda are no more than spectators to the savagery which aid workers say has seen the massacre of 15,000 people.[44]

In fact the UN mission was among the first victims of the attack when ten Belgian paratroopers were tortured to death by the *genocidaires*. One Rwandan official explained that the mutilation of the corpses, whose genitalia were hacked off and stuffed in their mouths, was inspired by the effect on western resolve following the Black Hawk incident. 'We watch CNN too you know,' he commented.[45] Dallaire lacked sufficient troops to mount a rescue operation and the Belgians subsequently withdrew their 400 soldiers, who were the key component of the UNAMIR force. UNAMIR was reduced to a rump force of about 270 ill-equipped Canadian, Ghanaian, Tunisian and Bangladeshi soldiers, who are nevertheless credited with saving up to 30,000 lives.[46] France and Belgium evacuated their nationals from the country and left the Rwandans to their fate. Dallaire has subsequently estimated that a total of 4,000 well-equipped troops would have given him enough leverage to stop the slaughter. He believes that a number of different players share responsibility for what happened:

> The Rwandan genocide was the ultimate responsibility of those Rwandans who planned, ordered, supervised and eventually conducted it. Their extremism was the seemingly indestructible and ugly harvest of years of power struggles and insecurity that had been deftly played on by their former colonial rulers. But the deaths of Rwandans can also be laid at the door of the military genius Paul Kagame, who did not speed up his campaign when the scale of the genocide became clear and even talked candidly with me at several points about the price his fellow Tutsis might have to pay for the cause. Next in line when it comes to responsibility are France, which moved in too late and ended up protecting the genocidaires and permanently destabilizing the region, and the US government, which actively worked against an effective UNAMIR and only got involved to aid the same Hutu refugee population and the genocidaires, leaving the genocide survivors to flounder and suffer. The failings of the UN and Belgium were not in the same league.[47]

Once the genocide was underway the US government lobbied hard to prevent it being described as such by the UN Security Council, lest this require it to support a more forceful intervention. Belgium tried to persuade other troop-contributing countries to withdraw their contingents to minimize its embarrassment at pulling out.[48] It then stated that it was ready to redeploy its forces in a strengthened UN mission, but France vetoed the plan. Most humanitarian agencies also withdrew from the country, with the exception of the ICRC. In a reversal of roles from Biafra, a group of MSF doctors put themselves at the ICRC's disposal when their own organization pulled out.

MSF, Oxfam and a number of other agencies campaigned vigorously for international military intervention. MSF ran a series of adverts proclaiming that 'one cannot stop a genocide with medicines.'[49] What finally brought the slaughter to an end, however, was the military victory of Kagame's RPF forces, who controlled more than half the country by the end of May 1994. The UN finally agreed to deploy a second mission in early June, but this initiative foundered when the French government unilaterally announced that it was sending its own forces on a 'humanitarian mission' called Operation Turquoise. The French government offered to place them at the UN's disposal, a move the Security Council endorsed later that month. The French 'humanitarian intervention', however, was a partisan attempt to shore up an ally, and permitted many of those directly involved in the genocide to flee to neighbouring Zaire.[50] The majority settled in camps in eastern Zaire, which were increasingly used as bases for continuing attacks on Rwanda.[51] While the beleaguered UN Secretary-General Boutros Boutros-Ghali publicly welcomed the initiative, Dallaire privately threatened to shoot down the French force's planes.

UNHCR and the other humanitarian agencies were soon criticized for 'feeding killers' in the camps in Zaire while ignoring the survivors of genocide inside Rwanda.[52] Some international NGOs, such as MSF, IRC and CARE, withdrew from the camps in September 1994, citing their concerns over the misuse of relief. Within one year of the refugees arriving in the Zaire city of Goma, bordering Rwanda, the number of relief agencies had dropped from 150 to five.[53] The continued existence of these camps, both inside and outside Rwanda, became an acute source of embarrassment to the international community. UNHCR supported publicity campaigns in the camps encouraging the inhabitants to return home voluntarily – despite credible evidence of revenge killings inside Rwanda.[54] One aid worker has claimed that the camp authorities reduced food rations and refused to treat any new cases of TB or AIDS in order to pressurize people to return.[55] Ultimately many of the camps were forcibly closed by the Rwandan army; in one such operation, around 2,000 internally displaced civilians were massacred.[56] Thousands more were arbitrarily arrested or 'disappeared', and many are believed to have been killed.[57] UNHCR's director of planning, policy and operations, Sergio Vieira de Mello, failed to condemn the operation, though, as Ian Martin (a former secretary-general of Amnesty International now serving with OHCHR) stated, the principles of *non-refoulement* and refugee law were 'abused and brushed aside to a degree never seen before'.[58]

The Rwandan government held one of the non-permanent seats on the UN Security Council in 1994, and so participated in all the debates before, during and after the genocide. The RPF's seizure of power during the course of this year obviously brought a dramatic change in the perspective it was to adopt at the Security Council, though, ironically, the new government remained opposed to external intervention; it also voted against the establishment of an international criminal tribunal to try those accused of carrying out the genocide. RPF troops were soon facing accusations that they had committed war crimes and crimes against humanity, within the country itself and in neighbouring Zaire (soon to become the Democratic Republic of the Congo).

The horrors of Rwanda and the conflict in the Balkans (discussed in the next chapter) had a huge impact on the humanitarian interventions debate during the 1990s, with many observers blaming the UN for its failure to act firmly enough. However, that failure needs to be set in the context of what had happened in Somalia, and, in some ways, the failure of this intervention was more significant. The Somali mission had been authorized by the UN, was properly funded and had a sufficiently robust mandate, yet it ended in ignominy and its failure directly contributed to the disasters that followed elsewhere.

Some of the participants in the UN mission in Somalia believe it should have been more forceful, while others think it strayed too far from its humanitarian mandate.[59] A US military spokes-man summed up what many in the international community thought had gone wrong: 'We fed them, they got strong, they killed us.'[60] A review ordered by the incoming US president, Bill Clinton, concluded that the 'Somalia syndrome' meant western public opinion would not tolerate the deaths of any of their soldiers engaged in humanitarian work. Many US critics blamed 'UN incompetence' for its failure and this became a standard excuse for the US government's lacklustre support for future missions. The US ambassador to Sierra Leone, John Hirsch, says that the US effectively withdrew from UN peacekeeping opera-tions in Africa as a result.[61] Spyros Economides and Paul Taylor have noted, in *United Nations Interventionism*, that it also led to a wild oscillation in Clinton's foreign policy during the conflict in Bosnia-Herzegovina. The US often seemed prepared to 'fight to the last Fijian' UN peacekeeper to oppose any settlement that legitimated ethnic cleansing in the former Yugoslavia, but it refused to countenance deploying its own ground troops in the region to stop it.[62] For the rest of the 1990s the US government refused to provide adequate support for UN missions to prove effective, and then used their resulting failures as retrospective endorsement of this policy.

Most observers agree that the key turning point in Somalia was not the shift from US to UN command of the mission in May 1993, but the response to Aidid's attack on the Pakistani soldiers the following month. The subsequent decision to take a harder line against Aidid was unanimously backed by all members of the UN Security Council, including the US government, and most of the leading personnel responsible for implementing this policy were closely linked to the US administration. Clearly the human rights violations committed by UN soldiers were a major factor in alienating ordinary Somalis, and Human Rights Watch published a report urging that future UN missions should have an explicit human rights component. This was generally accepted and one of the first acts of the new UN High Commissioner for Human

Rights was to despatch OHCHR observers to Rwanda in May 1994. The Human Rights Watch report also warned against future attempts to tackle humanitarian problems through military means, but failed to spell out what this might mean in practice.[63]

The decision to intervene in Somalia was the direct result of a campaign by a number of humanitarian organizations and, despite its debacle, they continued to argue in favour of similar interventions elsewhere. Some, such as Weiss and Collins, argue that the main failure was that the intervention came too late – as if the same strategy would have been more successful had it been implemented twelve months earlier. Others continue to use Somalia as an example of how the indiscriminate delivery of aid can increase human suffering by 'feeding the war economy'.

An alternative view would be to say that giving out food in a famine is a sensible course of action. Famines usually occur because an excess of demand over supply causes prices to rise, while incomes often simultaneously fall. Most people die not because of a lack of food but because they cannot afford to buy what little is available.[64] Of course, in an ideal world food should be delivered where it is most needed, but Somalia was not ideal in any sense. The ICRC approach of flooding in as much as possible, even if it meant paying off the various militias, was probably the most suitable for the conditions since it was better to distribute food indiscriminately than not at all. Another alternative, proposed by Andrew Natsios, a senior USAID official, was to sell the food at cut-prices to local merchants and allow market mechanisms to help with the distributions. This would also have increased supply, and so lowered prices, and he felt that the merchants would be more effective in delivering food to places the humanitarian agencies could not reach. However, when he presented this to a meeting of donors and UN officials he was met with disbelief:

The notion that humanitarian organisations would sell food in a famine mystified some and appalled others . . . The UN field staff of the World Food Programme and the UN Development Programme initially resisted the concept: they opposed the scheme because they thought it was abusive to sell food to starving people (which, of course, was not what the plan proposed to do) and they were uncomfortable with the practical mechanisms for carrying it out. Because of these misgivings they slowed the implementation in its formative months.[65]

Such schemes would also have been difficult to justify to a sceptical western public that has become increasingly used to hearing media reports of the waste and inefficiency of humanitarian relief. It also cuts against a number of prejudices about humanitarianism, such as the idea that food should only be given to the 'deserving' and that benevolent centralized agencies are better at allocating scarce resources than leaving the task to market mechanisms. Instead, the World Food Programme left its supply in Mogadishu's warehouses for months because it could not figure out how to distribute it, while UNDP failed to spend any of the $68 million it budgeted for Somalia because it could not get a signature from the appropriate minister in the country's non-existent government.[66] Of the $1.6 billion spent on Operation Restore Hope in 1993, it is estimated that only 4 per cent reached the people of Somalia and this mostly fell into the hands of the warlords, whose operations the UN ended up subsidizing to a far greater degree than the ICRC had ever done.[67]

Perhaps the main lesson of Somalia is that humanitarians should have argued more forcibly against the militarization of the mission. Mohamed Sahnoun was forced out of office largely because he took this position, but he received little support from the other main humanitarian organizations. He has stated that while some military force might have been justified, it should have been much more limited and 'capable of being absorbed by the local environment'. The huge US-led force deployed in

Somalia was intended to overawe the militias, but it ended up taking over the logic of the whole mission. In calling for the military intervention, and then relying on it for their security, the humanitarian agencies lost any possibility of maintaining their neutrality or building links with Somali civil society.

Sahnoun also urged humanitarian organizations to 'achieve enough solidarity amongst themselves so that they are able to resist the imposition – for instance, by the deployment of security assets – of political-military priorities in the deployment of humanitarian goods and services'.[68] This sound advice was basically ignored by humanitarian agencies as they increasingly allied themselves to the cause of western intervention, both through their advocacy and operational activities over the next decade.

Chapter Three

Kosovo

ON MONDAY, 22 April 1996, a group of Serbs in the western Kosovan town of Dečani was gathered in a local restaurant when masked gunmen with semi-automatic weapons burst in and opened fire indiscriminately, killing three people and wounding others.[1] They threw a grenade into the building as they fled. About half an hour later two Serbian policemen were shot and wounded when they tried to check the identification papers of a group of armed men in the town of Peć. The same evening, another policeman was killed near the Kosovan capital Priština, while gunmen ambushed another police car, wounding the officer inside and killing his female prisoner.

These attacks were the first co-ordinated actions of the Kosovo Liberation Army (KLA), a previously unknown guerrilla group, which faxed to the world's media claims of responsibility from the Albanian capital of Tirana. The killings were denounced by the mainstream Democratic League of Kosovo (LDK), which foreswore violence and whose leader, Ibrahim Rugova, initially blamed on Serbian agents provocateurs. However, the subsequent heavy-handed actions of the Serbian security forces boosted the KLA's credibility and its attacks continued. By January 1998 it had managed to ignite a low-level insurgency with a dozen or so killed on both sides. Their stronghold, the mountainous Drenica region of western Kosovo, was becoming a no-go area for the Serbian security forces.

Weapons started to flow across the border from Albania following the collapse of the country's government in 1997, and the KLA's ambition of winning independence from Yugoslavia — now comprising effectively Serbia, Montenegro and Kosovo — for the Serbian province of Kosovo through military action began to seem less far-fetched.

In February 1998, Yugoslav security forces launched a major counter-insurgency operation in Drenica, killing twenty-six people. In March they attacked the home of the regional KLA commander Adem Jashari, killing fifty-eight members of his extended family. This proved the spark for a major uprising and the KLA activated its network of 'sleeping' members. Other Kosovan Albanians went to the mountains to join up and the KLA soon declared much of western Kosovo 'liberated territory'. The security forces abandoned their positions without much of a fight but counter-attacked in July 1998 with a large-scale 'scorched earth' operation in Drenica, burning villages and displacing up to 200,000 people from their homes. In Orahovac, fifty-five Serbs were reported kidnapped and murdered by the KLA when they captured the town, while anywhere between fifty-eight and 200 Albanians were killed when the Serbs retook it.[2]

This offensive did little damage to the KLA who simply withdrew their forces, but it was a propaganda disaster for the Serbs. Human rights organizations condemned the attacks and the international media portrayed it as a repeat of the 'ethnic cleansing' that had marked the wars in Bosnia-Herzegovina and Croatia. International observers arrived to monitor the situation that autumn, and by the spring of 1999 NATO launched a military action against Serbia. This action, which was not approved by the UN Security Council, was justified by its supporters as a humanitarian intervention, but its more immediate impact was to cause a dramatic increase in the conflict.

There is a common dictum about the Balkan wars that 'it all started with Kosovo and it will end with Kosovo.' The roots of the crisis that broke Yugoslavia apart can be found in the political changes that swept the old Soviet Union and Eastern Europe at the end of the 1980s, but they were also due to various specifically local factors. On 24 April 1987, Slobodan Milošević, then a Serbian Communist Party leader, travelled from Belgrade to Kosovo Polje to listen to the complaints of the Serbian community who said they faced discrimination and intimidation from the Albanian majority in the province. Outside the meeting hall scuffles broke out between the crowd and the police, who used their batons against the protesters. Milošević came out to remonstrate with the police. 'No one should dare to beat you,' he told the crowd, in front of the television cameras, before launching into a speech about the historical significance of Kosovo to the Serbian nation.[3]

This event was to propel Milošević from obscurity to national and then international prominence as he used his new-found role as the saviour of the Kosovo Serbs to wrest control of the Serbian League of Communists and then the Yugoslavian state. Kosovo's autonomy was abolished two years later and its parliament suspended. In 1989, Milošević addressed a victory rally at the site of the historic battle of Kosovo Polje, where Serbian forces had suffered a 'glorious defeat' at the hands of the Ottoman Empire six hundred years before.

The move also changed the political arithmetic within the federal structure of Yugoslavia's collective presidency, which after the death of its former dictator Josip Tito had been carefully devised to ensure no single republic could dominate decision-making at federal level. Its six republics had one vote each, as did Kosovo and Vojvodina, provinces within Serbia. Although Serbs were the largest ethnic group within Yugoslavia as a whole, the borders of the six republics were drawn to include substantial Serbian minorities in Croatia and Bosnia-Herzegovina.

By abolishing the autonomy of Kosovo and Vojvodina, Milošević gained two extra votes within the collective presidency, which, once he also secured that of Montenegro, gave him four out of the eight, enough to play the other republics off against each another. Slovenia and Croatia, Yugoslavia's two richest republics, became increasingly critical of the federation's financial arrangements, which meant that they were subsidizing its poorer regions. Along with Bosnia-Herzegovina, these countries had elected anti-communist governments, and all three began to move towards secession from what they dubbed 'Serbo-slavia'.

The parliaments of Slovenia and Croatia voted for independence in June 1991. Macedonia declared independence in January 1992, followed in April by Bosnia-Herzegovina. The Yugoslav army made a half-hearted attempt to prevent Slovenian secession, but it was first Croatia and then Bosnia-Herzegovina that descended into civil war. The Yugoslav military intervened directly in both places, and then provided covert support to the paramilitary forces of ethnic Croatian Serbs based in Krajina and Bosnian Serbs in Banja Luka. The Bosnian conflict became the bloodiest war fought in Europe for fifty years.

The authority of Bosnia's president, Alija Izetbegović, a Muslim with Islamic nationalist sympathies, was hampered from the outset by the fact that Muslims only made up about 40 per cent of Bosnia-Herzegovina's population, and that he had no effective military force to counter the insurrection of his well-armed opponents. Between 1992 and 1995, Bosnian Muslims were driven out of large areas of the country by Serbian and, to a lesser extent, Croatian paramilitaries. The term 'ethnic cleansing' was soon used to describe the mass burning of houses, rape, torture, transportation, threats and murder by which Bosnian Muslim civilians were terrorized from their homes. The siege of Sarajevo – and other Bosnian cities in which people sought refuge – also horrified international public opinion.

The UN imposed an arms embargo on the whole of the former Yugoslavia during the conflict in Croatia, which made it even more difficult for the Bosnian government to defend itself. International peacekeeping soldiers were deployed to guard aid convoys, but their mandate effectively prevented them from doing anything to stop the killing. A number of Bosnian cities were declared 'safe areas' for the Muslim population, but it did not prevent Srebrenica being overrun by Bosnian Serb forces in the summer of 1995 and the ensuing massacre of up to 7,000 captured men and boys.

The image of the 'well-fed dead' of Srebrenica had an important impact on the subsequent strategic thinking of those involved in humanitarian work. Many aid agencies were involved in supplying the 'safe areas' during the conflict and, by encouraging civilians to stay in areas where they could not be protected, some believe they contributed to the scale of the slaughter.[4] The UN itself has since recognized its own failure to respond more assertively to Serbian aggression.[5] The journalist Misha Glenny described the UN force in Bosnia-Herzegovina as 'outgunned, demoralised, and subject to the most inflexible bureaucracy in military history, this force became a convenient scapegoat for everybody.' He concludes that responsibility for this lay with the five permanent members of the UN Security Council who denied the force sufficient support and constricted it with an imprecise mandate that was impossible to implement.[6] Francis Briquemont, the former commander of the UN forces, complained publicly about the 'fantastic gap between the resolutions of the UN Security Council, the will to execute these resolutions and the means available to commanders in the field'.[7]

But even without the failures of leadership it displayed, the UN faced a virtually impossible task. Bosnia's ethnic diversity meant that the conflict was mainly fought through small-arms encounters between neighbouring communities. The battle lines were spread out along small pockets of conflict, hence an intervening force could never have physically positioned itself between the two sides. All the peace plans put forward proposed some form of internal administrative division of the country, in which local 'cantons' or 'entities' would have substantial autonomy, so, for the most part, there was no clear line of territory the UN forces could defend.

In August 1992, the UN Security Council adopted resolution 770 under its Chapter VII powers threatening to use 'all measures necessary' to protect humanitarian aid convoys. The wording deliberately echoed that of the resolution which sanctioned the use of force against Iraq following its invasion of Kuwait in 1990. However, the members of the council had no intention of implementing this resolution by force; rather, they were hoping that the threat itself would be a sufficient deterrent. The following August it adopted Resolution 836, extending its mandate to 'deter attacks against the safe areas', an extremely vague formulation that clearly stopped short of an instruction to defend these areas should the deterrence fail.

One of the strongest denunciations of the UN's role in the Bosnian war was written by Adam LeBor who, in *Complicity with Evil*, cites it as evidence of the UN's 'repeated failure to confront genocide'. This is over-simplistic on a number of levels. He refers, for example, to the decision of the UN field mission not to disarm the Bosnian fighters with the safe havens as 'one small victory', but fails to make the obvious connection between the fury with which the victorious Serbs eventually fell upon its population and the subsequent indictment of its Bosniak commander for war crimes.[8] The Bosnian Government was a party to the conflict and, although its armed forces were initially much weaker than its opponents, they were not merely passive victims. By failing to mention the atrocities these forces committed, LeBor presents not only a distorted picture of the conflict itself but a flawed analysis of the dilemmas facing those involved in the humanitarian operation.

The UN mission was humanitarian, and this dictated its fundamental character. It gradually became more militarized as the conflict wore on, and by early 1994 UN commanders were increasingly prepared to use air strikes against the Serb forces. Each 'military victory' of the Serbian forces further outraged international public opinion, while the defeats suffered by the Bosnian government strengthened calls for more forcible intervention. The UN's response remained confused and reactive, and this lack of consistency brought the worst of both worlds.

The policy of designating strategically significant areas of territory as 'neutral and free of belligerent activity', for instance, was fundamentally flawed because the UN did not have the will or means to accomplish it. As Karin Landgren, UNHCR's former chief of mission in Bosnia-Herzegovina, has noted, the safe areas were created partly to keep would-be refugees within the borders of the former Yugoslavia and partly as a 'principled' way of preventing the UN from being used as an agent of ethnic cleansing. However, by failing to demilitarize these areas, the UN sealed the fate of their inhabitants. 'The "safe areas" provided a degree of sanctuary from the slaughter,' she says. 'They also provided relief, recuperation and other forms of bases for the military; potential bargaining chips for later negotiations on territory; and effective and continuing symbols of oppression in a war which counts CNN among its fronts.'[9]

Indeed, while Yasushi Akashi, head of the UN mission in Bosnia, and the Dutch UN peacekeepers stationed at Srebrenica have rightly been excoriated for their passivity during this massacre, the Bosnian Government also emerges with little credit. It evacuated all its top commanders out of the town before it was overrun and then ordered the remainder of the garrison to mount diversionary attacks to help lift the siege of Sarajevo. Its army then failed to advance to save the town, or even try and link up with a column of soldiers and civilians fleeing from the slaughter.[10]

The Bosniak army, which was initially forced to recruit from criminal gangs and radical Islamic groups, finally became a more effective fighting force by the start of 1995, and that summer drove the Serbs back across the country. A number of human rights and humanitarian organizations, including World Vision and Human Rights Watch, set aside their traditional reservations regarding the use of military force and called on western governments to mount air strikes against Serbian forces besieging the remaining Muslim enclaves.[11] NATO did indeed carry out a few air strikes that helped the Bosnian advance, but were probably not militarily decisive.

The Croatian Government, in an on-off alliance with the Bosnians throughout the war, also used the aftermath of Srebrenica as political cover for its Operation Storm, which retook Krajina causing 100,000 Serbs to flee from their homes. Under pressure from the international community, in November 1995 the Bosnians agreed to a peace deal at Dayton which recognized Bosnia-Herzegovina as a single entity but divided it administratively into a Bosniak-Croat federation on the one hand and Republika Srpska on the other. A high proconsul with executive powers was appointed to administer the new entity.

However, the Dayton agreement failed to address the situation in Kosovo. This proved a huge blow to Ibrahim Rugova and his LDK, which had hoped a campaign of passive resistance, begun in 1989, would shame international opinion into putting pressure on Milošević. The LDK's boycotts were met with the wholesale dismissal of Albanian police, teachers, doctors and other civil servants. Protests were forcibly suppressed and thousands arrested and tortured. Albanian language newspapers were banned and teaching children in Albanian was effectively prohibited. By the end of the 1990s, the KLA was becoming the focus of the resistance which led to the offensives and counter-offensives over the spring and summer of 1998.

The upsurge in fighting came three years after the end of the Bosnian conflict, and some in the west saw it as a basic extension of the same war. As the full extent of the horror of Srebrenica's genocide became known, many condemned the previous attempts to resolve this conflict through diplomacy as a latter-day form of appeasement. There was a growing determination that 'never again' should the Serbs be allowed to get away with such atrocities. On 23 September 1998, the UN Security Council adopted Resolution 1199 calling for an immediate ceasefire in Kosovo, an international presence to monitor it, the withdrawal of 'security units used for civilian repression' and dialogue on the future of the province.[12] The Resolution was adopted under Chapter VII of the UN Charter, which permits the use of force, although both Russia and China indicated they were opposed to military intervention. Eventually a deal was worked out in October 1998 in which the Serb forces pulled back and the Organization for Security and Co-operation in Europe (OSCE) deployed a team of international observers to gather evidence on what was happening in the province.

A few days later the mutilated corpses of a family were discovered outside the village of Gornje Obrinje. They were presumed murdered by Serbian paramilitaries and the discovery caused an international outrage, increasing the pressure for military action by NATO. The arrival of OSCE's international observers postponed this, but in January 1999 the head of this delegation, Ambassador William Walker, was ordered out of the country after publicly accusing the authorities of responsibility for the murder of forty-five Albanian civilians in the central Kosovo village of Račak.

Milošević was eventually indicted by the International Criminal Tribunal for the Former Yugoslavia (ICTY) for his role in the Račak killings, which the tribunal classified as a war crime. It was the bloodiest single incident before the start of NATO's intervention and followed a string of KLA attacks in the area. ICTY's chief prosecutor, Carla Del Ponte, attempted to enter Kosovo to investigate the killings two days later but was refused access by the Yugoslav authorities. Many Serbs still maintain that Račak was a legitimate police action and that most of the dead were KLA fighters. There was also dissatisfaction within the OSCE team over how quickly and definitively Walker had declared that all those killed were civilians. The OSCE's mission is widely believed to have gone beyond a simple monitoring of human rights issues since it also included 'reporting on troop movements and more generally providing intelligence information'.[13] A number of its former members later told me they thought some of their colleagues had links to the CIA.

After the arrival of the OSCE monitors, the KLA moved its forces back into the areas the security forces had left and continued to terrorize the local Serbian population. Serbian paramilitaries responded with their own brutalities and the Serbian police and army were also accused of perpetrating massacres throughout the autumn and winter. With all sides talking about a 'spring offensive', the countdown to western military intervention had begun.

In February 1999, a last attempt was made to find a diplomatic solution to the crisis at a conference at Rambouillet, where delegates were presented with a plan that would involve disarming the KLA, withdrawing most Yugoslav security forces and in their place deploying a 30,000-strong NATO force in the province. Kosovo would have its autonomy restored for a three-year interim period, after which 'final status' negotiations would be held to determine its future. Various mechanisms would also be put in place to safeguard the rights of its non-Albanian ethnic minorities. The Kosovan Albanian delegation eventually agreed, in principle, to sign a document based on these proposals, but the Serbs refused.

Critics of the deal have pointed out that it contained an annexe that would have given NATO peacekeeping forces 'free and unrestricted access' throughout the whole of Serbia's territory, something which would never have been acceptable to the Serbian Government. Its chapter on the future of Kosovo's economy also called for the privatization of state-owned assets, which some cite as evidence that there was a hidden political agenda behind the professed humanitarian concern of the international community.[14] In fact, the first is a fairly standard provision in UN peacekeeping agreements, while the second was due to the fact that Yugoslavia's former states were going through a privatization process at the time, and it was necessary to specify how assets previously owned by the state would be dealt with by its successor. A better criticism of Rambouillet is that none of the participants seemed to approach it as a serious attempt to resolve the crisis through diplomatic means, viewing it instead as a piece of political theatre.

All OSCE international staff withdrew from the province after the failure of the talks and NATO's bombing campaign started on 24 March 1999. The US and UK were the strongest supporters of military intervention and they initially hoped that a few days of 'surgical strikes' would be sufficient to force Milošević to back down. Instead the crisis escalated massively and the Serbs began a policy of systematically burning down villages, executing suspected KLA members and deporting civilians. An estimated 800,000 Kosovar Albanians were driven from their homes in the space of a few weeks after the bombing campaign started. NATO decided not to send ground troops into Kosovo to try and halt the killing and instead relied on an aerial campaign of attrition to weaken the Serb forces. Although western public opinion demanded military action, western governments were not convinced that they would tolerate military casualties among their own forces. US General Wesley Clarke, NATO's supreme allied commander in Europe, stated the first objective of the campaign in Kosovo was the 'avoidance of Allied losses' to enable the air war to 'persist as long it was needed'.[15] NATO gradually widened its list of targets to include civilian infrastructure, such as electricity power plants, as well as government buildings and a television station.

Finally, on 10 June, Yugoslav security forces started to withdraw from the province in accordance with provisions laid out in UN Security Council Resolution 1244, which was adopted on the same day. This included a plan for Kosovo's administration similar to that proposed at Rambouillet: military withdrawal of Yugoslav security forces, disarmament of the KLA and the deployment of a 50,000-strong international peacekeeping force.

Kosovo legally remained part of Serbia, but was to be adminis-
tered by a UN mission. The mission's acting head was initially
Sergio Vieira de Mello, soon to be replaced by Bernard Kouchner, who stayed for over a year. The mission, the largest ever of
its kind, was assembled through a combination of various UN
agencies and directly recruited staff.

I was working as a mid-level manager at Amnesty International UK during the Kosovo war and received a phone call that
May from the Council of Europe asking if I could go to the
region at very short notice to run training courses on international human rights law. There were media reports that up to
100,000 Kosovar Albanians were missing and presumed dead. It
seemed likely that ICTY would soon issue more indictments for
war crimes and investigators would need help from Kosovan civil
society activists in gathering evidence. Milošević was in fact
indicted at the end of May. I pleaded with my boss, who
reluctantly granted me emergency leave, and caught the first
plane to Tirana. I spent two weeks in Albania and Macedonia
and returned for a week, in August 1999, to Kosovo itself. I made
another trip in October that year, and was then appointed to a
seconded post in UNHCR the following September.

From my first direct contact with refugees in Albania and
Macedonia during the war I saw the conflict through the eyes of
Kosovo's Albanian majority. One woman I spoke to saw her
neighbour's son beheaded by Serbian paramilitaries. Others lost
family members who were either dead or among the missing. No
one really knew what was going on in the country at the time of
my first visit and, after Srebrenica, it seemed reasonable to fear
the worst. However, even at that point it was clear there were
important differences between Kosovo and Bosnia-Herzegovina,
which meant that any external intervention would have a crucial
difference on the eventual resolution of the conflict.

The two main points at issue during the wars in the former
Yugoslavia concerned self-determination and minority rights. A
people have a right to self-determination under international

law, but this right includes respect for the territorial integrity of their state. Minorities are not permitted to threaten this territorial integrity through secession, hence there is an obvious conflict between the two principles. The federal states of Yugoslavia had been created with administrative borders, and Croatia and Bosnia-Herzegovina contained significant Serbian populations who argued that they had as much of a right to self-determination as the majorities within the republics who wished to secede. Milošević backed these demands but in Kosovo he applied the opposite logic. Although the Kosovar Albanians constituted around 90 per cent of the population within the province, Kosovo was legally part of Serbia, who in turn treated the Albanian population as an ethnic minority.

The implications of allowing Kosovo to secede also worried many western diplomats because of the destabilizing impact it might have elsewhere in the region. If Kosovo's Albanians were allowed to secede then surely the Serbs in Croatia and Bosnia had an equal right to do so. There were also sizeable Albanian minorities in neighbouring Macedonia and Greece, as well as in southern Serbia and parts of Montenegro. During the war, I remember being rather taken aback when my Albanian driver explained why Corfu should be included in a new Greater Albanian State.

Two UN resolutions were passed in the autumn of 1998 condemning acts of violence by both parties and demanding that the Serb forces halt aggressive military action in Kosovo, but they did not authorize NATO's subsequent intervention. Russia indicated it would veto a Chapter VII resolution endorsing it, hence none was ever tabled to this effect.

The Serbian Government argued that this meant the intervention was illegal and sought to bring a case against the individual members of NATO before the ICJ, which dismissed the suit on the procedural grounds that Yugoslavia was not at the time a member of the UN and so was not a party to the Court's statute. The ICJ also rejected the argument that a case could be brought under Article 9 of the Genocide Convention, which Serbia had ratified and which allows parties to submit disputes relating to this to the Court.[16] Serbia only invoked the Genocide Convention in order to gain jurisdiction for its case, but some supporters of the doctrine of humanitarian intervention have argued that this could provide a legal basis for military action where the UN Security Council fails to act.

A Russian resolution condemning the action, cosponsored by India and Belarus, was voted down at the Security Council on 26 March 1999. The British Government also justified the intervention by citing the 'doctrine of humanitarian intervention', which is discussed in more detail in chapter six.

No one can put a precise figure on the number of victims in the Kosovo war, although everyone agrees that the vast majority of the deaths came after the start of NATO's bombardment. The previous autumn, the best estimate Amnesty could make was that 'several hundred ethnic Albanians and a smaller number of Serbs have been reported as killed since the conflict began in February 1998 between police and armed ethnic Albanians.'[17] NATO claims that before the bombing started, in March 1999, over 1,500 Kosovans were killed. The Serbs put the figure much lower. In her biography of Sergio Vieira de Mello, *Chasing the Flame*, Samantha Power claims that 3,000 Kosovar Albanians were killed before the start of NATO's intervention, though this is implausibly high.[18] Assuming both the Amnesty and NATO figures are broadly credible means that a significant number of the killings took place between September 1998 and the end of March 1999. Anecdotal testimony suggests that the spike in the death rate occurred in February and March, after the departure of the OSCE mission and by the time war seemed inevitable.

Two years after the war ended Human Rights Watch documented a total of 3,453 killings by Serbian or Yugoslav government forces, while the International Criminal Tribunal for the former Yugoslavia (ICTY) exhumed approximately 4,300 bodies. Kosovo is a fairly small place and it is unlikely that there are that many more corpses undiscovered: many researchers put total deaths at around 5,000 Kosovans killed by Serbian forces plus a further 500 civilians killed by NATO's bombardment. Other estimates, such as the Brookings Institute's, claim the figure is twice as high at around 10,000.[19] As in all conflicts, the numbers are disputed but clearly much lower than the predictions made at the time. The day before the bombing campaign started, President Clinton likened Kosovo to the Holocaust,[20] while US Defense Secretary William Cohen claimed that during the conflict 'up to 100,000 ethnic Albanian men in Kosovo of fighting age have vanished and may have been killed.'[21] Both these predictions turned out to be very far off the mark.

During 1998, Yugoslav and Serb forces conducted a counter-insurgency campaign of extreme brutality. This certainly killed hundreds and displaced tens of thousands, and was rightly condemned on human rights grounds. But could such coun-ter-insurgency operations really be described as genocide? Since the immediate impact of NATO's military intervention was to increase the suffering of civilians, the humanitarian justification for the action remains controversial. Most of the civilians who died during the war were killed by Serb forces, but NATO was also responsible for a number of fatalities. On 12 April, for example, NATO struck a passenger train just south of Belgrade, killing thirty civilians. Two days later it hit a convoy of refugees killing sixty-four. On 23 April, NATO deliberately bombed a Serbian television station killing ten. On 10 May a cluster bomb went astray and hit a hospital and market killing fifteen. A mistaken missile strike on the Chinese Embassy the same day killed three.[22] Most of these were mistakes for which NATO apologized, but clearly such incidents pose questions about the circumstances in which it is justifiable to use force on humani-tarian grounds.

Independence for Kosovo was never a 'war aim' on NATO's part; indeed most European leaders viewed with undisguised horror the spur this might give to a Greater Albania project.

There was also considerable unease at NATO's forming an effective military alliance with the KLA. Many regarded it as a terrorist organization, known to finance itself through drug trafficking, and drawing part of its political inspiration from the late ultra-Stalinist Albanian dictator Enver Hoxha. Yet as the campaign progressed it became clear NATO was effectively acting as the KLA's air force, while the guerrillas functioned as 'proxy troops' on the ground, drawing out the Serb forces so they could be bombed from the air.

The Security Council subsequently endorsed Resolution 1244, which laid the basis for the UN administration of the province. This resolution attempted to preserve the international consensus on the province's future by insisting on treating Kosovo as a humanitarian rather than a political issue. It condemned 'all acts of violence against the Kosovo population as well as all terrorist acts by any party', and reaffirmed 'the sovereignty and territorial integrity of the Federal Republic of Yugoslavia'. It called for the demilitarization of the KLA and established 'an interim administration for Kosovo under which the people of Kosovo can enjoy substantial autonomy within the Federal Republic of Yugoslavia'. It also provided 'for the safe and free return of all refugees and displaced persons to their homes', and called on the international community to promote Kosovan self-government pending an ultimate decision on its final constitutional status.[23] This wording may have been a feat of international diplomacy but it created what was in practice a completely unworkable and contradictory strategy.

Arriving in Priština in August 1999, I found a city celebrating its liberation. NATO's laser-guided missiles had been remarkably precise and, while a number of strategic buildings around the city were reduced to rubble, there was little of the collateral damage I have come across in other war zones. There was obviously considerable looting, and I passed thousands of burned-out houses on my journey through the countryside. Without knowing the province's intimate ethnic geography, it was difficult to tell whether the destruction was caused by Serb or Albanian forces or, as I later found out, a mixture of the two.

The majority of Serbian civilians had already fled with the retreating Yugoslav forces, and those that remained were gradually hunted down by Albanian extremists. On my second visit, two months later, a newly arrived international aid worker was lynched when he stepped outside our hotel. Valentin Krumov, a 38-year-old Bulgarian, arrived in the province on the same day as me to join the UN mission. Walking down Priština's main street with two colleagues, he attracted the suspicion of a group of Albanians who decided he looked Serbian. One asked him the time in Serbo-Croat and he glanced at his watch before replying. He was beaten up and then shot in the head, while his two colleagues escaped with injuries. Krumov might in fact be counted as the only US casualty of the Kosovo conflict,[24] since he had settled in America after studying for his doctorate.

By the time I returned in the autumn of 2000, Kosovo was a mono-ethnic province. Estimates of the number of Kosovan Serbs who fled their homes after the war vary between 100,000 and a quarter of a million. The only Serbs still there were living in enclaves under 24-hour protection from NATO troops. The KLA had also targeted Roma, who they accused of collaborating with the Serbs. In the northern town of Mitrovica the entire Roma quarter had been burned to the ground and was still a ghostly ruin a year later.

I was based in UNHCR's Protection Unit, a term that comes from the organization's mandate to provide refugees with the 'protection' their own government no longer offers them. UNHCR is also mandated to co-ordinate international action to protect refugees and resolve refugee problems. This led to it developing a large field presence both in places where refugees have fled to and the areas they are fleeing from, and to which they may return. My main role was a sort of political outreach officer with the NGOs delivering UNHCR's assistance – often a challenging task given the controversial political circumstances in which we were trying to work. The organization was criticized at the start of the crisis for its failure to respond quickly enough to the massive outflux of refugees. It was then criticized again as the refugees returned home far more rapidly than anyone had expected. UNHCR was originally designated as the first pillar of the UN mission in Kosovo (UNMIK), which effectively became the province's interim government, charged with the reconstruction of houses after the war. By the time I arrived it had taken responsibility as the lead agency protecting Kosovo's minorities and was, theoretically, preparing the ground for their eventual return.

Resolution 1244 provided 'for the safe and free return of all refugees and displaced persons to their homes', but, of course, this was nonsense. A couple of weeks after I got there, four Albanian-speaking Roma returned from exile. Some of their extended family had KLA links and one woman had been raped by Serbian paramilitaries. Nevertheless they were threatened by Albanian extremists, and fled the province in 1999. The four men arrived on their own to 'test the water' for a larger group return. UNHCR staff interviewed them and provided them with a standard 'return package' of food and non-food aid, including a tent. When my colleagues went to visit them the next day all four were dead, murdered execution-style with a bullet to the back of the head.

UNHCR ran a bus service between the different Serb enclaves, which helped people get to the markets and enjoy more social contact. The service travelled under military escort but was still frequently attacked. A few months before I arrived one bus was hit with a rocket-propelled grenade that killed two people. A couple of months later an elderly couple were beaten to death with a shovel in Obilic, the nineteenth such incident in this small municipality. Albanian extremists would often snipe at vehicles travelling in and out of the enclaves, or throw hand grenades into them. Once when I was visiting the area a grenade was thrown into a school playground. The Serbs increasingly took their frustrations out on the international community and several of our offices and vehicles were wrecked during riots. Many international organizations adopted a conscious policy of hiring non-Albanian ethnic minorities, particularly for programmes aimed at Serbs and Roma. During one human rights training seminar I was conducting in a café, a man pulled a gun on a young Serbian woman. Her Albanian colleagues immediately surrounded her for protection. The humanitarian agencies went to ever more elaborate lengths to protect their own staff's safety, but, month by month, more and more left.

It was a strange atmosphere to work in because we were completely surrounded by violence but as international workers were largely insulated from its effects. The sound of bomb blasts or automatic weapon fire became routine and colleagues frequently complained about their windows being blown out during the night or seeing a shooting in the street. 'Death by AK' was a common expression in our morning security briefings. Yet the violence only touched us personally when it affected our national colleagues, some of whom lost friends and relatives during the attacks.

As the autumn of 2000 turned to winter, the failings of our efforts became increasingly apparent. The destruction of homes during the war created a housing crisis exacerbated by a huge influx of international aid workers. Rents shot up, making even modest apartments an extremely valuable asset, thus the issue of property ownership assumed an economic as well as political significance. Most of the homes abandoned by the hundreds of thousands of minorities who had fled at the end of the war were now either occupied by neighbours or seized by other homeless people or KLA fighters. An early decision was taken to remove disputes over property from the jurisdiction of the local court system on the grounds that Albanian judges were likely to be biased against Serbs or too easily intimidated by thugs. UNMIK created a Housing Property Directorate to deal with these cases, but the regulation required to allow it to start processing claims was not signed until more than a year later, and its work was further delayed by organizational problems. A decision was made to verify all claims individually and for the whole process to be overseen by international staff. Since the impartiality of local staff was considered suspect, each statement and document had to be translated. In practice this meant that for several years no one displaced from their home had any effective remedy. Even when the formal legal system began to function properly there were further problems in enforcing court decisions.

Despite its being the most expensive mission of its kind, UNMIK was a disaster, at least in its early years. Some individual UN agencies functioned well, but the overall governance mechanisms proved a hopeless way of making and implementing decisions. UNMIK was thrown together by staff from a wide variety of backgrounds and on various kinds of contracts, often recruited by word of mouth and with extremely variable levels of competence. Young UN volunteers intermingled with retired judges and policemen, seconded civil servants, friends of UN staff from other missions and people who turned up in Kosovo on speculation. It was difficult to make appointments or promotions on the basis of experience, because nothing like this had been done before, hence lop-sided systems were created where managers had little authority.

OSCE was given responsibility for monitoring and oversight and expanded from a temporary small-scale mission to a fully fledged bureaucracy with staff drawn from throughout Europe and North America. Everyone was on six-month renewable contracts, and pay-scales, which varied wildly, were based on people's country of origin rather than their seniority within the organization. This obviously impacted on the quality of the staff recruited and made it impossible to create a proper career structure. With no common culture or work ethic, different departments were soon consumed by internal office politics with little thought for the original mission and minimal effectiveness in achieving anything beyond their immediate environment.

UNMIK's most notorious failure came in its efforts to re-establish the province's electricity supply. Hundreds of millions of dollars were poured into the restoration of the aging power plants in Obilic, but they remained hopelessly erratic. Usually we would get electricity for only a couple of hours a day, but there was not even a rationing system that would have allowed for preplanning. Instead the lights would go out at any time and stay out for anything from five minutes to ten hours. Most international staff in Priština lived in 1970s-style council estates, where it was impossible to rig up generators without deafening our neighbours. This meant we could not cook, watch television or pretty much do anything at all, except trudge around darkened streets and stairwells by torchlight or strain our eyes reading by candlelight. In winter the temperature dropped to minus 40 degrees, which froze everyone's water pipes. Some people were unable to wash for weeks on end, and in the coldest months of the winter we could not take our clothes off at all.

During the decade in which they suffered under the Serbs, Kosovo's Albanian population built their own parallel structures to administer education, health and other social services, staffed by professionals sacked by the official system. This parallel system now became the only effective way of getting anything done in the province. However, as well as being exclusively Albanian, the parallel system was overtly politicized to support the goal of Kosovan independence, against which the UN had officially set its face.

According to UN Resolution 1244, Kosovo was still legally a Serbian province with its final status to be determined at some point in the future. One argument often used against giving it independence was the presence of an ethnic minority population opposed to this goal. The KLA was not a signatory to the peace accords and, though its leaders eventually agreed to a disarmament process, many saw no reason to give up now, with their stated goals still not yet accomplished. A plan was drawn up for 3,000 former KLA fighters to be absorbed into a new Kosovo

Protection Corps, an unarmed civil defence force charged with disaster response, search and rescue and helping with reconstruction. A cross between the Boy Scouts and the St John's Ambulance was how some diplomats must have envisaged it. The Albanian abbreviation of its title was TMK, which soon attracted the nickname 'Tomorrow's Masters of Kosovo'. It adopted a uniform and insignia similar to that of its KLA predecessor, occupied the barracks of the departing Yugoslav armed forces and organized itself on overtly military lines. No one doubted that it would form the basis of Kosovo's new national army.

TMK members were heavily implicated in the campaign of intimidation and violence against Kosovo's remaining ethnic minority population which, according to one Human Rights Watch report, resulted in the death or 'disappearance' of up to 1,000 people in the months after NATO assumed responsibility for security in the province. Former KLA members were also at the forefront of the upsurge in criminality and gangsterism that followed the withdrawal of the old Yugoslav police force. UNMIK took responsibility for training a new police force from scratch, along with new judges to administer the legal system. In practice, however, few dared act against the new mafia now taking control of the province. The corpses of over-conscientious public officials soon started turning up in back alleys, along with Kosovo's ethnic minorities.

In spring 2001, conflicts broke out in neighbouring Macedonia and southern Serbia, with former KLA members joining local Albanians to mount terrorist attacks in support of their separatist demands. I was on leave in the part of Macedonia where the fighting was fiercest and got stuck on the wrong side of the border for several days until we were allowed back into Kosovo. A huge amount of international diplomacy, combined with promises of western aid and other economic incentives, were necessary to prevent the war-weary Serbian and Macedonian authorities from striking back.

The KLA's political wing, the Kosovo Democratic Party, fared badly in the province's first elections in the autumn of 2000. Its leader, Hashim Thaci, was widely regarded as a sinister figure and most Kosovans returned their allegiances to Ibrahim Rugova and his LDK. The KLA responded by hiring a former Labour Party spin-doctor to improve its public image. When we bumped into each another in Priština I remember suggesting that she tell them to 'drop the extortion rackets, fascism and murdering old age pensioners'.

A number of former KLA members were indicted by ICTY, including one of Thaci's rivals, Ramush Haradinaj, who had broken away to form his own political party. He was made prime minister under Rugova, but soon replaced by Agim Çeku, the KLA's former military head. Most Kosovar Albanians I met disapproved of many of the KLA's actions and agreed that the Serbs and other ethnic minorities had a right to return. However, they were united in their support for Kosovan independence and complete rejection of Serb rule. UN inertia over the next few years strengthened the extremists and Thaci was elected prime minister in November 2007. In February 2008, Kosovo declared independence unilaterally, which led to more clashes as Serbs in Mitrovica tried to split away from the province. Had the UN offered Kosovo some form of independence earlier, in return for guaranteed respect for minority rights, it might have provided an incentive for more moderate voices, but the wording of Resolu-tion 1244 precluded this. The international community managed to convince itself that Kosovo was a human rights issue, when it was really a dispute over sovereignty and territory.

NATO intervened to prevent war crimes and ethnic cleansing, but these dramatically increased as a direct result of the interven-tion. The UN pledged to create an administration to provide an effective interim governance of a multi-ethnic province that would uphold human rights and the rule of law, but Kosovo remains a mono-ethnic state, mired in corruption and largely dependent on international subventions. Neither outcome can be remotely regarded as a success. The international community fudged the most vital issue of Kosovo's future sovereignty, since it did not know how to deal with it. Keeping the province in a state of suspended animation resulted in the worst of both options.

The failure of the international community to resolve the conflicts in the Balkans has generated much subsequent debate. Some stress the failure of diplomacy when it could have made a difference before the conflicts erupted. The international community could have tried harder to insist on a comprehensive settlement, addressing both self-determination and respect for minority rights, before recognizing the independence of the new republics in 1991. Kosovo's status could also have been addressed in the Dayton Accord in 1995 and further efforts at diplomacy might have worked at Rambouillet in February 1999. Others focus more narrowly on the military responses once the conflict began, with some blaming the lack of a coherent internationally co-ordinated response, while others argue that too much effort was put into trying achieve an international consensus.

Prior to NATO's intervention, Blair seemed to have had serious doubts about the wisdom of air strikes as a means of resolving the problem. Alistair Campbell, his former head of communications, recalls a discussion among his senior advisers in January 1999, in which 'they agreed we could not bomb at the moment because there was no political process and the KLA were not much better than the Serbs and looking to NATO to bomb Milošević for them . . . TB [Blair] said that everyone accepts that Milošević is a dreadful man, but what is the process that we are trying to bring about? If the KLA move back in and take over, what then?'[25] Campbell, who was subsequently drafted into NATO to help improve its public presentation, recalls the start of the campaign as a catastrophe. His diary entries for 29 March 1999 states: 'The refugee situation was getting worse and there wasn't much sign that the military campaign was getting better,' while the following day he notes that: 'Kosovo was not looking good. The humanitarian crisis was becoming a disaster.'[26]

However, as NATO's campaign continued, Blair began to argue that it presented a model for a new western foreign policy based on what came to be known as 'liberal intervention'. In a speech in Chicago on 24 April 1999, he argued that: 'We have learned twice before in this century that appeasement does not work . . . Just as I believe there was no alternative to military action, now it has started I am convinced there is no alternative to continuing until we succeed.' The rhetoric echoed that of his predecessor but one, Margaret Thatcher, and the conflict coincided with his embrace of the 'Atlanticism' she had also favoured.

Although Blair was elected on a strongly multilateralist platform, he began to move away from seeking to develop a common European foreign policy and support for the UN in favour of the 'special relationship' with the US, praised in the speech as the world's 'strongest state'. His speech specifically bracketed Saddam Hussein and Slobodan Milošević as two of the biggest threats to world peace, and suggested that new rules should be developed for when the 'doctrine of non-interference' should be set aside. He set out five basic considerations in which interventions could be justified: right cause, exhaustion of diplomacy, practical achievability, long-term commitment and national interest. Approval by the UN Security Council was noticeably absent from his list.[27]

After Kosovo, Britain and the US began to co-operate increasingly closely in planning military interventions, marginalizing other members of the UN Security Council in the process. The US basically withdrew from participation in UN peacekeeping missions after the Somali debacle of 1993 and, when the British Government sent troops to Sierra Leone in 2000, it also refused to place them under UN command. A recurring theme of the liberal interventionists since then is the supposed 'weakness' of the UN compared to the 'strength and decisiveness' of British and American forces. This policy survived the election of a strongly unilateralist US president, George Bush, in 2000, and seemed to have been based on a calculation that the military might of the two countries could decisively reshape international relations. Blair returned to the same theme in the aftermath of the 9/11 attacks in his speech to the Labour Party conference in October 2001:

> When Milošević embarked on the ethnic cleansing of Muslims in Kosovo, we acted. The sceptics said it was pointless, we'd make matters worse, we'd make Milošević stronger. And look what happened: we won, the refugees went home, the policies of ethnic cleansing were reversed and one of the great dictators of the last century will see justice in this century. And if Rwanda happened again today, as it did in 1993 [sic], when a million people were slaughtered in cold blood, we would have a moral duty to act there also . . . The starving, the wretched, the dispossessed, the ignorant, those living in want and squalor from the deserts of northern Africa, to the slums of Gaza, to the mountain ranges of Afghanistan: they too are our cause.[28]

Chapter Four

Afghanistan

I WAS IN Kosovo on 11 September 2001, the 'turning point in history' to which Blair referred in his Labour Party conference speech. Some of my colleagues from UNHCR were dispatched to Afghanistan almost immediately in anticipation of the refugee crisis that was to come. I returned to Britain instead to study for a Masters degree in law, and met my future wife, Glaucia, a Brazilian judge. We spent a few months in Brazil after I graduated, before I started looking for work again. I was offered a job in Iraq with OHCHR in April 2003, but had already accepted a post in Afghanistan.

The first thing I remember was how arid the country looked. Afghanistan mainly consists of mountains and deserts and while its terrain is beautiful it is also extremely harsh, which is one of the reasons the country has been so difficult over the centuries for invaders to subdue. Our small UN plane circled over Kabul airport and then swooped down to land. This was May 2003, before planes had to corkscrew to avoid Taliban missiles, but it was still a bracing descent. I emerged into the chaos of noise, smell and confusion that is Afghan society, and my home for the next fifteen months.

It took me three days to get there from Brazil, but the exhaustion and jet lag were matched by a strange sense of belonging. I had worked with my new boss, Polly Truscott, in Kosovo and then studied with her at the Human Rights

Centre in the University of Essex. She took me to a Thai restaurant on my first night in Kabul and the owner, who has made a successful business out of following UN missions around the world, remembered me from Priština. I spent my first three months based in the northern town of Mazar-i-Sharif where I worked for the International Rescue Committee (IRC) developing a training course in refugee, human rights and humanitarian law for Afghan public officials. I then moved down to Kabul to manage a legal aid project for the Norwegian Refugee Council (NRC). Both programmes were supported by UNHCR's Protection Unit, and its staff were my main counterparts during my time in the country.

The problems facing those engaged in the post-war reconstruction of Afghanistan can be summed up by the dilemma of the US pilots who began returning to base with full payloads on the second day of the air campaign against the Taliban. The destruction of one of the poorest countries in the world over the previous twenty-two years was such that it was difficult to find anything left to bomb. Military commanders regularly complained, 'There's not much point dropping a million-dollar missile on a ten dollar tent.' As Afghanistan's National Development Strategy states:

From Sawr 1357 (April 1978) until the signing of the Bonn Agreement on 14 Qaws 1380 (5 December 2001) [the] conflict killed over a million Afghans, most of them civilians; over a million Afghans were orphaned, maimed or disabled; a third of the population was driven into exile as refugees, and many more were displaced from their homes; the villages where most of the population lived were devastated; and much of the country's educated class was forced into exile. Much agricultural land and pasture had been mined and was therefore unproductive. Fragile systems for managing the country's scarce supplies of water were devastated. Most basic infrastructure was destroyed, including roads, bridges, irrigation systems, and electric power lines, and that which remained was not maintained. Afghans were unable to use many schools and clinics, many of which had degenerated into crumbling structures, unsuitable for their intended purposes. One generation or more lost the chance for education. The printing of worthless money to fund militias sparked hyper-inflation, which reduced the value of salaries to almost nothing. Demoralized government staff received neither genuine salaries, training to meet new challenges, nor the leadership and equipment they needed to do their jobs. Licit agricultural production fell by half.[1]

The western military intervention in Afghanistan began on 7 October 2001, when both the US and its key ally the UK reported to the Security Council that they were taking action under Article 51 of the UN Charter in response to an armed attack by Al-Qaeda on 9/11. NATO evoked similar provisions under its own Charter. Two UN Security Council resolutions adopted immediately after 9/11 drew on the language of both Article 51 and Chapter VII of the UN Charter in framing the international response.[2] President Bush, elected on an 'isola-tionist' platform, consciously re-engaged the US Government with the international system – at least initially – paying off a substantial part of its debts to the UN and seeking to build a broad-based coalition in support of its intervention in Afghani-stan.

Much of the discussion about Afghanistan has been overshadowed by the subsequent invasion of Iraq. However, Afghanistan was neither 'liberated' nor 'conquered' by the west through a conventional invasion. The US-led Operation Enduring Freedom (OEF) mainly consisted of air strikes and the provision of logistical support to the Taliban's Northern Alliance opponents in the country's long-running civil war. According to the journalist Bob Woodward: 'In all, the US commitment to overthrow the Taliban [was] 110 CIA officers and 316 Special Forces personnel, plus massive airpower.'[3] Although air strikes played an important role, it was bribes rather than bombs that broke the back of the Taliban's resistance. US operatives flew in with suitcases full of cash and simply bought the allegiance of many commanders.

One consequence was that as the Taliban fled they left a power vacuum that was soon filled by local warlords. They were the mujahedin forces who had fought the Soviet Union after its invasion in 1979 and then fought among themselves when the Russians left ten years later. Afghanistan's civil war did far more damage to the country than the original invasion and made the mujahedin deeply unpopular, particularly among the educated middle class. The Taliban were initially welcomed in some areas because their tough policies at least restored basic security.

Afghanistan is a multi-ethnic state in which no single group forms a clear majority, although Pashtuns are the largest of these minorities and were the traditional rulers in Afghan society. A key part of the Taliban's ideology was based on a Pashtun ultra-nationalism and a contempt for 'lesser races' such as the Hazara, who they massacred in great numbers. This meant that the Taliban could never credibly claim to 'represent' the Afghan nation as a whole. Their complete neglect of social welfare programmes and a medieval fundamentalism made them increasingly unpopular, even among their original supporters. The intervention to overthrow them was widely welcomed, and by early 2002 they seemed finished as a significant force.

The framework for Afghanistan's governance arrangements was agreed at a UN-sponsored conference in Bonn, Germany, in December 2001. This established an Interim Authority which governed the country until an Emergency *Loya Jirga* (grand council) selected a Transitional Authority, which would govern the country until a new government could be sworn in following national elections. Presidential elections took place in October 2004, and a new parliament was elected in September 2005.

President Hamid Karzai was effectively appointed as Afghanistan's president at Bonn and his position reaffirmed by the subsequent arrangements. Although he is a Pashtun, most members of his first new administration were not.[4] Critically, a number of key positions were taken by a small group of Tajiks from the Panjshir valley, the dominant grouping in the Northern Alliance. Most of these mujahedin fighters were former commanders under the late, charismatic General Ahmad Shah Massoud and they constituted themselves into a powerful inner circle within the government. Internal power struggles within the new administration, and the reluctance of the international community to fill the security void, meant that the incoming administration's writ of authority did not extend much beyond the outskirts of Kabul.

In a report published in early 2002, the International Crisis Group estimated that it would take at least 25,000 peacekeepers to secure Afghanistan.[5] A UN-mandated International Security Assistance Force (ISAF) was deployed, but it consisted of only 4,500 troops and remained confined to Kabul for the first few years of its existence. The warlords consolidated their grip elsewhere and as late as 2004 an estimated half of Afghanistan's provincial governors and security force commanders were self-appointed. Despite appeals by Karzai and the UN, the US Government initially opposed enlarging ISAF, concerned that it would interfere with the OEF hunt for 'high value' Al-Qaeda and Taliban targets.[6] President Bush was also reluctant to become too deeply engaged in nation building. At a White House press briefing in February 2002, his spokesperson stated that: 'The President continues to believe that the purpose of [the] military is to be used to fight and win wars, and not to engage in peace-keeping of that nature.'[7]

The UN civilian mission (UNAMA) was also kept deliberately small and denied the kind of executive powers its counterparts in the Balkans and East Timor were granted. It was intended to operate with a 'light footprint', which in its own words would restrict its presence 'to the minimum required, while our Afghan colleagues are given as much of a role as possible'.[8] In establishing UNAMA, the Security Council Resolution stressed that: 'while humanitarian assistance should be provided wherever there is a need, recovery or reconstruction assistance ought to be provided through the Afghan Interim Administration and its successors'.[9] The US government consciously decided to co-opt the local political forces and the patronage networks they relied on. A decision to allow a group of 100 warlords to participate as delegates in the Emergency *Loya Jirga* in 2002 was followed by a failure to vet candidates for the 2005 parliamentary elections to exclude those guilty of serious human rights violations and drug trafficking.[10] Time and again the international community failed to challenge land-grabbing, extortion and corruption rackets by public officials in the new administration.

Although the western military intervention in Afghanistan was not carried out on humanitarian grounds, the tasks facing aid and reconstruction workers were similar to those in other post-conflict countries. What Afghanistan needed was massive long-term investment and a large international peacekeeping force to help secure the country until it built up its own national army, combined with serious efforts to root out corruption and tackle impunity. Instead, the US gave indiscriminate support to any militia or warlord it identified as anti-Taliban, while donors reneged on their promises to fund a reconstruction programme and international attention was diverted by the invasion of Iraq. At a conference in Tokyo in January 2002, donors pledged $5.1 billion in international assistance, but by the summer of 2003 only a tiny amount of this money was delivered. Meanwhile, President Karzai called for a quadrupling of this pledged financial aid, saying that the country needed between $15 and $20 billion over the next five years to rebuild vital social and economic infrastructure and to combat terrorism and drugs production.[11]

Humanitarian assistance was used to plug the gap, but we were operating with a fraction of the resources available in the Balkans while dealing with problems that were far, far greater. Almost two million refugees returned home in 2002 in a process supported by UNHCR, but the country's infrastructure was simply not developed enough to support them. Early on, a decision was made to tie a significant amount of the distribution of aid directly to the military through the formation of Provincial Reconstruction Teams (PRTs), which consisted of uniformed soldiers accompanied by civilian aid workers.[12] One of the first of these teams was sent to Mazar-i-Sharif, where I was based. As a DFID note explained: 'The concept of Provincial Reconstruction Teams has been developed as an alternative to a full-scale ISAF expansion . . . The *primary purpose* of PRTs are [*sic*] to extend the authority of the Afghan Transitional Authority and to promote a secure, stable environment in the North. The *secondary purpose* is to promote diplomatic dialogue, reconstruction and security sector reform.'[13] Another project, the National Solidarity Programme (NSP), worked through village institutions to deliver aid with the aim of weakening the influence of the warlords and strengthening the authority of the central government. Most humanitarian aid workers had mixed feelings about both the NSP and the arrival of the PRTs. We welcomed anything that could bring greater security to Afghanistan's anarchic countryside, but we could also see that aid was being used to promote explicitly political objectives – indeed, similar programmes were being introduced in Iraq at the same time – which could compromise the way we were viewed by the various protagonists.

The main political tensions in northern Afghanistan centred on rivalry between General Dostum and his Jonbesh militia and General Atta, who commanded the Jamiaat. They frequently skirmished for position, causing the international community to scurry to their bomb shelters. On the day I arrived in Mazar-i-Sharif, there were clashes between Jonbesh and Jamiaat forces, and a policeman guarding the UN compound was shot dead. The small UN civilian force there was headed by Michelle

Lipner, a formidable American woman with whom I had worked in Kosovo. GOAL, an Irish NGO, had about ten expatriate staff, and there were also a number of French NGOs, including MSF. The PRT, which arrived that summer, consisted of a few dozen British soldiers and made very little difference to the security situation.

Security was an overriding concern and made for a rather claustrophobic existence. Every day I would get up at dawn, have breakfast with my colleagues, work a thirteen-hour day and then be driven back to our compound where we would watch a video and collapse into sleep. Our curfew was 10p.m., which made our weekly parties rather tame affairs. However, the atmosphere was friendly and we were often invited to the homes of our local staff and to weddings and other gatherings. The integration was not as easy as it was in Kosovo, but this was mainly because of our very different cultural backgrounds. In one of my first letters home I wrote:

> The sexual apartheid is really difficult to get used to (and I hope I never do). When you see a group of women talking among themselves they are often very lively and animated. There are educated women here – although they are few and far between – and quite capable of holding their own in conversation. However, for the most part, women 'know their place', which is generally out of sight and out of mind. This segregation affects the men as well. Our young, male staff are visibly embarrassed in the presence of their female colleagues and discussions about sexual relations are very much taboo. Our staff were shocked when Polly and I hugged and kissed when we said goodbye.

The last sentence says much more about my own naiveté. I soon grew to admire many of my Afghan women colleagues and their understated strength and resilience. Most international workers recognized that they were guests in Afghanistan and adapted their behaviour accordingly. There is some truth in the cultural stereotype about aid workers being middle-class western liberals, but an increasing proportion are recruited in the field with a rather different profile. Many are ex-soldiers, whose experience makes them well suited to the job, and increasing numbers started out as local staff, often refugees in their own countries.

Allan Mukuru, one of my flatmates at IRC, who was later killed in an air crash in Sierra Leone in June 2004, was typical of the best kind of worker the humanitarian aid community can produce. A Ugandan, he joined IRC in Zaire during the Great Lakes crisis of 1994, before becoming head of programmes in Tanzania in 2001. He came to Afghanistan to sort out a huge administrative mess before going on to head the organization in Sierra Leone. He never hid his suspicion of the liberal values that underpin much of the human rights discourse and his unease that our work was being used to legitimize a misguided western foreign policy. Some of the views put forward in this book are directly based on the discussions I had with him during this time.[14]

At its best, aid work involves a relationship based on mutual respect and understanding by people from an increasingly wide variety of backgrounds. This is obviously not without difficulties. Soon after my arrival in Afghanistan we faced a dilemma when we were approached about the case of a thirteen-year-old girl who had recently fled a forced marriage to a much older man. The girl was abducted from her parents by an uncle who took her to Herat when she was nine. After Mazar-i-Sharif fell to the Taliban in 1998, he told her that her parents had been killed and sold her into marriage. Her father subsequently went to Herat to find her and she fled with him. Her husband had connections to the local militia, who threatened to kill her family if she did not come back. My first instinct was that we should physically rescue the girl, while other IRC staff worried, quite rightly, whether our 'humanitarian mandate' permitted us to intervene at all.

We eventually solved this case together with the local Afghan Human Rights Commission, who convened a meeting of the various elders and obtained their agreement that the girl should go back to her parents. When I became programme manager of Norwegian Refugee Council's (NRC) legal aid project shortly after, this mechanism became one of the main ways we dealt with many of our cases. The dilemmas we were grappling with were similar to those that have confronted many other humanitarian aid workers on both a theoretical and practical level. How far could we intervene in Afghanistan's internal affairs while maintaining our neutrality, and how far could we stray from our mandate by failing to protect people from violations of their basic human rights?

The legal aid project of the NRC limited its caseload to civil rights issues linked to the return of refugees, which in practice meant dealing mainly with land and property cases. We represented women in inheritance disputes and divorce and custody cases, using both the formal and customary legal system, but steered clear of criminal cases or the sort of human rights violations organizations like Amnesty deal with. It soon became clear that the self-imposed limits of our mandate provided us with sufficient challenges.

Land rights are a sensitive and deeply controversial subject in Afghanistan: land ownership is starkly inequitable and a significant proportion of the rural population is landless.[15] Frustration at the slow pace of land reform was a significant factor in the ousting of King Zahir Shah by his cousin General Mohammed Daoud in 1973 and the subsequent seizure of power by the communists in 1978. The sweeping land reform measures the communists introduced provoked a conservative backlash that plunged the country into civil war, and then, after the Soviet invasion in 1979, a national liberation struggle. Since then, successive governments have used land policy as a way of rewarding their own supporters.

A quarter of a century of conflict and the natural growth of the population only added to the problems. Only a small part of the land in Afghanistan is fit for farming and large numbers of people

were returning after years in exile, which gave us a huge
caseload. There were disputes over inheritance within families
and conflicts over borders between different plots of land. Prices
had risen sharply, particularly in urban areas, and returnees often
found themselves entangled in property disputes, or fell victim to
extortion rackets. In rural areas, rival clans and villages fought
over large strips of land and humanitarian agencies often found
themselves drawn into attempts at mediation.

When I arrived NRC already had one legal aid centre in
Jalalabad, in eastern Afghanistan, and we opened more during
the course of 2003 and 2004 to cover the west, north and centre
of the country. I was mostly on my own for the first six months,
but in early 2004 I was joined by Simon Russell, a former
colleague from Amnesty who had spent the previous year
working for another organization in the southern Afghan city
of Kandahar. Later on a young Scottish lawyer, Jennifer Escott,
worked for us as a volunteer, but the full quota of international
staff I had been promised did not arrive until after I left the
country.

We took a deliberate decision not to establish any centres in
the south of Afghanistan, since the security situation was clearly
deteriorating as 2003 wore on. Attacks on the UN and ICRC in
Iraq forced most aid organizations to withdraw from the country
that autumn and 'security awareness' suddenly became the new
buzz-term from our various headquarters. I noted in my diary in
late August:

> It is difficult to know whether the revival of the Taliban in
> recent months is directly connected with events in Iraq, but
> President Karzai's boast of a few months ago that the Taliban
> were a spent force looks increasingly hollow. The Govern-
> ment has announced that it is postponing the *Loya Jirga*, which
> was scheduled for the start of October, and is supposed to
> adopt a new constitution and pave the way for elections. No
> one believes the official version, that it has been put back

because it clashes with a religious celebration, and opinion is split as to whether they are more scared of the security situation or the current political mood. Most ordinary Afghans still seem grateful to the international community for rescuing them from the Taliban and the warlords, but that goodwill is fast dissipating and this seems, at least partly, due to Iraq. A hundred people were killed here last week during the independence day celebrations (that is independence from Britain) which were marked by audacious attacks by the Taliban. Last night American Special Forces in the south were involved in a major gun battle that left eighty people dead. There are more and more warnings about security threats in Kabul.

Most of my tasks for the NRC project were administrative. It was basically a management job that involved getting systems up and running and ensuring that my staff adopted simple and transparent procedures. I opened offices, wrote reports and proposals, attended meetings, hired staff and sometimes had to fire them as well. These are the sort of routines to which anyone who has been in a management position anywhere in the world quickly becomes accustomed. The main problem facing our legal aid centres was that there were practically no legal mechanisms with which to work. Few people possessed official title deeds, and most used customary documents to prove ownership. There was no up-to-date cadastral record and the courts suffered from a serious lack of capacity, as well as widespread corruption. Missing deeds, widespread forgery and the fact that disputed land has often been sold many times over made it difficult to determine who owned what.

The absence of rule of law in much of the country also meant that even when the courts issued fair judgments, there was no guarantee of their enforcement. NRC's lawyers instead relied primarily on convening *Shuras* and *Jirgas* (traditional meetings of elders) to mediate settlements. In other cases we confronted outright instances of land-grabbing, either by rival clans or people linked to the warlords and commanders. These were obviously the most difficult cases and we had to approach them sensitively. I noted in my diary in September:

> I met my first Afghan warlord, Commander Qara Beg, yesterday. We are pursuing a complaint on behalf of 300 returned refugees who live near his compound and who claim that he has recently cut off their water supply. They have complained to him on two occasions and both times he promised he would restore it. The supply was not restored, however, and on the third occasion they sent a delegation. The soldiers beat some of them and imprisoned them in his compound for eight hours. The people further complain that Qara Beg's soldiers have threatened to shoot anyone who crosses the wire of his compound. When they attempted to collect water from a broken pipe, soldiers beat up a woman, confiscated their water vessels and a cart, and fired over their heads and at their feet.
>
> It was fairly obvious, as we were ushered into his spacious office, that Commander Qara Beg had had a 'good war'. His fingers were fat and clammy to the touch and he had a well-fed, confident air about him that is noticeably rare in this hungry and insecure country. The head of our Kabul office introduced me and then made a short presentation on NRC's legal aid programme. I nodded and smiled a lot. Qara Beg praised the Norwegian Government's humanitarian assistance and material support, but signalled that much more aid was needed, for his organization in particular. And then we got down to business.

Qara Beg claimed that he was forced to cut off the water supply to the surrounding area because of the many returned refugees and a big increase in demand for water. His compound had no electricity and they needed fuel for the generator to work the water pump, and extra piping to carry the water from his compound to further up the mountain where the returnees had settled. All of this cost money, which he did not have, so he suggested that NRC might be able to help. My staff countered by asking him about the reports of beatings and shootings. Was it true? Yes, according to Qara Beg. The people attacked his compound and his guards defended it, what was wrong with that?

Perhaps the biggest thing wrong with it was that Commander Qara Beg was secretary-general of the Red Crescent Society and the compound we were sitting in was marked by the 'hallowed emblems' of the world's oldest humanitarian relief agency. Qara Beg was formerly deputy minister for internal security in President Rabbani's Government of 1992–1995. This was the period when Afghanistan descended into such chaos that many people were glad to welcome the Taliban forces that eventually overran most of the country. Like so many other well-connected warlords, Qara Beg believed he could operate with complete impunity.

Afterwards we went up the mountain to talk to the returnees, and they showed us where their pipe was cut and where the soldiers shot at them. Some of the bullets had ripped holes in people's trouser legs. A woman in a burka, who had been beaten, told me that this was not what she expected from the Red Crescent Society. The pipe in question was not much bigger than a household outlet, with a little water trickling pathetically into the sand. It was incredible to think that this was what 300 people relied on to supply all their water needs. It was also incredible to imagine how these families were able to survive living halfway up a mountain, with no proper roads, half-an-hour's walk away from anywhere, completely exposed to the summer heat, the winter snows and the biting, arid wind. I could still feel the sand and dirt in my eyes, ears and nose as we drove back to the city.

It took several more meetings, but we eventually reached a settlement to the dispute, partly because of the leverage that Beg's position with the Red Cross gave us. Other cases were more difficult, although the ingenuity and perseverance of our legal counsellors was positively inspiring. I once had to jump in a car and drive to Jalalabad to confront a local commander who had threatened to kill one of my staff. On other occasions we had to evacuate staff facing security threats and redeploy them in different parts of the country. My Afghan colleagues used my status as an international to give them more protection, and every time I visited our offices in the field they would take me out to shake hands and drink tea with the local notables. Most of these threats against us came from public officials, who were nominally part of the government, though we were becoming increasingly aware that another looming menace was overshadowing our work.

In September 2003, the Taliban stopped a car belonging to a Danish aid agency. The Afghan aid workers were forced from the car at gunpoint and their hands were tied behind their backs. They were then roped together, lined up on the road and shot. Four were killed and one survived by playing dead. He said the gunmen shouted that the attack was in retaliation for the mistreatment of detainees in Guantánamo Bay. In November I recorded in my diary:

> The grim news came last night of the murder of a colleague in Ghazni. Bettina Goislard, a UNHCR protection officer, was shot dead as she drove through a bazaar in the city centre. Two gunmen on a motorbike drove up beside her vehicle and shot her six times in the chest at point-blank range. The attack took place at midday in an area we had previously considered relatively safe. She was only twenty-nine years old and had formed a very strong attachment to Afghanistan during her time here. She spoke fluent Dari, had many Afghan friends and was deeply committed to the country. She had told her parents that, in the event of her death, she would like to be buried here and they are now flying out for the funeral on Thursday. It really is a terrible loss.

This was the first killing of a UN staff member in Afghanistan and came a week after a bomb blast at UNAMA's headquarters in Kandahar. No one was injured in this attack but one of my former colleagues, Peter Deck from UNHCR Kosovo, said that he was literally blown out of his chair. The week of Bettina's funeral was difficult. Lisbeth Pilegaard, my boss, who was mainly based in Pakistan, was on leave which meant that I had to take responsibility for making a security assessment for the programme. I temporarily shut down the Jalalabad office, which was our most vulnerable, and did my best to calm the nerves of our local staff and those at our headquarters in Oslo who wanted to suspend the entire programme. Coincidentally, I also had to fire my most senior national staff member on the day Bettina was buried, and make a grant-funding proposal to a donor, which is always nerve-wracking. Polly took me out for a meal that evening to cheer me up, and we heard a rocket slam into the Intercontinental Hotel while we were eating.

Prior to Bettina's death, life had settled into a pattern that seemed quite normal. I had started playing tennis in Kabul at the weekend and we formed an opera appreciation society, taking it in turns to organize DVD screenings. Steve MacQueen, my tennis partner and fellow opera devotee, was later shot dead as he drove home from one of our favourite restaurants. Another friend, Clementina Cantoni, with whom I had worked in Kosovo, was subsequently kidnapped, though she was released unharmed. Both events happened after I left the country, by which time Afghanistan was sliding further into a full-scale conflict.

Bettina's killing had a huge emotional impact on her friends and colleagues. It was followed by a three-month 'lock-down curfew' in which all UN staff were forbidden to leave their compounds at night. The upside of this for NGO workers was that it became possible to get seats in Kabul's growing number of swanky restaurants. However, the claustrophobia for those thrown together for so long was intense. Security restrictions also made it increasingly difficult for people to do their jobs, particularly out in the field. 'What am I doing here?' was a question I heard repeatedly.

Aid workers get little help in dealing with stress, which we are no better or worse at coping with than most people. Some showed remarkable fortitude while some cracked up or left the mission. I was very glad to get away for a break that Christmas.

The Afghanistan we returned to in 2004 was clearly a different mission to the one most of us had joined: to all intents and purposes the humanitarian effort had become part of a wider counter-insurgency operation. This was not what the majority of aid workers had signed up to, but we could hardly claim ignorance of the developments. President Bush announced at the start of military operations that 'as we strike military targets, we will also drop food, medicine and supplies to the starving and suffering men and women and children of Afghanistan',[16] while neglecting to mention that the food packages were the same colour as the cluster bombs, which resulted in a number of children blowing themselves up.[17] US Secretary of State Colin Powell referred to humanitarian NGOs as a 'force multiplier for us, such an important part of our combat team'.[18]

The main reason the military involves itself in humanitarian work is to win the support of local populations' 'hearts and minds'. This was taken to new lengths with the formation of the PRTs, which, as described earlier, were partly formed owing to the reluctance of ISAF to expand its reach beyond Kabul. Both the US and British Governments appear to have decided that by linking the delivery of aid to the military it could be integrated into a counter-insurgency effort. The British Government announced that ISAF and the PRTs could bid for funding from its humanitarian assistance budget.[19] Some of the PRTs did a great job. In the central mountainous region of Bamiyan, for example, a tiny contingent of fourteen troops from New Zealand provided visible reassurance to the local population. One soldier told me that he always made a point of ostentatiously marking the GPS co-ordinates of the homes of all the local warlords, an implicit way of reminding them of the threat of air strikes. Running a legal aid programme in a country where there is so little law and order, I was personally glad to know that there were PRTs located near some of our isolated offices and encouraged my staff to make contact with them.

One problem, however, was that it was sometimes difficult to distinguish aid workers from soldiers since they often drove the same white vehicles as us, dressed in civilian clothes and concealed their weapons. There were allegations that some American PRTs used humanitarian assessment missions as a front for intelligence-gathering operations. On one occasion, US forces handed out leaflets encouraging people to inform on insurgents and threatening to withdraw assistance to such areas if the insurgency continued.

The bigger problem was that the military intervention in Afghanistan was now taking over the logic of the whole mission. While some aid workers complained about the 'mixing of military and humanitarian mandates', the simple fact was that we were becoming objectively indistinguishable. We both wanted to strengthen law and order, weaken the warlords, combat corruption and support human rights. These were all worthy objectives – and it is difficult to see how Afghanistan can attain a reasonable future without them – but they were also clearly political, which meant that we were taking sides in what was turning into a bitter conflict. In a diary entry in March 2004 I noted:

> Life goes on here as usual. Last week I was woken by a call from our Jalalabad office to say that six to eight missiles had struck the city earlier that morning. One landed inside the IRC compound, but did not explode. There was also an attack on the governor's house in Laghman in which a guard was killed. More missiles dropped on Kabul on the same day but caused very little damage. The US has just started a spring

offensive against the Taliban in the south and east of the country and the latest attacks may have been in response to this. The commander of the police in Jalalabad has recently been sacked and some people think he bombed his own city in retaliation. The governor of Laghman seemed to have his own share of domestic enemies when I visited him a couple of weeks ago, so perhaps both these incidents were of a localized nature.

Returning from that trip we passed a truck recently damaged by a landmine. The front of the vehicle was almost intact but its rear was blown out across the road. A couple of US military helicopters buzzed us as we slalomed past the smoking wreckage. My diary recorded:

> I flew down to Jalalabad the following week. I was planning to drive back to Kabul at the end of the week and make a stop-off in Laghman to have another look at one of our land disputes. In the event our meeting with the governor was postponed so often that I had to cancel this plan and fly back instead. It turned out to be just as well as there was a massacre on the road the day before in which five Afghan aid workers were killed. Four de-miners were killed outside Herat a few days before, a Turkish engineer was shot dead on the Kandahar-Kabul road and an Australian helicopter pilot was shot a couple of days later. Taking yesterday's murder of a Red Crescent worker into account, this brings the death toll of humanitarian aid workers to about a dozen in the past fortnight.

In April 2004, photographic evidence emerged confirming the rumours of systematic abuse of detainees in Abu Ghraib prison in Iraq. Although supporters of the Bush administration dismissed this as the work of 'a handful of petty sadists', I heard similar stories about detention facilities in Afghanistan. Our legal aid centres also began to receive requests for help from people whose family members were missing, and possibly taken into custody by US forces. We referred them on to the ICRC since I could not see how we could provide them with a legal remedy. The Americans had made it very clear by now that they considered themselves to be above the law. Afghanistan was full of secret prisons and one senior UN official once told me that the US Government refused to tell even him of all their locations. On another occasion, I asked an Afghan judge why he did not take further action after he described a complaint he received from two people who alleged they had been tortured in the US Bagram air base facility. 'I didn't want to end up in Guantánamo Bay myself,' he said, only half-joking.

Afghanistan was not Iraq and opinion polls continued to register support for the presence of foreign troops in the country, just as decisively as Iraqis were supporting their withdrawal. But by now the Americans were losing the battle for public opinion. 'When they arrived here they had the support of 80 per cent of the population' in the predominantly Pashtun south and east, one of my staff told me. 'It is probably down to about 20 per cent now.'

By the spring of 2004 my diary was mainly a list of security incidents. In April, my colleague Simon got caught up in faction-fighting between Jonbesh and Jamiaat forces in the north-west and had to spend a couple of days in the bunker of the local UN compound after the building was surrounded by an armed mob. In June, I narrowly missed being caught in a bus bombing aimed at UN election workers in Jalalabad. I had stopped to talk to someone before getting in my car and saw the blast up ahead of me a few minutes later. Three women were killed and several more seriously wounded, including two children who had been on the bus with their mothers. The Taliban subsequently stated that anyone who registered to vote would be considered a target.

Later that same month, MSF suffered the biggest single loss of life in its history when five of its staff were murdered near Herat. The attacks might have been the work of the Taliban, but were more probably related to faction-fighting within the region between supporters and opponents of Ismail Khan, then the governor of Herat.

Although we refused to accept military escorts, we relied on their security information on when it was safe to travel. We ripped the humanitarian emblems off our vehicles since they helped to identify us, and my national staff travelled in local taxis for many journeys. The programme itself was becoming increasingly well-respected, but as the date for my departure, the end of July, grew closer it became difficult to remain focussed on dealing with some of the bigger issues. Staff shortages left me exhausted and irritable. I noted in my diary:

> Our headquarters in Oslo have already publicly stated that they will consider shutting down the programme if it gets too dangerous, and at least half the security measures I am now taking are aimed at reassuring them that we have things under control. We were supposed to have two new international staff this month but one has just pulled out, citing security concerns (as if he had not realized that Afghanistan is a dangerous place when he applied for the job!). Instead, Oslo has sent me an interactive CD to test my 'security awareness', which is apparently going to take me about five hours to work through. I have forwarded it up north for Simon to do first so I can find out if it is going to be as much of a waste of time as I expect.

It is stating the obvious to say that aid workers make mistakes, get over-excited and sometimes find ourselves out of our depth. Maintaining personal relationships is difficult in hardship-posts like Afghanistan and Iraq, which restricts the potential number of staff aid agencies can recruit. We were working crushingly long hours in stressful and insecure conditions, for which most of us had received no preparation. Yet we had become part of the front line in what the liberal interventionists now regarded as a global war to bring a radical transformation to these conservative and traditional societies.

I left Afghanistan in August 2004 and travelled to Brazil, where Glaucia and I got married at the end of the year. I have worked as a freelance consultant since then, mainly involving shorter assignments in a variety of countries, some of which are discussed in subsequent chapters. It was not until early 2008 that I had an opportunity to return to Afghanistan for a short-term research project.

I arrived in Kabul in mid-January, travelling on a commercial airline, which was a smoother and safer experience than my previous flights. Many things about the country have improved. The city's infrastructure is visibly better and wide roads have been constructed with new shops and gleaming wedding halls built on each side. There was even a new shopping mall with escalators. Signs of conspicuous consumption among Kabul's foreign and domestic elite were everywhere. The luxury Serena Hotel was doing a brisk trade until a few days before I arrived, when it was the target of a Taliban attack. A friend of mine who worked for UNHCR was leaving when gunmen burst in. Her car was riddled with bullets in the crossfire. She survived unscathed, but her driver was hit in the shoulder and she was obviously shaken by the experience.

The city was tense and jittery while I was there. One night I was woken by the sound of an explosion. While such attacks were nothing new in the Kabul I remembered, everyone assured me they were becoming increasingly frequent. Suicide bombings, practically unknown when I was there, are often targeted at rush hour traffic. The public line of both the Afghan Government and western diplomats was that the Taliban were driven to this type of attack due to the defeats it was suffering at the hands of NATO forces. But in private, officials painted a much gloomier picture.

Around 8,000 people were killed in Afghanistan in 2007, making it by far the deadliest year since the overthrow of the

Taliban. The anti-government insurgency, once confined to a couple of pockets, now stretched across the entire southern belt of the country to Kabul's outskirts. ISAF increased almost ten-fold during this period, reaching a strength of over 50,000 troops, but the role they were expected to play underwent a complete transformation from peacekeeping to mounting a fully-fledged anti-insurgency campaign. There is a huge difference between these two roles, but there seems to have been little public debate in the troop-contributing countries. Rather than admit that the previous strategy had failed and then analyze the reasons for it, western governments have portrayed the extension of the military mission in humanitarian terms.

The British military went to Helmand in July 2006 with the stated aim of 'providing a secure and stable environment in which the reconstruction of the province can take place'.[20] Before the deployment, Britain's defence secretary, John Reid, said that he hoped they could fulfil their mission in three years and leave the country without a single shot being fired. The army later admitted they had fired over four million rounds of ammunition in their first year in the province, and military strategists began to predict that the mission could last up to thirty years.[21] An inquest into one of the first British fatalities returned a verdict of 'unlawful killing' after hearing that the soldiers were completely unprepared for the resistance they would face. 'To send soldiers into a combat zone without basic equipment is unforgivable, inexcusable and a breach of trust between the soldiers and those who govern them,' the coroner said.[22]

Most aid organizations pulled out of the south and east of the country, or sought informal permission from the Taliban to continue operating. While the Afghan National Army and international troops might control these places during the day, the Taliban patrolled at night and had their own checkpoints on many roads. Over the same period more bombs have been dropped in Afghanistan than Iraq, and the parallels between the two countries have become increasingly apparent.[23] While western governments publicly boasted of their success in bolstering the capacity of the Afghan national police and army, it was not reflected in private conversations. More than 900 Afghan policemen died in ambushes in 2007, a rate of attrition that means they are being killed or deserting faster than their replacements can be trained. Some progress was made in building a professional army, but every single person I spoke to was scathing about the police, who were variously described as 'an absolute mess', 'universally hated' and 'responsible for instigating the vast majority of crime in the country'.

Time and again I was told that 'things were going backwards' and that the international community had 'got the template wrong' for the country. None of the mistakes people mentioned were particularly surprising, since they were the same ones we had been commenting on for years. The international community's presence was too weak, little attention was paid to building functioning judicial and policing systems, corruption and impunity went unchecked. Signs of corrosion and neglect were everywhere. Parliament was dominated by warlords, the state lacked legitimacy and the rule of law was practically non-existent. It was no surprise that the Taliban, initially swept to power in reaction to such lawlessness, was making such a come back.

My Afghan friends were unanimous in their opinion that this was an unwinnable war and that the only road to peace was through a reconciliation that included a place for the Taliban in a broader-based government. President Karzai had already offered the Taliban's leadership direct talks, a full amnesty and a couple of government ministries; the only question was how many more concessions he would make to sue for peace. Although in public western governments continued to talk about defeating terrorism and upholding human rights, in private their diplomats conceded that the search was on for an exit strategy.

The similarities between the failures in Afghanistan and Iraq are striking. The planning cycle for both operations consisted of initial over-confidence, poor preparation, lousy follow-through, inertia, drift and then panic and delusion. A huge increase in troop numbers and attempts to buy the allegiance of local militia forces brought some breathing space for western forces in Iraq and a similar strategy could conceivably achieve short-term success in Afghanistan. However, the long-term prospects for both countries are bleak. Neither intervention can be described as humanitarian, since the expressed primary motivation of the intervening powers was not to relieve the suffering of the people in the countries concerned. However, the use of such rhetoric by Bush and Blair has impacted on how other potential interventions have come to be regarded. They also set a precedent for the way humanitarianism has been integrated into counter-insurgency strategies.

In March 2008, a group of aid agencies released a report noting that $10 billion of the $20 billion assistance promised to Afghanistan had never arrived, and 40 per cent of the money delivered went on corporate profits and consultancy fees.[24] Oxfam produced a similar report a few months earlier stating that the delivery of aid by the PRTs had proved wasteful and inefficient.[25] The problem was that by linking the delivery of aid so closely to the counter-insurgency strategy donors were increasingly pouring money into areas, not on the basis of where it was needed or could do any good, but solely because of its supposed ability to buy the allegiance of local populations to stop them killing western soldiers. The US Government, by far the biggest donor, was spending over half its aid in the four southern provinces that were effectively under the control of the Taliban. This money bypassed Afghanistan's central government, which weakened its ability to build up national capacity, and was instead being given to US private contractors. Other countries were also channelling most of their support into areas where they had PRTs.

The strategy was failing on its own terms, and the main reason for the big under-spend was that donors were having problems finding sensible projects to fund. But it also showed how the debate over military interventions and humanitarian assistance has gone full circle. In previous conflicts critics of humanitarian aid have complained that it was used as an excuse for not taking the military action needed to save lives. Now in Afghanistan, instead of discussing whether and when military force should be used to support the relief and reconstruction effort, aid was being used to support the military. Most aid agencies refused to accept grants on these terms, which was why the US became so reliant on commercial contractors, but the experience has given a new urgency to the deliberations on whether humanitarians should ever compromise their principles of neutrality and independence.

Chapter Five

Sri Lanka and Indonesia

ON 26 DECEMBER 2004 an earthquake occurred in the Indian Ocean, off the west coast of Indonesia. It literally shook the world as the longest and second strongest ever recorded, and triggered a series of devastating tsunamis that engulfed coastal communities in neighbouring countries with waves up to 100 feet. The tsunami killed more than 225,000 people, with the worst devastation in Indonesia, Sri Lanka, India and Thailand.

The tsunami sparked a huge worldwide humanitarian response. Many of the places it hit were tourist resorts, hence its impact on western public opinion was enormous and immediate. Everyone seemed to know someone who was there and it was mainly tourist video cameras that captured the images that were soon broadcast around the world. After the first few days of frantic phone calls, people started digging deep into their pockets to fund a massive relief and reconstruction effort. Billions were pledged in donations, making it by far the best-funded humanitarian response operation to a natural disaster.

The scramble to respond to the tsunami reveals some of the tensions within modern humanitarianism. The public's unprecedented generosity was matched by far greater scrutiny over how their money was being spent, fed by a steady stream of media reports about inefficiency and waste by the humanitarian agencies responsible. The total funding for the tsunami worked out at more than $7,100 for every affected person, compared to about $3 per head for those affected by floods in Bangladesh the previous year.[1] Aid workers often complain about the way some emergencies attract far more money than others, but while it is true that the current system for funding such responses bears little relation to actual needs, it is difficult to see how an alternative could be constructed. People have a right to donate money where they want and democratic governments need to respect public opinion when allocating official assistance. It may be wrong for people to care more about a tragedy in one place rather than another, and human sympathy can be manipulated by the way a crisis is reported, but aid organizations themselves often collude in such manipulation as part of their work.

An estimated 80 per cent of the adult population of Britain made a donation to the tsunami relief effort, and the vast majority of this money was 'new', in that it would probably not have been given to another crisis.[2] If the tsunami diverted resources from elsewhere it was mainly due to the action of humanitarian agencies who understood its fund-raising potential from a business point of view. Aid agencies need to follow the high-profile disasters because it is what their supporters expect. They may well know they are duplicating the efforts of others, but it would be impossible to ignore a disaster on the scale of the tsunami. Indeed, some argue that by intervening in high-profile crises they can raise funds that help cross-subsidize work on the lower-profile ones. MSF went further than most when it told its supporters it would spend some of the money it received for tsunami relief on more deserving crises elsewhere.

A major problem for most humanitarian agencies is that they only have what is called reactive capacity. Like most aid workers in the field, I am usually employed on short, fixed-term contracts and go wherever I am sent for as long as I am needed – or until I feel I have had enough. Outside the UN system there is very little career structure in humanitarian aid work, meaning that staff turnover is high and many agencies have to rely on recruiting whoever they can get hold of when a crisis breaks. Many of the international aid workers deployed for big crises, or for work in particularly difficult or dangerous countries, are therefore likely to be young and inexperienced. They will also probably be unfamiliar with the local culture and unprepared for what they may face. Of course this limits their effectiveness and makes preplanning and disaster preparedness difficult. What aid organizations really need is a pool of experienced staff on standby, combined with predictable flows of steady income with no strings attached, so they can choose to spend the money entirely as they see fit. Unfortunately, this is the exact opposite of what usually happens.

One of the regular criticisms of humanitarian aid organizations is that they waste too much money on staffing costs and overheads. Some benefactors go out of their way to try and ensure that aid gets to where it is really needed. The problem with this approach is that it involves attempts by people even further removed from the crisis trying to make decisions about how it should be dealt with. After a recent flood in Mozambique, for example, the head of the local Red Cross told me that she had to leave tons of donated food and medicine in a warehouse for weeks until she could raise enough money to buy petrol for the trucks needed to distribute them.

I got married in Brazil the week before the tsunami and was on holiday on the island of Fernando de Noronha when I first heard about it. 'How soon can you get to Sri Lanka?' said an email from the Norwegian Refugee Council (NRC) in Oslo. 'I am on honeymoon,' I replied. 'Yes, but you are probably going to be married for ages; we only want you for a few months,' said the next one. I eventually agreed to go for six weeks, arriving at the end of January 2005. Later that year I went to Aceh, Indonesia, for a four-month post-tsunami project with the International Rescue Committee.

There is an obvious need for aid agencies to get their staff on the ground as fast as possible to start planning responses, but this is also strategically important in the rush to get funds. Strong, dramatic images showing the work an agency is doing are vital for public fund-raising, and agencies openly compete for 'visibility' in their front line activities. Sometimes they are tempted to exaggerate either the scale of the crisis or their ability to respond to it in order to boost their fund-raising efforts.

The amount of aid donated for the tsunami significantly exceeded that which could be sensibly spent, overwhelming some agencies and leading to waste and inefficiency. Shortly after I arrived in Sri Lanka, I remember reading an appeal in a British national newspaper that specified the exact costs and dimensions of the new houses it was promising to complete within a matter of weeks. By chance I was sitting with a group of bored construction engineers who told me that it would be months before they even got permission to start work. In the meantime, their agency was paying their salaries and living costs to do nothing. Further down the beach a group of displaced people started a fire with a pile of donated clothes because they could not see any other use for the woolly jumpers and mini-skirts they had been given.

Despite the waste, the tsunami relief operation deserves to be remembered as a qualified success. It is doubtful that the aid organizations could have scaled up their operational activities any faster, and a sounder criticism would be their failure to manage public expectations. The tsunami came with virtually no warning and hit a dozen different countries simultaneously. The two worst affected countries, Sri Lanka and Indonesia, had also endured long-running internal conflicts that hampered access to the affected populations. And it was Christmas, which meant most agencies had shut down their headquarters and their staff were on holiday. As one aid worker commented, it was far beyond even the worst-case planning scenario.[3] Two million people were displaced by the disaster and there were initial fears of a second catastrophe through the spread of infectious diseases. But no public health emergency occurred and within days the majority of people affected received food, water, sanitation, shelter and healthcare. Within a month, the emergency response phase geared to saving lives was completed, and the focus moved to recovering livelihoods and getting children back to school.

Considerably more problems arose with the transition from relief to development, and international organizations have been rightly criticized for their failure to support the priorities of local communities. Although donors pledged to 'build back better', there was little sign of this by the time I arrived in the devastated region of Aceh, eight months after the disaster. Aceh was at the tsunami's epicentre and around half a million people had been displaced; however, according to the World Bank, only 10,000 new homes had been built by October 2005.[4] The view expressed by some that it would have been more effective to divide the amount spent on the operation by the number of people affected and give them cash handouts is not entirely unreasonable and is discussed further later in this book.

The tsunami is one of the most effectively analyzed disaster response operations. Eight weeks in, a group of humanitarian agencies joined together to form the Tsunami Evaluation Coalition (TEC), which commissioned a series of studies on the response as it unfolded.[5] The principal aim of these reports was to 'improve the quality of humanitarian action' and to 'provide accountability to both donor and affected-country populations for the overall response'. On one issue, however, it was noticeably evasive:

> The tsunami and the tsunami response have had an impact on the armed conflicts in Sri Lanka and Indonesia (Aceh). While the TEC studies provide a variety of perspectives, the impact of the international presence on the peace and governance situation in Aceh is deemed to have been positive. This is irrespective of whether or not this was explicitly planned and commensurate with the funding available to international organisations to achieve positive change. However, the pre-

dominant factor in these conflicts was, and continues to be, the ongoing political and military processes. Overall, the international response has probably had a limited impact, at best. Demonstrably, in the case of Sri Lanka, the impact has not been positive.

Other observers have offered a far more forthright analysis. In her book *The Shock Doctrine*, Naomi Klein claims that the tsunami in Sri Lanka 'scrubbed away intractable hatreds, blood feuds and the tally of who last killed whom' and provided a basis for peace and reconciliation in the country. She argues that: 'The enormous outpouring of generosity after the tsunami had held out the rare possibility of a genuine peace dividend – the resources to imagine a more equitable country, to repair shattered communities in ways that would rebuild trust as well as buildings and roads.'[6] But within a year Sri Lanka slid back into war. In Aceh, by contrast, the peace process held, and aid appears to have made a positive contribution to resolving the conflict.

Sri Lanka and Aceh would seem to offer an interesting case study of how aid can impact on conflicts. Both locations had experienced decades of brutal civil war between government and rebel forces. The immediate aftermath of the disaster saw a reduction in violence and agreements were signed between the governments and guerrillas for the delivery of huge amounts of aid. International observers were also deployed and some of the aid was delivered to support peace-building activities in both places. Was something done right in one place and wrong in the other and, if so, what and why? Or does the assertion, by Klein and others, that aid was a significant factor in the conflict, simply overstate the political influence of humanitarianism?

Arriving in Sri Lanka in early 2005, the first thing that struck me was how peaceful the country seemed. After leaving Afghanistan I spent a month in Colombia and became used to the idea, in both places, that some people would consider me a 'legitimate target'. It took a while to adjust to driving around the capital city in an open tuk-tuk or heading into the field in a thin-skinned vehicle. Unlike most humanitarian agencies, NRC's decision to establish a presence in Sri Lanka was linked not to the tsunami but to attempts at ending its long-running civil war. Direct peace talks between the government and the Tamil Tiger rebels began in September 2002, following two years of international mediation by the Norwegian government. Scandinavian countries, led by Norway, deployed a group of unarmed observers, the Sri Lanka Monitoring Mission (SLMM), earlier that year to help build mutual confidence. Many other countries also offered substantial financial support if peace could be achieved, and the decision to establish an NRC project was taken in this context. The organization had enough money to carry out reconstruction work on houses and schools damaged during the conflict, and was planning to establish a small legal aid project to help returning refugees and displaced people.

The tsunami obviously meant a lot more money would be available, and the reason NRC wanted me in the country so fast was not to help out with the front line operation, for which I have no specialist skills, but to position the organization more advantageously with donors by designing a bigger legal aid programme. There was an evident and pressing need for such a programme and some donors, such as UNHCR and the European Commission's Humanitarian Aid Office (ECHO), were prepared to define 'tsunami-affected areas' quite flexibly to include many parts of the country where most of the displacement had been caused by the war. Unfortunately, others took a less enlightened view and it was common to see brand new camps with piped running water, for 'tsunami IDPs [internally displaced persons]', right next to squalid camps where many 'conflict IDPs' had been living for years.

Sri Lanka's civil war has cost the lives of nearly 70,000 people and displaced over a million in a country slightly smaller than Ireland. The conflict, now some twenty-five years old, pitted Sri Lanka's majority Sinhalese population against its minority Tamils, seeking a separate state in the north and east of the country. Led by Velupillai Prabhakaran, the main guerrilla group, the Liberation Tigers of Tamil Eelam (LTTE or Tamil Tigers), has gained a fearsome reputation through its attacks on rival Tamil groupings and eliminating internal dissent.[7] The LTTE has carried out large-scale massacres of civilians and deliberate acts of ethnic cleansing. It recruits child soldiers and was one of the first terrorist groups to use suicide bombers. For its part, the Sri Lankan Government is accused of arbitrary executions and torture and failing to protect Tamil civilians from attacks by Sinhalese extremists.

The conflict began to attract international attention in July 1983 when up to 1,000 Tamil civilians were murdered in mob violence following an LTTE attack on the Sinhalese-dominated Sri Lankan army. Hundreds of thousands of Tamils were driven from their homes and either fled abroad or became internally displaced within the country. India became involved in the conflict in the late 1980s, parachuting food and medicine into LTTE areas besieged by government forces. India's then prime minister, Rajiv Gandhi, also pressurized Sri Lanka into making a number of concessions, including the devolution of power to the provinces and official recognition of the Tamil language. In 1987, India deployed a peacekeeping force (IPKF), which took control over most of the north and east of the country. The IPKF was deployed with the Sri Lankan Government's acceptance rather than with UN approval, but in other ways it resembled a military humanitarian intervention. All Tamil insurgents initially agreed to surrender their weapons to the IPKF and, when the LTTE refused to do so, an attempt was made to disarm it forcibly.

The Sri Lankan Government agreed to the IPKF deployment because this enabled it to redeploy its armed forces in the south to crush a rebellion by the Janatha Vimukthi Peramuna (JVP), a Marxist and ultra-nationalist Sinhalese political party whose supporters were previously involved in acts of anti-Tamil violence. However, as the occupation continued the Sri Lankan Government publicly opposed the IPKF's presence. In a move that seems incomprehensible to outsiders, it also covertly armed the LTTE forces fighting the Indian occupation force, thereby resupplying its former deadly foes. Over 1,000 IPKF soldiers and 5,000 Sri Lankans lost their lives in this conflict, which ended with India's ignominious withdrawal in early 1990. The following year a female LTTE suicide bomber killed Rajiv Gandhi, who had been voted out of office partly because of the unpopularity of his Sri Lankan policies.

The LTTE moved to occupy the positions vacated by the IPKF and established many political and social institutions, including courts of law, in the areas under its control. It also destroyed rival Tamil groups and, in an organized act of ethnic cleansing, deported almost thirty thousand Muslims from the Jaffna peninsula in the north of the country to Puttalam in the south-west. In June 1990, the LTTE murdered over 100 Sri Lankan policemen; the army responded by killing up to 250 Tamil civilians. The war continued for more than a decade, despite various peace initiatives. The LTTE carried out more massacres of Muslim and Sinhalese civilians and the army trained 'home guard units' to respond with attacks on Tamil villages. Large-scale pitched battles were fought for control of the Jaffna peninsula, and LTTE suicide bombers took the conflict south, killing hundreds of people including, on 1 May 1993, Sri Lanka's President Ranasinghe Premadasa. Meanwhile unofficial government death squads hunted down, kidnapped or killed Sinhalese and Tamil youths suspected of being JVP or LTTE sympathizers.

Norway began to mediate a negotiated settlement to the conflict in early 2000 and the LTTE called a unilateral ceasefire at the end of that year. This broke the following April, but was reinstated in December 2001. A formal ceasefire agreement was signed in February 2002, which led to the deployment of the SLMM observers and then to substantive talks in the autumn of 2002. Both sides agreed to the principle of a federal solution, with the LTTE dropping its demand for a separate state. In return, the government agreed to considerable devolution of power to the provinces, giving the Tamils effective autonomy in their majority areas. The talks broke down in April 2003 but the ceasefire held and there were hopes that further progress could be made. Prabhakaran, the LTTE leader, formally apologized for the expulsion of Muslims from Jaffna and some began to return home. Many displaced Tamil and Sinhalese villagers also wanted to go home; this was the context in which NRC set up its programme.

I spent six weeks travelling round Sri Lanka, discussing where to open offices, what type of caseload we could expect and how to establish relations with local organizations. It was hardly long enough to gain much insight into the intricacies of Sri Lankan politics, but it was sufficient to see that the peace process was under strain and that if a breakdown came it was likely to centre on the north-east coast of the country, near the town of Trincomalee.

Sri Lanka's east coast is the most ethnically mixed part of the country, and one of the reasons many aid organizations had trouble obtaining permission to start rehousing people after the tsunami was that this ethnic balance had political implications for the borders of the new state entity the LTTE was trying to create. The LTTE suffered the most serious split in its history in March 2004 around Trincomalee, when its eastern commander, Colonel Karuna, led 5,000 guerrillas out of the organization, claiming that easterners were bearing the brunt of the fighting but were under-represented within the LTTE's power structures. The leadership hit back immediately, attacking the dissidents and driving them into hiding. Sporadic fighting continued, and there were claims that the army was helping Karuna's forces to mount attacks on the LTTE, which escalated dramatically in the short time I was there.

The spring of 2004 also saw the election of a new Sri Lankan government in which the extremist Sinhalese JVP was represented as a coalition partner. Although it favoured continued negotiations, the JVP advocated a harder line towards the Tigers, and by the end of the year the previous political momentum towards a settlement was ebbing. Hitting the island at a time when most observers agreed the country's leaders were facing a political crossroads, the tsunami's immediate effect was a reduction of violence and the agreement of a Post-Tsunami Operational Management Structure (P-TOMS) for the delivery of aid. The LTTE established its own humanitarian agency, the Tamil Relief Organization, through which it tried to control aid deliveries. While these arrangements became a source of friction with many international agencies, they caused even greater resentment among the Sinhalese population who complained of the pro-LTTE bias of the international community. The JVP withdrew from the government in protest at the P-TOMS agreement, which was eventually ruled unconstitutional by the courts.

Tensions continued to escalate during 2005 and the SLMM reported a growing number of ceasefire violations, including the murders of Sri Lanka's foreign minister by the LTTE, and a journalist and a politician with Tiger sympathies by unknown assassins. The general elections at the end of 2005 resulted in the narrow victory of a Sinhalese hardliner after LTTE intimidation prevented a huge number of Tamils from voting for her opponent. There was an attempt to revive the peace talks in early 2006, but by the spring the country plunged back into all-out war.

In August 2006, seventeen Action Against Hunger staff were shot at close range in their office in north-east Sri Lanka, the biggest single act of murder perpetrated against humanitarians since the Baghdad bombing three years earlier. The victims were found lying face down on the floor, still wearing T-shirts indicating their humanitarian status. The area had recently been captured by government forces and SLMM observers originally blamed the Sri Lankan security forces for the attack. The government issued denials and established a commission to investigate the incident, which many saw as a delaying tactic. Three witnesses, who also blamed the Sri Lankan security forces, have since been killed and others have gone into hiding.[8] More than thirty aid workers have been murdered in Sri Lanka since the conflict resumed, making it one of the most dangerous countries in the world for humanitarian staff. The death toll included an NRC staff member working as a driver who was killed after he refused to give a lift to some Sri Lankan soldiers a few days before.

I handed over to my successor, Ulf Edqvist, well before this and I remember my shock at hearing him describe the situation when we met at a seminar in the summer of 2006. Ulf had worked in Bosnia-Herzegovina and Nepal and we brought him to Afghanistan and Pakistan for a couple of short-term consultancies to deal with our staffing crisis. I had been away from conflict zones for a while by the time we met up again, but it was easy to relate to the stress he must have been under.

Although the NRC legal aid programme involves advocacy work, it remains neutral within humanitarian terms. It has consciously avoided speaking out on contentious political or human rights issues which could jeopardize its existence in countries such as Sri Lanka and Afghanistan. This is a pragmatic decision, but it also rests on the traditional concept of humanitarian neutrality, which has come under increasing criticism in recent years. Uniting its critics is the belief that humanitarian neutrality leads aid workers to concentrate on treating the symptoms of suffering while ignoring the root causes. This, they maintain, is both wrong on principle and counter-productive in practice. If the delivery of aid can make a significant difference in determining whether a conflict worsens or abates, then surely it is morally indefensible not to use it to protect rights and promote peace and justice.

Of course humanitarian aid can be used in ways that support ongoing peace processes, and many programmes are designed to support initiatives such as the disarmament of former combatants and reconciliation of divided communities. A badly designed or ill-thought out programme might cut across such objectives, and a case can be made that the delivery of aid might negatively impact on particular conflicts at the micro-level. However, it is more difficult to sustain the case, now made with increasing frequency, that aid makes a real difference between peace and war in a country or region.

Naomi Klein, for example, suggests that the Sri Lankan president used the tsunami as an excuse to push through a proposal for economic reform, supported by the World Bank, the US Government and the country's business lobby. The centrepiece of what she describes as 'a new kind of corporate *coup d'état*' was a plan to construct a string of beachside hotels to boost Sri Lanka's tourist industry. In the immediate aftermath of the tsunami, the government proposed a buffer zone in tsunami-affected areas that would have prevented people living in coastal areas from returning to their homes. Some also suspected it could have resulted in the land being handed over to corporate developers. Following local objections, the buffer zone plan was never enforced, and there is no serious evidence to support Klein's claim that this led to a growing estrangement between aid workers and local people. Nevertheless, she concludes that aid agencies became unwitting agents of a process she labels 'shock therapy' and this, combined with their 'lavish lifestyles', made them increasing targets of local resentment:

> Seeing this resentment build, I couldn't help wondering how long before Sri Lanka went the way of Iraq and Afghanistan, where the reconstruction looked so much like robbery that aid workers became targets. It happened shortly after I left: seventeen Sri Lankans working on tsunami relief for the international NGO Action Against Hunger were massacred in their office near the east coast port city of Trincomalee. It sparked a new wave of vicious fighting, and tsunami reconstruction was stopped in its tracks.[9]

In attributing what was almost certainly the work of a death-squad within Sri Lanka's security forces to a spontaneous outburst of popular anger, Klein spreads a particularly nasty piece of propaganda by the ultra-chauvinist Sinhalese parties and the armed forces themselves. Almost everything in the rest of her account is also inaccurate. The civil war was well underway by then and the massacre had very little impact on tsunami operations, which were mostly in the south of the country. Nevertheless, by linking a broad criticism of the post-tsunami humanitarian aid effort to the specific roots of the conflict in the north and east, Klein reinforces a widely-held assumption that aid can and does play a decisive role in the dynamics of conflicts such as Sri Lanka's. Yet, beyond this grossly inaccurate anecdote, she provides no empirical evidence to support her thesis.

A few months after leaving Sri Lanka in August 2005, I travelled to Aceh where I worked on developing a land rights project for the International Rescue Committee (IRC). Aceh's conflict began with the formation of Free Aceh Movement (GAM) in the mid-1970s. The rebels declared independence for Aceh from Indonesia, protesting against the centralizing tendencies of President Suharto, the military general who seized power in 1965, and his policy of 'transmigration', the settling of migrants from central Indonesia on its outer-lying islands. Aceh has a higher proportion of Muslims than the rest of Indonesia and it had been granted special status allowing Islamic traditions and laws greater prominence.[10] The Acehnese separatists argued that their religion and culture were under threat and that they were not receiving a fair share of the province's natural resources. Their revolt came shortly after Indonesia's illegal annexation of East Timor and coincided with other separatist campaigns within the country.

The Indonesian Army (TNI) repeatedly claimed to have crushed GAM but the province remained under military occupation throughout the 1980s and 1990s, during which time there were allegations of widespread human rights violations committed by both sides. Despite the fall of President Suharto in 1998, and Indonesia's withdrawal from East Timor the following year, the conflict in Aceh continued as more government soldiers were deployed. The government claimed to have badly damaged GAM in a series of military offensives between 2002 and 2004 which resulted in several thousand civilian deaths. Two days after the tsunami, GAM declared a unilateral ceasefire to facilitate the distribution of aid. The Indonesian Government also temporarily suspended restrictions of movement to allow for rescue efforts in the area.[11]

Aceh suffered the greatest damage of all the regions affected by tsunami fall-out. Up to 200,000 people were killed on its western coast and half a million driven from their homes. The tsunami even changed the province's physical geography, ripping large chunks of land from coastal areas and tossing them into the sea. On a trip to the beach a couple of weeks after I got there, one of my national colleagues got lost when he could not find his bearings in the new landscape.

Negotiations for a comprehensive agreement between GAM and the Indonesian Government began in February 2005 in Finland, moderated by former Finnish president Martti Ahtisaari. The final peace accord was signed on 15 August and implementation of its provisions began immediately. An Aceh Monitoring Mission (AMM) was set up by the European Union and the Association of Southeast Asian Nations (ASEAN) to oversee the process and report on any violations.

I arrived in Aceh just before the peace agreement was signed. We watched as TNI soldiers began to evacuate and GAM fighters handed in their weapons at special collection points. A presidential decree granted amnesty to around 500 former GAM members in exile and unconditionally released 1,500 GAM prisoners. My diary after a month there noted:

The tsunami seems to have swept up the Indonesian Government, the separatist rebels of the Free Aceh Movement (GAM) and the Indonesian National Army (TNI) and de-

posited them together at the peace table in Helsinki. After a
few months of fairly intensive on-again-off-again discussions,
a Memorandum of Understanding was signed in August, by
which GAM has agreed to disarm, demobilize and turn itself
into a political party. In return it gained an amnesty for its
prisoners and a reintegration package for its former guerrillas.
The TNI and security police are also beginning a phased
withdrawal which should halve their numbers . . . Already the
first batches of prisoners have been released from Indonesian
prisons and groups of guerrillas are coming down from the
hills to hand in their weapons. After nearly thirty years of
conflict there is a visible sense that people are beginning to
relax a bit: political exiles are returning home and human
rights activists are becoming more open in their activities.
Soldiers play football with local kids who would not have
dared to venture anywhere near them a year ago. While it
may be simplistic to give all the credit to a big wave coming
out of the sea, every single person I have met sums up the
reason for the change with the single word 'tsunami.'

In what was one of the most contentious issues in the negotiations, the government agreed to recognize Aceh-based political
parties, which participated in the local elections that December.
GAM split into two factions during the election campaign, but its
former chief negotiator, Irwandi Yusuf, was eventually elected
governor of the province. On 27 December, GAM's leadership
announced that the group had disbanded its military wing, and
the international monitoring mission withdrew from Aceh at the
end of the year, its mission successfully accomplished.

The other two main areas covered by the agreement were a
proposal to establish a 'Truth and Reconciliation Commission'
to investigate past atrocities, and a deal on how to split the
income derived from the province's natural resources. Land
rights, the focus of my consultancy work, could also become
a controversial post-conflict problem in Aceh since displaced

GAM supporters and other indigenous Acehnese might clash with more recent settlers brought into the province by the transmigration programme.

Human rights and humanitarian organizations have a potentially valuable role to play in these areas in strengthening Aceh's governance, rule of law and civil society to help ensure that the province does not slip back into conflict. Many agencies have considerable experience in implementing demobilization, disarmament and reintegration (DDR) programmes, by which former combatants are paid to hand in their weapons. These programmes are often backed by education and training projects for former combatants to acquire new skills, as well as other income-generating and micro-finance schemes to build a peacetime economy. Psychosocial programmes aimed at former combatants, particularly child soldiers, also help societies move on from conflicts.[12] Other conflict victims may need counselling and support. Criminal violence often increases in post-conflict societies where many have been exposed to violence and the rule of law has collapsed. Women and children are particularly vulnerable to sexual violence and other forms of abuse.

All this fits within the broad category of 'peace-building', an accepted part of the work of humanitarianism. However, there was nothing controversial about implementing such programmes in Aceh as we were supporting a locally-driven peace process. We were also under no illusions about the modest impact of our activities. My memories of my time there are summed up in a somewhat culturally insensitive diary entry shortly before I left:

> Aceh is a very, very boring place if you are an expatriate aid worker. The population is overwhelmingly Muslim and the Indonesian Government introduced Sharia law here a couple of years ago as an earlier concession to separatist sentiment. This means alcohol is completely banned and the lack of any clubs or bars means there is nowhere much for internationals to meet up in the evening. There is nothing at all to do on

those evenings apart from read by candlelight (if the power goes down) and curse the heat and flies. Most of the toilets are squat. Showers and hand basins are non-existent. I wash using two buckets of cold water in the morning and clean my teeth by spitting into the squat hole . . . The only real danger comes from earthquakes. We get about two or three a week and some of them can be quite violent. People say that it is just the earth settling down after the tsunami, which makes them seem slightly less threatening, although one in March killed several hundred people. It is difficult to complain since even the boredom is a cause for optimism. The reconstruction effort is making slow but steady progress and is helping to lay the basis for a lasting peace. It is a shame that 'aid workers actually do some good somewhere in the world' does not seem to make for an interesting story anymore.

This is basically how I remember Aceh; nothing glamorous, but good projects doing good work. There were no doubt many specific mistakes made by the international humanitarian community in relation to the peace process in Sri Lanka and Aceh, but there is little evidence that any of them made a decisive difference to the overall outcome. It might seem fairly obvious to point out that what distinguishes Aceh and Sri Lanka was the political situation on the ground rather than anything the international community could have done, but in light of the repeated criticisms made of humanitarianism's interventions elsewhere it bears repeating. In Aceh the government agreed to grant autonomy and the rebels agreed to accept it. In Sri Lanka, though the outlines of a similar agreement may be in sight, neither side has shown itself prepared to make sufficient concessions at the same time in order to achieve it. Neither the presence of international observers nor the efforts of the humanitarian community had a fundamental impact on these developments.

Sri Lanka had already experienced a military humanitarian intervention in the shape of the Indian peacekeeping force at the end of the 1980s, and few would recommend repeating the experiment. There was never any prospect of an external intervention in Aceh along the lines of the Indian force in Sri Lanka, but there are interesting lessons to be learned from the UN's 1999 mission to East Timor, which show what the international community can achieve as well as its undoubted limitations.

Indonesia annexed East Timor in 1975, brutally crushing all resistance to its rule. The US backed President Suharto's dictatorship as a 'bulwark against the spread of communism', but he was eventually overthrown by his own people in 1998. At that point, the new reforming government asked the UN to help it supervise a referendum in which it seems to have thought that the East Timorese would accept a proposal for autonomy rather than independence.[13]

The UN agreed to supervise the vote and its mission consisted of a team of unarmed observers led by Ian Martin, the former head of Amnesty International.[14] The TNI remained responsible for security in the territory during the vote and it soon became obvious that they were arming militia groups to intimidate people into voting against independence. Despite the threats, the turnout was high and the vote for independence overwhelming. In the weeks that followed, the TNI and its militias unleashed a wave of violence during which an estimated 1,300 people were killed and most houses and buildings destroyed. The violence was only brought to an end by the arrival of an international peacekeeping force consisting of 11,000 troops led by Australia. Indonesia reluctantly agreed to accept this force under massive diplomatic pressure. A UN Chapter VII Resolution 1272 created a transitional administrative body, headed by Sergio Vieira de Mello, which handed over to an independent government in 2002.

Human rights and humanitarian organizations campaigned vigorously for an 'effective UN presence' during the weeks of September 1999 when the violence was at its height. The Chinese threatened to veto a resolution authorizing an intervention without the Indonesian Government's consent. It took precious days of shuttle diplomacy and pressure to obtain, and during this time many innocent people died. Nevertheless, a deal was reached and a fair assessment should concede this as a victory rather than a defeat for the UN's efforts.

The referendum was held on 30 August 1999. The Indonesians agreed to accept the multinational force on 12 September and it arrived in the capital, Dili, on 20 September. Some have argued that the UN should never have agreed to organize the referendum without the deployment of UN peacekeeping troops to prevent violence, but Indonesia would never have accepted the deployment of foreign soldiers on its territory before the result of the referendum was known. Australia and New Zealand raised the possibility of an unauthorized intervention if UN approval was not forthcoming, and, as discussed in the next chapter, this could be one of the cases where it might have been justified. However, putting together a mission of that size in under three weeks would have been a huge logistical challenge and it is doubtful that it could have been done much sooner, even without the initial diplomatic impasse.[15]

Nevertheless, the delay was seized on by the UN's critics. A few days after the arrival of the multinational force, the French philosopher Andre Glucksman wrote: 'The UN lured the Timorese into an ambush: it offered them a free referendum, they vote under its guarantee, it delivers them to the militia's knives . . . the UN knows, the UN keeps quiet, the UN withdraws.'[16] Bernard-Henri Levy echoed these sentiments the following day, claiming that: 'The time of the UN has passed. We have to finish off this macabre farce that the UN has become.' Vieira de Mello responded with a furious 'Retort to Two Intellectual Show-offs' who 'caricatured, ridiculed and defamed' the UN 'from the comfort of their Parisian homes'.[17]

The human rights lawyer Geoffrey Robertson also maintains that the bloodshed, which he claims cost several thousand lives 'was all the UN's doing' and makes a rather scornful reference to how the mission 'quickly evacuated itself to Darwin' when the violence started.[18] In fact, sixteen of the UN's local staff were massacred by the militias and, despite this, a group of the UN's international staff refused to be evacuated unless provision was made to protect 1,500 East Timorese civilians seeking shelter in their compound. Led by Martin, they stayed during the height of the violence until 14 September, by which time the Indonesian Government agreed to accept the presence of a multinational peacekeeping force. A year after this crisis, in September 2000, three UNHCR international staff were murdered in West Timor when their office was stormed by militia forces. Some of their team were later redeployed to Kosovo where I was working at the time. They told us that staff safety precautions consisted of an escape ladder propped against the back wall. It seems reasonable to ask how many of the UN's armchair critics would be prepared to work in such conditions themselves.

A stronger criticism could be made of the performance of the UN Transitional Administration in East Timor (UNTAET) which replicated many of the mistakes made in Kosovo and anticipated those made in Iraq. According to Robertson, UN-TAET 'helped the East Timorese to prepare for civil society and self-governance under a new constitution, taking care not to impose its own solutions over the sometimes unfathomable preferences of local leaders'.[19] But this is not how most people who worked there remember it. Many UN staff were horrified when they read the text of UN Security Council Resolution 1272, which appeared to have been written by simply replacing the word 'Kosovo' from Resolution 1244 with 'East Timor'. Lakhdar Brahimi, who would serve as UN representative in Afghanistan and Iraq, turned down an offer to lead the mission, telling Kofi Annan, 'I know nothing about either Kosovo or Timor, but the one thing that I am absolutely certain of is that they are not the same place.'[20]

Unlike Kosovo, almost all countries accepted East Timor's right to self-determination through the establishment of an independent nation-state. Indonesia's invasion was denounced at the time as an act of aggression and the UN Security Council resolution establishing the transitional administration explicitly noted that the East Timorese people had expressed their clear wish to 'begin a process of transition under the authority of the United Nations towards independence'.[21] The East Timorese leaders were therefore outraged that the Security Council resolution gave 'all legislative and executive authority' to an unaccountable foreign administrator, a sentiment the Iraqis were soon to share when the US and UK made a similar decision.[22]

Most of the core members of the UN team that followed Vieira de Mello to East Timor came straight from Kosovo. The staff's general view was that the mission there had failed to stand up sufficiently firmly to the KLA's thuggery, which initially led them to take a fairly authoritarian approach with the local Timorese political leadership. Eventually a more consultative style was adopted, partly due to Vieira de Mello's diplomatic skills, though much political goodwill was squandered in the intervening period. Jose Ramos-Horta, later the country's prime minister, complained that members of the interim government were 'caricatures of ministers in a government of a banana republic'.[23] Xanana Gusmao, the country's first president, noted their experience of the UN 'was limited to watching hundreds of white four-wheel drive vehicles driving around Dili and receiving a succession of regulations drafted by the UN administration'. He also noted:

> We are witnessing another phenomenon in East Timor, that of an obsessive acculturation to standards that hundreds of international experts try to convey . . . we absorb standards just to pretend we look like a democratic society and please our masters of independence. What concerns me is the non-critical absorption of [universal] standards given the current stage of the historic process we are building.[24]

A related problem was that UN rules forbade it from spending its peacekeeping funds on local reconstruction, which meant the impoverished Timorese people saw few economic benefits from the huge international presence. As one critic observed, the $27 million UNTAET spent in a year on bottled water for international staff was approximately half the total budget of the embryonic Timorese government.[25] UNTAET cost an estimated $692 million in total yet virtually none of this brought any economic advantage to the country. Vieira de Mello complained in vain to the Security Council and subsequently wrote that 'the rules make the UN appear arrogant and egotistical in the eyes of those who we are meant to help.'[26]

Timor-Leste's stability since independence in 2002 has been fragile. A poorly implemented demobilization of former guerrilla fighters by UNTAET stoked up strong resentment. Donors concentrated on building a new Timorese police force, many of whose members had served the previous Indonesian regime, while a large number of former guerrillas ended up unemployed. This fed into existing tensions between Gusmao and Ramos-Horta on the one hand and a group of exiled political leaders on the other. An outbreak of violence in the spring of 2006 displaced more than 100,000 people from their homes. In February 2008, there was an attempted coup by a group of rebels during which shots were fired at Gusmao, who escaped unharmed, and Ramos-Horta, who was seriously injured. The International Crisis Group has warned that the underlying problems leading to the crisis were not tackled and that the country faces a bleak future unless they are addressed.[27]

The best that can be said about the UN intervention in East Timor is that it probably provided the least bloody route to the country's independence. Blaming the observer mission for the violence of 1999 is like blaming the international monitoring mission in Sri Lanka for the fact that its civil war soon resumed. There are legitimate criticisms to be made of the way humanitarian aid is often used in the aftermath of a conflict or natural disaster, but it is equally important to recognize how limited its impact is likely to be on the dynamics of a particular conflict.

A broader criticism of military interventions on humanitarian grounds and the type of international relief operations mounted after the tsunami is that their effects will almost always be messy and unpredictable. A sudden, large influx of resources will invariably distort the local economy and the arrival of an international mission will have a destabilizing effect. However well-intentioned, the intervening participants will almost always be inadequately informed regarding specific local politics and culture. Even the worst-paid international aid workers are likely to earn several times more than the average local salary, since agencies would otherwise find it impossible to recruit and retain staff. In his book *Lords of Poverty*, Graham Hancock lashes out at 'the freewheeling lifestyles, power, prestige and corruption of the multibillion dollar aid industry' and the criticisms he makes have been echoed by many before and since.[28] US Secretary of Defense Donald Rumsfeld, for example, set out a critique of previous UN interventions, in February 2003, in which most aid workers would recognize some truth:

> East Timor is now one of the most expensive cities in Asia. Local restaurants are out of reach for most of the people. They cater to international workers who have salaries that are some 200 times the average local wage . . . Take Kosovo where a driver shuttling international workers around the capital can earn ten times the salary of a university professor in that country. A recent *Wall Street Journal* story described how three years after the war the United Nations still runs Kosovo really by executive orders. They issue postage stamps, passports, driver's licenses and the like and decisions made by the local parliament are invalid without the signatures of the UN administrators.[29]

The legitimacy of these criticisms is ironic given that the spectacularly incompetent administration the US imposed in Iraq was to replicate the same problems and cause many more besides. The 'lighter footprint' of the UN mission in Afghanistan also proved inadequate in tackling the problems the country faced, precisely because it was not prepared to challenge the warlords and corrupt political elites. The broader lesson from a range of international interventions in recent years is that it will always be difficult to impose governance and assistance mechanisms from the outside because there is a clear tension between the 'doctrine of international community' and the demand for local accountability and self-determination. There is a good reason why the principle of self-determination is enshrined not only in Article 2 of the UN, but as the first Article of the twin international covenants on civil and political and social and economic rights. As the discussion in the following chapter illustrates, this tension is a recurring feature in the discourse on the relationship between national sovereignty and international law during humanitarian crises and the circumstances in which the international community can set the former to one side by claiming that it has a 'responsibility to protect' people's basic human rights.

Chapter Six

A Responsibility to Protect

O N 17 MARCH 2003, the British attorney general, Lord Goldsmith, published a short statement, in response to a parliamentary question, claiming that the forthcoming invasion of Iraq was legal under international law.[1] He argued that the Iraqi Government was in breach of three previous UN Security Council Resolutions: 678, 687 and 1441. The first two dated back to the first gulf war of 1991 and set out the conditions for restoring peace and security in the region, including an obligation on Iraq to eliminate its weapons of mass destruction (WMD). The more recent Resolution 1441, of November 2002, 'revived' this demand and warned Iraq of 'serious consequences' if it did not comply. According to the attorney general: 'It is plain that Iraq has failed to comply' and this, he maintained, was sufficient legal grounds for a military invasion, even without the explicit authorization of another UN Security Council resolution.

This legal opinion was enough to head off a rebellion within the British Government against the war. Clare Short, a minister who threatened to resign over the issue, voted in favour of the war in Parliament the following day. In a letter sent to every Labour MP, she gave the attorney general's legal opinion as the first reason for changing her mind, and also said that it would be 'cowardly' to 'leave the situation as it is with Saddam Hussein defying the UN and the people of Iraq continuing to suffer'.[2]

The opinion was also enough for Sir Admiral Michael Boyce, the chief of defence, who had demanded a clear assurance of the war's legality to ensure military chiefs and their soldiers that they would not be 'put through the mill' at the International Criminal Court (ICC).[3]

Ten days before his opinion was published, the attorney general sent a longer, private and secret, memorandum to the prime minister setting out the legal arguments in more detail. This was shared with the Foreign Office and defence chiefs and appears to have been what alarmed Boyce into demanding the clarification. In it he noted that the three legal grounds for the use of force were 'a) self-defence (which may include collective self-defence); b) exceptionally to avert overwhelming humanitarian catastrophe; and c) authorisation by the Security Council acting under Chapter VII of the UN Charter'.[4] He stated that he did not believe the invasion could be justified on either of the first two grounds, but that an arguable case could be made for it on the third. This argument was controversial, he said, and 'not widely accepted amongst academic commentators' so 'the safest legal option would be to secure the adoption of a further resolution to authorise the use of force.'

The attorney general said that 'a reasonable case' could be made that Resolution 1441 'revived the authorisation to use force in resolution 678', but that 'the UK has consistently taken the view . . . that, as the cease-fire conditions were set by the Security Council in resolution 687, it is for the Council to assess whether any such breach of those obligations has occurred.' He also noted that the 'revival' argument would 'only be sustainable if there are strong factual grounds for concluding that Iraq has failed to take the final opportunity [to get rid of its WMDs]. In other words, we would need to be able to demonstrate hard evidence of non-compliance and non-cooperation.' The memo also drew attention to the recent reports of the weapons inspectors who had not found hard evidence that Iraq still possessed WMD. Without a second resolution, 'we would need to consider urgently at that stage the strength of our legal case', and the memo discussed the possibility of action against the British Government at the International Court of Justice, by the ICC or through the domestic courts. He concluded that while UK forces had participated in military action in Kosovo 'on the basis of advice from my predecessors that the legality of the action under international law was no more than reasonably arguable. But a "reasonable case" does not mean that if the matter ever came before a court I would be confident that the court would agree with this view.'

The difference between the two opinions is striking and has led many commentators to suggest that the attorney general was 'leaned upon' to come up with his second statement. Elizabeth Wilmhurst, the deputy legal adviser at the Foreign Office, resigned in response to the second statement, saying that: 'I regret that I cannot agree that it is lawful to use force without a second Security Council resolution . . . an unlawful use of force on such a scale amounts to the crime of aggression.'[5] Most international lawyers also rejected the reasoning of the second statement, with many arguing that the attorney general demeaned his office by issuing it.

The subsequent failure to find any WMD in Iraq obviously removed the only legal justification for the invasion that the attorney general was prepared to support. In September 2004, Kofi Annan publicly joined the growing number of international experts who declared it to be illegal. Many of his colleagues at the UN urged him to speak out against the invasion sooner, and Ruud Lubbers, the head of UNHCR, tried to rally the other heads of agencies into condemning it. Both Annan and Sergio Vieira de Mello refused to do this on the grounds that it would play into the hands of those in the US Government who, they believed, wanted to use the war as part of a wider strategy to weaken the UN and other multilateral institutions.

The Bush administration's attitude to international law was summed up by John Bolton, who was subsequently appointed as its UN ambassador. 'It is a big mistake for us to grant any validity to international law even when it may seem in our short-term interest to do so because, over the long term, the goal of those who think that international law really means anything are those who want to constrict the United States.'[6] Although Bush described the invasion of Iraq as 'liberation', his main case for it was the doctrine of 'pre-emption', by which the US claims the right to attack any state which might threaten what it defines to be in its 'national interests'. One of the persistent criticisms that US Republicans had made of the Clinton administration was that it got involved in conflicts where the US had no 'national interests' at stake, while failing to act more decisively in places that it had.[7]

While Iraq did not pose a credible direct threat to the US, it could have threatened Israel, the US's strategic ally in the Middle East, as well as Kuwait and Saudi Arabia, its principal oil suppliers. Imposing a pliant pro-western regime in a country that remains one of the world's biggest potential producers of oil has long been a goal of some ultra-hawks within the Bush administration, and this fitted easily into the pre-emption doctrine developed after 9/11. Most of the evidence presented to show that Iraq posed an 'imminent threat' to peace turned out to be unreliable, and some was based on fairly blatant lies and forgeries. The Iraq Study Group, headed by former US Secretary of State James Baker, was later to comment that: 'Good policy is difficult to make when information is systematically collected in a way that minimises its discrepancy with policy goals.'[8]

As the original justification for the invasion disappeared, Blair shifted his ground. In February 2003, he had stated that: 'ridding the world of Saddam would be an act of humanity. It is leaving him there that is in truth inhumane. And if it does come to this, let us be clear: we should be as committed to the humanitarian task of rebuilding Iraq for the Iraqi people as we have been to removing Saddam.' However, he distinguished between 'the moral case for removing Saddam' and the actual 'reason we act . . . [which] must be according to the UN mandate on weapons of mass destruction'.[9] Later, in a speech to the US Congress in July 2003, he stated that 'history will forgive' the invasion even if Iraq turned out not to possess WMD because 'we will have destroyed a threat that at its least is responsible for inhuman carnage and suffering.'[10] He has returned to this theme several times since, often borrowing the language used in the debate on 'the responsibility to protect' to justify his actions. In a speech in 2004, for instance, he argued that it was international law that was at fault in not permitting such invasions because: 'a regime can systematically brutalise and oppress its people and there is nothing anyone can do, when dialogue, diplomacy and even sanctions fail, unless it comes within the definition of a humanitarian catastrophe [though the 300,000 remains in mass graves already found in Iraq might be thought by some to be something of a catastrophe]. This may be the law, but should it be?'[11]

This attempt to repackage Iraq as a 'humanitarian intervention' has infuriated many. During discussions on Darfur in 2007, the pro-interventionist International Crisis Group despairingly dubbed Blair a 'false friend of the responsibility to protect doctrine'.[12] However, it has tapped into a broader sentiment among some political humanitarians and partly explains why a section of liberal-left opinion in Europe and North America backed the war. In November 2007, his former chief of staff, Jonathan Powell, stated that: 'We should have been clear we were removing Saddam because he was a ruthless dictator suppressing his people. But the lawyers said there was no legal basis for proceeding on these grounds, and so we were not able to make this case as wholeheartedly as I would have liked.'[13]

In his book *The Duty of Intervention*, Bernard Kouchner identified four stages of humanitarianism: the 'Red Cross' approach, in which relief is provided, on strictly neutral terms, via the state authorities wherever possible; the 'borderless doctors' approach, where respect for the authorities may be flouted in order to help victims; the 'safety zone' or 'humanitarian corridor' approach, where UN-authorized operations may intervene in a territory as far as is strictly necessary to protect lives; and, finally, intervention to help free oppressed people from their tyrants.[14] This is a polemical rather than a legal argument, though it builds on a set of concepts found in international human rights and humanitarian law.

The starting point, which almost all humanitarians accept, is that while states are primarily responsible for protecting people within their jurisdiction, there are circumstances in which this protection might not be sufficient to guarantee their basic rights. Refugee law, for example, recognizes that people who have fled across a border due to fear of persecution can no longer be said to enjoy the protection of their own state. Where one country occupies another, the occupying power must assume some responsibilities for protecting the rights of the people in the occupied territory. During an armed conflict a state may no longer be able to protect its own people against its military opponents, or it may itself pursue counter-insurgency strategies that violate their rights. As an increasing number of conflicts take place within, rather than between, states, this latter concern has become a particularly pressing issue.

In its Chapter VII resolutions authorizing military interventions, the UN Security Council has explicitly recognized the destabilizing effects that humanitarian crises can have on neighbouring countries. The Genocide Convention additionally recognizes circumstances in which the UN Security Council can directly intervene to protect people's rights against their own government. It is becoming increasingly accepted that the doctrine of national sovereignty should no longer be used as a shield behind which states can violate the rights of their own people with impunity. As Kofi Annan put it, shortly after the Kosovo crisis, 'if humanitarian intervention is indeed an unacceptable assault on sovereignty, how should we respond to a Rwanda, to a Srebrenica – to gross and systematic violations of human rights that affect every precept of our common humanity?'[15]

This view rests on the premise that states derive their legitimacy from the way they treat people within their jurisdiction.[16] As Professor Marc Weller has argued: 'After all, the state which the government claims to represent, and whose right to non-intervention it invokes, is nothing other than the legal abstraction of the population and the competencies it has transferred to the state organs. A government which seeks to destroy that population, or a constitutionally relevant segment thereof, cannot at the same time claim to represent it.'[17] According to Professor David Forsythe, 'if a state fail[s] to meet its responsibility to protect internationally recognized human rights standards, then the UN Security Council or some other entity might override traditional notions of state sovereignty and try international *direct* protection of rights.'[18] This may be achieved through the use of force because, as Annan has commented, 'the reality is that there are situations when you cannot assist people unless you are prepared to take certain [military] measures.'[19]

UN Security Council authorization is widely regarded as conferring international legality on a humanitarian intervention, but this poses the question as to whether intervention is legitimate purely because the Security Council has declared it to be so, or whether some independent principles exist against which the legitimacy of an intervention can be judged. If the latter is the case then is the Security Council under an *obligation* to intervene in certain circumstances to protect people's human rights and, if it fails to discharge this, does the responsibility then pass to others? Are there circumstances, in other words, in which a humanitarian intervention can be justified without UN sanction?

It is not difficult to think of a hypothetical situation in which there is an ongoing humanitarian crisis but the UN Security Council fails to act because of the veto power of one of its members. In such circumstances there is at least a moral case for an individual state or group of states to take action where the gravity of the situation demands it, and the action has a reasonable prospect of resolving the crisis and saving more lives than it costs.

It is less easy to think of real-life situations where this has actually happened,[20] although, given the UN's undoubted failures in some interventions, it is not surprising that many humanitarians support such 'unauthorized interventions' as a potential measure of last resort.

Others go even further and argue that the UN should be bypassed from the decision-making process entirely. Professor Henry Shue, for example, states that 'an authorizing body for military intervention needs to be either democratic or impartial or both. The [UN] Security Council is neither.'[21] He also, however, attacks the UN for constraining itself to the principle of 'impartiality' and says that 'it is especially obtuse to think . . . that the intervention should be impartial between victims and victimizers.'[22] Geoffrey Robertson also argues that decisions on intervention 'cannot be the sole prerogative of the UN, because its defective procedures have blocked it [intervention] on many appropriate occasions'.[23] He maintains that there is an 'evolving principle of humanitarian necessity' in which states may, in exceptional, conscience-shocking situations use 'proportionate force' to intervene in other states' internal affairs in order to uphold certain basic rights or end gross violations. Applying this to NATO's intervention in Kosovo in 1999, he states that while this 'was plainly a breach of Article 2 (7) of the [UN] Charter' it was legally justified for the following reasons:

> In the three months before the air strikes evidence emerged of massacres of ethnic Albanians by Serb troops, directed from Belgrade, going far beyond what could ever be justified as reprisals for some terrorist killings committed by an insurgent Albanian group, the Kosova Liberation Army. Evidence mounted that Serbia was engaged in a plan to terrorise the ethnic majority in the province, to 'ethnically cleanse' it by persecuting the Albanian majority so severely that they would flee, creating a refugee crisis for neighbouring States. This would amount to a crime against humanity under Article 7 of

the Rome Statute which set up the International Criminal Court. The legal justification for NATO's attack without security council approval was that a) the Serbian State was engaged in an ongoing conspiracy to commit a crime against humanity; b) this conspiracy was producing a humanitarian emergency which threatened international peace and c) military intervention in the form of air strikes was a proportionate deterrent, offering a reasonable prospect of avoiding the tragedy, or at least punishing its perpetrators.[24]

This is a reasonable summary of how its supporters justified NATO's intervention in Kosovo; however, all the supposed facts on which it is based are contestable. The massacres perpetrated by Serbian forces were on a relatively small scale and were mainly carried out by local forces in retaliation for KLA actions. Although they involved clear violations of human rights, there is no evidence that these murders were part of a systematic campaign of 'ethnic cleansing'. The first mass displacement of Albanians from their homes came in the summer of 1998 and was part of a military counter-offensive against the KLA, not an attempt to change the province's ethnic demography. The second did not occur until after the start of NATO's action. There is evidence that the latter was indeed directed from Belgrade as part of a deliberate plan to create a refugee crisis intended to put pressure on NATO to stop the bombing, and, as such, it can rightly be described as a 'crime against humanity'; its timing, however, invalidates the rest of the argument.

NATO's intervention in Kosovo can legitimately be described as humanitarian because its basic war aim was to bring the suffering of civilians to an end. However, air strikes could never have provided direct protection to the civilian population, only ground troops could have done so. Indeed, the most direct consequence of removing the human rights observers was to increase the vulnerability of civilians, which inevitably led to a spike in the killings. NATO's strategists were fully aware of this in advance, and the key decisions governing the operation were taken on political rather than humanitarian grounds. Although Milošević subsequently ended up in the custody of the ICTY, his arrest was not directly linked to the intervention and was not a condition of the end of hostilities.

Shortly after the war, Richard Goldstone, a South African judge who became ICTY's first prosecutor, chaired an International Commission on Kosovo that produced a well-researched and balanced assessment of the crisis.[25] The Commission concluded that while a political case could be made for the intervention, it could not be justified on legal grounds. It further stated that earlier intervention by the international community could have resulted in a peaceful solution to the crisis, but that 'by the early part of 1998, the options for a peaceful settlement had disappeared.' According to the Commission, NATO's military intervention was illegal because it did not have the consent of the Security Council, but legitimate because it 'succeeded in liberating the Kosovo Albanian population from the oppression that they were suffering'. The report stated that the gap between these two concepts needed to be bridged, but that NATO's apparent success should not be used as a precedent for sidelining the UN in the future. It was 'an unfortunate but necessary and reasonable exception' to the basic rules about interventions and international law. The report observed:

> Collective intervention blessed by the UN is regarded as legitimate because it is duly authorized by a representative international body; unilateral intervention is seen as illegitimate because self-interested. Those who challenge or evade the authority of the UN as the sole legitimate guardian of international peace and security in specific instances run the risk of eroding its authority in general and also undermining the principle of a world order based on international law and universal norms.[26]

A group of leading international scholars on humanitarian intervention argue the opposite, that Kosovo should be regarded as a precedent.[27] They propose that a 'coalition of liberal-democratic States' should draw up a new treaty containing criteria in which military interventions on human rights grounds are permissible, which 'would violate existing UN-based law'. They should then attempt to 'create a new norm of customary international law' through repeatedly acting outside the framework of the UN Charter and stating that they believe they have a right to do so (to establish the *opinio juris*).[28] According to one of these scholars, 'The phrase "UN-based law" is chosen deliberately. Proponents of reform . . . would stress that the UN is not identical with international law. Rather, it is only one, historically contingent, institutional embodiment of the idea of an international legal system. International law existed before the UN and may exist after the UN's demise.'[29] Another scholar specifically blamed international law for the failure of the UN commander in Bosnia, General Bernard Janvier, to prevent the Srebrenica massacre:

> He could have saved those 7,000 victims, but chose not to act. Now let us assume that General Janvier is an educated officer of the French Army. Very likely he took international law classes as part of his instruction. If so, very likely he was told that humanitarian intervention is prevented by international law by the same people who argue for that proposition today in France and elsewhere.[30]

Others have expressed similar views, albeit more cautiously. Antonio Cassese, the first president of ICTY who later chaired the UN inquiry into Darfur, has suggested that a new customary rule is crystallizing in international law that would legitimize such unilateral interventions.[31] Christopher Greenwood, who has often acted as an international legal adviser to the British Government, maintains that unilateral intervention to prevent 'another Rwanda, another Holocaust or even acts of mass killing that cannot be characterised as genocide, must be permissible under customary international law'.[32] But equally eminent international lawyers, such as Ian Brownlie and Michael Byers, disagree and the point remains contested. Opponents of the doctrine mainly base their concerns on its possible misuse and the damage it does to an international rules-based system.[33] Brownlie asked rhetorically how NATO's seventy-eight-day 'blitz with high explosives', which included non-military targets and the specific objective of putting pressure on a civilian population, can be described as a humanitarian intervention.[34] Helen Duffy notes that: 'As so few States have asserted a legal right to intervene on humanitarian grounds, it follows that the parameters of the concept remain undeveloped.'[35]

The strongest precedent for such an intervention, apart from Kosovo, was the establishment of the Kurdish 'safe haven' in 1991. This was backed by a Security Council resolution, albeit not one taken under Chapter VII of the UN Charter. Legal counsel for the UK Foreign Office has since cited both Kosovo and the Kurdish case as 'extreme circumstances [in which] a state can intervene in another state for humanitarian reasons'[36] and 'an exceptional measure on grounds of overwhelming humanitarian necessity.'[37] However, the Foreign Office has also stated that

> the best case that can be made in support of humanitarian intervention is that it cannot be said to be unambiguously illegal . . . But the overwhelming majority of contemporary legal opinion comes down against [it] . . . the case against making humanitarian intervention an exception to the principle of non-intervention is that its doubtful benefits would be out-weighed by its costs in terms of respect for international law.[38]

The International Commission on Intervention and State Sovereignty (ICISS), which was established after the Kosovo intervention and reported at the end of 2001, tried to weave a middle course through these various arguments. Its final report was endorsed at the UN World Summit in 2005 and led to the Security Council adopting a resolution the following year affirming its 'responsibility to protect' civilians in armed conflict from 'genocide, war crimes, ethnic cleansing and crimes against humanity'.[39] The doctrine of a 'responsibility to protect' (R2P) accepts both the logic of non-intervention and its permissibility in certain extreme circumstances. It states that: 'Intervention in the domestic affairs of states is often harmful. It can destabilize the order of states, while fanning ethnic or civil strife. When internal forces seeking to oppose a State believe that they can generate outside support by mounting campaigns of violence, the internal order of all States is potentially compromised. The rule against intervention in internal affairs encourages States to solve their own internal problems.' Nevertheless, it concludes, states must be held accountable for the way they treat their own populations:

> The case for thinking of sovereignty in these terms is strengthened by the ever-increasing impact of international human rights norms, and the increasing impact in international discourse of the concept of human security. International organizations, civil society activists and NGOs use the international human rights norms and instruments as the concrete point of reference against which to judge state conduct.[40]

The report argued for the development of a set of criteria for interventions based on 'just cause', 'right intention', 'last resort', 'proportional means' and 'reasonable prospect'. It states that: 'There is no better or more appropriate body than the United Nations Security Council to authorize military intervention for human protection purposes . . . Security Council authorization should in all cases be sought prior to any military intervention action being carried out.' However, if this council 'fails to discharge its responsibility to protect in conscience-shocking situations crying out for action, concerned states may not rule out other means to meet the gravity and urgency of that situation'. The report does not spell out what these 'other means' should be and, apart from raising the possibility of referring the issue to the UN General Assembly, contains no recommendation for circumventing the Security Council's authority. It also caustically notes that: 'Those States who insist on the right to retaining permanent membership of the UN Security Council and the resulting veto power, are in a difficult position when they claim to be entitled to act outside the UN framework as a result of the Council being paralyzed by a veto cast by another permanent member.'[41] As discussed in chapter one of this book, the report also floated the idea that NGOs should be formally incorporated into discussions of when military interventions on human rights ground are justified.

The report's recommendations for reform of the council were largely ignored by its permanent members and the wording they used to endorse the report's findings clearly stated that humanitarian interventions would need to be authorized by the Security Council to be considered legitimate. The UN Sub-Commission on Human Rights had previously declared itself: 'Deeply concerned at the intensified efforts to develop the concept of an alleged "duty" or "right" of certain States to carry out "humanitarian interventions", including through armed force, in situations unilaterally identified by themselves, as well as at the military operations undertaken using such justification, which have caused heavy loss of life among the civilian population and immense damage to civilian facilities.' It further expressed its 'firmest conviction' that such interventions were 'juridically totally unfounded under current general international law and consequently cannot be considered as a justification for violations of the principles enshrined in Article 2 of the Charter of the United Nations'.[42]

The ICISS and its R2P doctrine can be considered a small advance for the interventionist cause, although the UN's reaction shows that the issue is far from settled. Similar language to the ICISS report's can also be found in numerous UN speeches and reports throughout the 1990s, many of which also stress the significance of NGOs in the debate on intervention. The UN's *Agenda for Peace* report of 1992, for example, stated that NGOs' monitoring and advocacy work had turned them into part of the international community's 'early-warning' system for crises.[43] Boutros Boutros-Ghali similarly wrote in 1996, 'I know that it is sometimes difficult to convince states to commit themselves to essential peace-keeping activities. For them to commit personnel, materiel and money in the service of peace and in the framework of UN activities, it is often necessary for national public opinion to lead the way. Nongovernmental organizations, in most cases, have helped to clear the way.'[44]

Clearly humanitarian NGOs that engage in advocacy work can influence the debate about such interventions. CARE played a significant role in mobilizing support for the UN intervention in Somalia and also lobbied hard for military intervention to restore Haiti's elected government following a military coup against President Aristide in 1991.[45] World Vision joined Human Rights Watch and a number of other organizations in calling for military action against the Serb forces besieging the remaining Muslim enclaves after the fall of Srebrenica.[46] Oxfam also called for military intervention in eastern Zaire in 1996[47] and in Sierra Leone in 2000.[48]

Oxfam was one of the few NGOs to advocate military intervention in Kosovo when it released a statement in August 1998, regretting that 'the threat of military action by NATO over the summer has not prevented major offensives or the systematic abuse of civilians'. It stated that 'Oxfam believes action to enforce a ceasefire must be taken', and followed this up with a private letter to the British Government arguing for a credible threat of force as 'the only remaining option to uphold citizens' rights in war'. It said: 'this may not be an ideal option, but from Oxfam's perspective it is the least worst option.'[49]

Tony Vaux, who helped draft the letter, has subsequently written that he hoped the threat of force alone would be sufficient to force a Serbian climb down, and that once the conflict started Oxfam could not agree on any public position to take. It resisted pressure from its staff in Belgrade to condemn the bombing of civilian targets in Serbia, and felt unable to speak out against other alleged violations of international humanitarian law by NATO forces. Although its Belgrade office wanted a clear condemnation of attacks on non-military targets, staff at head-quarters responded that this could mean the organization would get drawn into a debate on what kind of bombs it was or was not legitimate to drop. As an organization based in one of the countries that was doing the bombing, this seemed too con-troversial a position to take.[50]

Most other aid agencies and human rights organizations remained silent on NATO's decision to take military action, using variations on Amnesty's 'neither supports nor opposes' formulation when questioned. However, there was a huge and highly publicized relief operation to assist the Kosovar Albanian refugees, during which aid workers closely co-operated with NATO military forces, accepting logistical support, travelling on military aircraft and helping build refugee camps alongside NATO soldiers. Although MSF refused to accept funds from governments involved in the NATO operation, most other agencies did so. CARE even accepted a grant from the Canadian Government to second staff into the OSCE Kosovo Verification Mission, which was suspected of involvement in intelligence-gathering activities. Three of CARE's staff in Belgrade were falsely accused of espionage and imprisoned by the Serbs during the bombing campaign.

Virtually every major humanitarian organization established programmes in Kosovo after the conflict, although we all knew of other places where people were in far greater need of assistance. Many of these programmes were entirely donor-driven, with the explicit aim of weakening 'extremist' political parties and promoting support for western liberal values and human rights. I was in Belgrade on the day Milošević was arrested, following his downfall in the 'bulldozer revolution' of October 2000, and remember the streets were plastered with posters depicting him as a corrupt war criminal. They were printed by a newly-created NGO which was heavily backed by USAID and other western donors. A similar group was also created in Kosovo and it ran a publicity campaign aimed at 'promoting tolerance' and weakening the influence of 'political extremists' during the province's first elections.

Oxfam had supported the use of force in Kosovo because it could not see any other way of preventing serious human rights violations, just as CARE in Somalia had called for military intervention on the grounds that there was no alternative for safeguarding its aid deliveries. Both believed that the concept of military action to protect the rights of civilians should override the principle of neutrality in these specific and narrowly-defined circumstances. Subsequently, a large number of organizations were involved in providing humanitarian assistance that was not delivered under conditions of neutrality.

Clearly the invasion of Iraq could not have been justified as an 'unauthorized humanitarian intervention' since there was no ongoing humanitarian crisis at the time. Unlike Kosovo, where UN Security Council authorization of the intervention was blocked by the veto powers of a minority, the majority of the Council was opposed to the invasion of Iraq. However, some claim that the interventionist doctrine could potentially be stretched to cover such cases. Human Rights Watch, for example, ran a long-standing campaign for the indictment of Saddam Hussein before an international criminal tribunal on crimes of genocide. Robertson argues that had the US and UK backed these efforts in the run-up to the invasion they could have invoked the provision in the Genocide Convention, which calls on its perpetrators to be brought before an international tribunal. The Security Council could have then 'dispatched human rights inspectors to gather evidence and to examine his prisons, police cells and court system'. By exposing the massive human rights violations the Iraqi Government had committed in the past, he argues, a case could have been made for military invasion which 'would have been more difficult for France and Russia and Germany to overlook'.[51] In his view, the combination of international human rights and humanitarian law provides a potential new dynamic. The former acts as a key 'to unlocking the closed door of state sovereignty', while the latter provides a mechanism for 'holding political and military leaders responsible for the evils they choose to visit on humankind'.[52]

> The global justice movement is a human rights offensive. In the past NGOs pleaded with tyrants to be less tyrannical and published reports which exposed state-sponsored torture and murder about which nothing could be done. Today, tyrants can be threatened, credibly, with international justice . . . We are beginning to call a savage a savage whether he or she is black or white. There will be less respect for old men with beards be they mullahs, or rabbis or patriarchs who ordain cruelty in the name of religion.[53]

During the US presidential campaign in 2008 the Republican candidate, John McCain, called for the creation of a 'League of Democracies', which could take military action in humanitarian crises 'where the UN failed to act'.[54] Robert Kagan, another prominent supporter of the invasion of Iraq, has called for the creation of such a league to 'promote liberal ideals in international relations'.[55]

While the initial impetus for this development came from within the humanitarian movement, many may now be dismayed by what their arguments are being used to promote. A year after the Kosovo intervention, a group of prominent international NGOs published a Humanitarian Charter as part of a project aimed at increasing the 'effectiveness and accountability' of their agencies.[56] The Charter states that it is 'based on two core beliefs: first that all possible steps should be taken to alleviate human suffering that arises out of conflict and calamity, and second that those affected by a disaster have a right to life with dignity and therefore a right to assistance. The Charter defines the legal responsibilities of states and parties to guarantee the right to assistance and protection. When states are unable to respond they are obliged to allow the intervention of humanitarian organisations.'

This last claim was dropped from a revised version of the Charter published in 2004. The idea that sovereign states are 'obliged to allow' humanitarian organizations to intervene in their countries is a quite startling proposition. It begs such obvious questions as: why, and what happens if they refuse?

In its original wording the Charter stated that 'international humanitarian law makes specific provision for assistance to civilian populations during conflict, obliging States and other parties to agree to the provision of humanitarian and impartial assistance when the civilian population lacks essential supplies.'[57] This obligation stems from the fact that the Geneva Conventions prohibit the use of starvation and the denial of life-saving supplies as a weapon of war against civilian populations.[58] According to the Geneva Conventions, if the civilian population of a territory that is either occupied or otherwise under the control of a party to the conflict is not adequately provided with food, medical attention and other necessary materials the party must agree to allow the free passage of relief supplies for purely humanitarian purposes.[59] Humanitarian organizations have the right to offer their assistance to parties to a conflict, without this being construed as an unfriendly act by the parties.[60] States must also not interpret the Conventions in such a way as to create obstacles to genuine humanitarian activity. The right of the ICRC to carry out humanitarian activities, and to be afforded the necessary facilities by state parties, is also explicitly acknowledged.[61] Occupying powers must also allow independent humanitarian evaluations of the situation and the needs of the civilian population.[62]

However, these provisions refer to international conflicts. The obligation on states to provide access in internal conflicts, contained in Protocol II of the Geneva Conventions, is much weaker. Starving civilians as a method of combat is prohibited[63], and the right of humanitarian initiative is also recognized.[64] Medical personnel must also be afforded freedom of movement 'whenever circumstances permit'.[65] But humanitarian organizations can only 'offer their services' and any activity is 'subject to the consent of the State concerned'.[66] Article 3 of Protocol II emphatically restates that:

1. Nothing in this Protocol shall be invoked for the purpose of affecting the sovereignty of a State or the responsibility of the government, by all legitimate means, to maintain or re-establish law and order in the State or to defend the national unity and territorial integrity of the State.
2. Nothing in this Protocol shall be invoked as a justification for intervening, directly or indirectly, for any reason whatever, in the armed conflict or in the internal or external affairs of the High Contracting Party in the territory of which that conflict occurs.

Since most wars, famines and other natural and man-made disasters take place entirely within the borders of a state, the laws of international armed conflict are not of much relevance here. It could be argued that states are obliged to grant access to relief supplies to affected populations, even during a purely internal conflict.[67] However, international law also recognizes that a state may derogate from certain human rights obligations in public emergencies which could legitimately permit it to impose various restrictions on the activities of aid organizations making deliveries. For example, freedom of movement could be suspended and suspected subversives interned without trial.

Organizations engaging in activities that provide indirect support for the political objectives of a rebel movement could be thrown out of the country and their staff arrested.

This is not a purely theoretical debate, as the experiences of the humanitarian agencies in Darfur, Burma, and elsewhere have shown. Governments frequently block aid workers from implementing projects and delivering supplies by citing vague considerations of 'national security'. More generally, the Federation of Red Cross and Red Crescent Societies have noted both government bureaucracy and national rules and regulations can be significant obstacles to getting aid to people in an emergency. Import duties for relief goods, visa requirements on staff, transit, over-flight and landing restrictions on supply flights all add significantly to the cost of an operation and slow down aid deliveries.[68] To what extent can a government legitimately impose policies that will prevent aid getting to its own people, and are there circumstances in which international agencies would be justified in flouting them? Is there a 'right', in international law, to deliver assistance against the wishes of the government concerned?

One of the only international legal cases to have considered this is contained within the ICJ's judgment on 'Nicaragua v United States', discussed in chapter two. The judgment rejected most of the US's arguments for interfering in Nicaragua's internal affairs, but ruled that not all the support the US extended to the contras was unlawful. It distinguished between the delivery of humanitarian aid and weapons and also stated that: 'The provision of strictly humanitarian aid to persons or forces in another country, whatever their political affiliations or objectives, cannot be regarded as unlawful, or as in any other way contrary to international law.'[69] The Court went on to define what constituted this type of aid:

An essential feature of truly humanitarian aid is that it is given 'without discrimination' of any kind. In the view of the

Court, if the provision of 'humanitarian assistance' is to escape condemnation as an intervention in the internal affairs of Nicaragua, not only must it be limited to the purposes hallowed in the practices of the Red Cross, namely 'to prevent and alleviate human suffering' and 'to protect life and health and to ensure respect for the human being'; it must also and above all be given without discrimination to all in need in Nicaragua, not merely to the *contras* and their dependents.[70]

Humanitarian aid agencies might argue that, since they are bound by their mandates to respond impartially to human need and suffering, they automatically fulfil these criteria, and the allocation of all humanitarian assistance involves some discrimination at the most basic level of how to share out finite resources. However, as the previous examples in this book show, there is an increasing trend towards using humanitarian aid to further certain political objectives, and organizations such as the ICRC, which have attempted to maintain the principles of humanitarian neutrality, have come under increasing criticism from a variety of commentators.[71]

The ICRC consistently refuses to allow its employees, past and present, to testify before any court or tribunal in respect of matters that came to their attention in their official capacities.[72] ICTY recognized that 'customary international law provides the ICRC with an absolute right to non-disclosure of information relating to the work of the ICRC.'[73] The ICRC also negotiated an exemption clause to the rules of procedure and evidence of the International Criminal Court (ICC) which provides that its information shall be regarded as privileged.[74] During the negotiations that led to the drafting of the UN Convention on the Safety of United Nations and Associated Personnel, the ICRC indicated that it did not want its own personnel to be protected under this convention since it feared its role as a neutral humanitarian intermediary could be jeopardized if it was perceived to be too closely aligned to the UN.[75]

Robertson has described this commitment to neutrality and confidentiality as a 'fetish' that requires its workers to 'turn a blind eye to human rights violations'.[76] As he points out, the ICRC's delegates knew for several months that prisoners were being abused in Guantánamo Bay and Abu Ghraib before it became public knowledge. The ICRC sent five specific complaints to the US Government about the abuse of prisoners in Iraq towards the end of 2003. Its full report was sent to the US and UK authorities in February 2004, yet the story did not become public until April of that year. 'In how many other prisons has the Red Cross found evidence of torture, and found its reports being consistently ignored, yet it still refuses to speak out knowing that torture is continuing,' Robertson asks rhetorically. The obvious answer to this is 'probably quite a lot', yet it is difficult to see any alternative being proposed. The ICRC is granted this access only because it guarantees to regard the information as privileged and such access would be withdrawn if it ceased to do so.

Organizations which can speak out against human rights violations – when speaking out will do some good and not jeopardize their access – will probably do so. The ICRC, for instance, denounced war crimes committed during the conflict in the former Yugoslavia, and one of its delegates has stated that it sees neutrality not as an end in itself but as a means of carrying out its mandate. 'The ICRC does not always abstain from denouncing humanitarian law violations,' she said. 'It subjects denunciations to certain conditions, notably the requirement that any such publicity be in the interests of the persons or populations affected or under threat.'[77]

On some occasions the ICRC was also prepared to operate without the consent of the authorities concerned. During the Ethiopian famine of 1984–5, for example, it was one of a number of humanitarian agencies that delivered aid to rural areas in Tigray and Eritrea against the expressed wishes of the central government, led by President Mengistu Haile Mariam, which had cut off all international aid to areas under rebel control as part of its counter-insurgency strategy.[78] In 1984, public exposure of the suffering caused by war and famine brought a worldwide surge in public interest and sympathy. The multi-venue Live Aid concerts and similar private fund-raising initiatives took place around the world. The Ethiopian Government at first tried to suppress the true scale of the famine, refusing to allow independent assessment missions to visit the regions most affected.[79] It then began to manipulate the aid for political purposes, transferring people out of the affected areas to 'new economic zones' in the south of the country. Humanitarian agencies became uneasy participating in this increasingly forceful population transfer programme, which seemed aimed at removing civilians from rebel-held areas rather than providing genuine famine relief.[80]

The bulk of the famine relief assistance provided by foreign donors went to Ethiopia's military government, and international NGOs such as Oxfam and World Vision continued to participate in the population transfer programme despite their increasing misgivings. MSF publicly condemned the programme and was expelled from government-controlled areas in December 1985.[81] An increasing number of donors began to channel cash contributions into rebel-held areas.[82] From the late 1970s onwards a cross-border relief operation was mounted by three different agencies: the ICRC; Emergency Relief Desk (ERD), a consortium of Scandinavian church-led organizations; and War on Want, a radical British-based NGO, both of which dramatically increased the delivery of aid in the mid-1980s.

The Ethiopian Government took military action in an attempt to prevent the deliveries, and the ICRC removed the humanitarian symbols from its vehicles after they were attacked by the Ethiopian military. War on Want made little attempt to remain impartial and championed its support for the rebel cause. Its reports on Tigray, *The Hidden Revolution*, and Eritrea, *Never Kneel Down*, were overtly propagandist and it donated trucks and helped build roads in the full knowledge that they could be used for military as well as humanitarian purposes.[83] ERD was far more discreet about its support; one of the reasons the consortium was created was to provide cover for the participating agencies. It effectively collaborated with the rebel-supporting relief associations but tried to do so covertly. The ICRC, by contrast, laid down strict conditions for the delivery of its aid in an attempt to ensure that neither side derived any significant strategic benefits through its delivery. However, in May 1987 it decided to suspend its deliveries, having failed to persuade both the government and the rebel groups to respect its impartiality.

The cross-border operation undoubtedly saved many people from starvation and also helped counter the Ethiopian Government's attempts to use food and famine as weapons of war. The EPLF and TPLF overthrew Mengistu in 1991, though the two guerrilla movements were to plunge Ethiopia and newly-independent Eritrea back into a conflict that claimed thousands more lives at the end of the 1990s. The aid operation also boosted the profile of War on Want's director, George Galloway, who was elected to the British Parliament in 1987. The ICRC again failed to persuade the two parties to respect its neutral status, but by withdrawing it reinforced the point that its neutrality was not up for negotiation.

The ICRC bases its work on the Geneva Conventions, which specifically refer to the activities of 'impartial humanitarian' organizations and define their role as providing assistance to certain victims of conflicts who are entitled to protection due to their status. The concepts of 'protection' and 'assistance' have a specific and legal meaning here but are also often used more loosely in discussions about humanitarianism and human rights. This can lead to considerable confusion since some human rights treaties also cover economic, social and cultural rights, which include the rights to food, clothing and shelter. Since these are of life-saving importance during a humanitarian crisis, it could be argued that governments are 'obliged' to accept such assistance if it cannot be provided through their own resources. Clearly if there is a 'right to assistance' it also implies an obligation that someone delivers it, and if there is a 'responsibility to protect' then mechanisms must be created to fulfil it. The broad tension between the concept of national sovereignty and the doctrine of international community is obvious, but the notion of a 're-sponsibility to protect' also raises specific issues related to notions of justice and accountability, which are further explored in the next two chapters.

Chapter Seven

Justice and Peace

CHARLES JJUUKO, head of the International Criminal Court's (ICC) outreach and information programme in Uganda, has one of the toughest jobs in his country. For more than twenty years northern Uganda has been ravaged by a campaign of terror by the Lords Resistance Army (LRA), making it Africa's longest-running civil war. The atrocities perpetrated by the LRA have succeeded in displacing 90 per cent of the people of northern Uganda from their homes. It has kidnapped around 20,000 children, some of whom have been forced to kill members of their own families, and systematically murdered, tortured, raped and maimed the people on whose behalf it claims to be fighting. The LRA's avowed aim is to establish a state based on the Bible's Ten Commandments, and it is led by Joseph Kony who proclaims himself a spirit medium and promises his followers that he can make them invincible to bullets. Many people who have met him conclude that he is completely mad.

In September 2005, the ICC chief prosecutor issued arrest warrants for Kony and four other LRA leaders on charges of war crimes and crimes against humanity. Three of the indictees are believed to be dead, including Josef Otti, Kony's deputy, who allegedly fell victim to an internal struggle within the LRA in October 2007, and Okot Odhiambo, believed to have died in a gun battle with government soldiers in April 2008. At the time that they were issued, Kofi Annan, the former UN secretary-general, said the warrants would 'send a powerful signal around the world that those responsible for such crimes will be held accountable for their actions'.[1] Groups such as Amnesty International also issued a more cautious welcome.

Inside Uganda itself, however, the move was met with outright hostility from a range of human rights and civil society organizations and traditional leaders. The condemnation was strongest in the north of the country, among those who have worked with people most affected by the conflict. I went to northern Uganda in September 2006 to work on a consultancy research project for UN-HABITAT, and it was a couple of months before I met Jjuuko. Everyone I spoke to expressed the same view, that the ICC's intervention was ill-thought-out and counter-productive. Jjuuko was nervous about me interviewing him. We met in a local café rather than at his office, and he asked me to put my questions in writing so he could clear his answers with the Court's headquarters in The Hague. His outreach and information programme was created as a specific response to the charge that the ICC was an out-of-touch international body meddling in affairs it did not understand.

The ICC prosecutor, Luis Moreno-Ocampo, had announced he was initiating the case at a January 2004 joint press conference in London with Uganda's President Yoweri Museveni.[2] Amnesty International's response to the announcement noted that 'any court investigation of war crimes and crimes against humanity in northern Uganda must be part of a comprehensive plan to end impunity for all such crimes, regardless of which side committed them and the level of the perpetrator.'[3] However, few outside the country commented on the obvious incongruity of a prosecutor jointly announcing the opening of an independent criminal investigation with someone who might turn out to be a chief suspect.

Moreno-Ocampo's office clarified that he would be investigating crimes 'by whomever committed', including by government forces, but the initial impression created was that he was acting on Museveni's behalf and focussing solely on the LRA. The implicit assumption was that only one side in Uganda's civil war had committed the kind of violations that fall within the ICC's jurisdiction.

The LRA responded to the September 2005 indictments by launching a series of co-ordinated attacks against humanitarian agencies in which two aid workers were killed and others wounded.[4] Two representatives of the ICC prosecutor had earlier been invited to address a meeting convened by the UN Office for the Co-ordination of Humanitarian Affairs (OCHA), without the foreknowledge of most attendees. MSF staff who attended complained this might have given the impression that aid organizations were co-operating with the ICC investigation at an operational level.[5] Most aid organizations have, publicly or privately, called on the ICC to drop its prosecutions in northern Uganda, and, for the reasons described below, it is increasingly likely that this may happen in the event of a peace agreement.

Many humanitarians initially welcomed the establishment of the ICC and the international tribunals that preceded it. Alex de Waal even suggested that their scope should be expanded to enable them to investigate 'famine crimes'.[6] In practice, however, their presence has further politicized the environment in which humanitarians work and posed them with a number of operating problems. Should they co-operate with its investigations and prosecutions, and if they do, what impact might such co-operation have on issues such as access and staff safety? Should they support its outreach activities and help dispel some of the myths and misconceptions developing about it? And are there occasions when they should publicly oppose its interventions on the grounds that it is damaging processes of peace and reconciliation? As discussed in the previous chapter, the ICRC negotiated an exemption for itself from the ICC, which provides that its information shall be regarded as privileged; other humanitarian organizations may decide to follow this example.[7]

The origins of the ICC lie in the Nuremberg Trials after the Second World War and the Genocide Convention of 1948. These events established that the way governments treat their own subjects is not solely a prerogative of national sovereignty, and that individuals can be held criminally accountable for certain human rights violations, that is, war crimes, genocide and crimes against humanity. The Genocide Convention's reference to prosecutions through 'an international penal tribunal'[8] anticipated the existence of the ICC, but it took fifty years before its statute was agreed to at a 1998 conference in Rome.

The 1998 statute needed to be ratified by sixty states before it came into force. A vigorous campaign by an alliance of human rights NGOs helped it achieve this remarkably quickly, allowing the Court to be established in 2002. However, the ICC has been bitterly opposed by the US Government, which has seriously weakened the Court's initial work. The US previously supported the *ad hoc* international criminal tribunals for the former Yugoslavia, Rwanda and Sierra Leone and, despite strongly expressed reservations, President Clinton signed the Court's statute in the final few hours of his presidency, on 31 December 1999. However, his successor, George Bush, withdrew the signature and has adopted an aggressively hostile approach towards the Court. The US Government demanded that its soldiers receive '100 per cent protection' from prosecutions. It even passed an act authorizing military action against Holland if any members of the US armed forces are ever sent to The Hague.[9]

It is probably no coincidence that the ICC's first investigations were launched in places of limited strategic significance to the major powers. The government of Uganda asked the ICC to investigate the situation in the north of the country in December 2003. This was followed by similar requests from the governments of the Democratic Republic of Congo (DRC) and the Central African Republic. Thomas Lubanga Dyilo, leader of a rebel group in the DRC, was the first suspect handed over in March 2006, followed by Germain Katanga, another DRC rebel leader, in October 2007. The Court has taken Charles Taylor, the former president of Liberia, into custody, though his case is being tried under the exclusive jurisdiction of the Special Court for Sierra Leone. It is also believed to be investigating Ange-Félix Patassé, former president of the Central African Republic.

In February 2007, the ICC prosecutor issued an indictment against a Sudanese government minister and a *janjaweed* militia leader over crimes committed in the Darfur region. This is the first case taken against a state that is not party to the ICC's statute, and follows a referral by the UN Security Council in March 2005. Sudan has signed but not ratified the ICC statute and its government has refused to hand over the two men. The Sudanese authorities also clamped down on the activities of a number of humanitarian aid agencies and arrested MSF's head of mission, which the organization believes was in retaliation for the ICC referral.[10] In July 2008, the ICC indicted Sudan's President Omar al-Bashir for crimes including genocide. The indictment of serving government ministers with crimes under the ICC's statute is clearly of great significance, as is the fact that the US did not veto the original referral of the case at the UN Security Council. While it was heralded as a victory by the Court's supporters, it also highlights the dilemma over what kind of body the ICC will turn out to be. While some claim that the Court marks a significant step towards a system of universal justice, it is developing into a quite different organization from the vision of its founders.

The idea of a court that can prosecute the gravest violations of human rights whenever and wherever they occur is undoubtedly inspiring. The ICC was envisaged as a body that would strike a blow against impunity by preventing dictators, warlords and gangsters absolving themselves from their crimes through granting 'self-amnesties' before they handed over power, or demanding such amnesties as the price for peace. The statute's preamble declares that 'the most serious crimes of concern to the international community as a whole must not go unpunished and that their effective prosecution must be ensured by taking measures at the national level and by enhancing international cooperation.' It could still fulfil this initial promise, but its first case in Uganda set some unfortunate precedents.

One problem with the ICC lies in the way it can gain jurisdiction over a case. As Geoffrey Robertson has noted, the Rome negotiations had two basic models to choose from.[11] The US, China and France wanted a court controlled by the UN Security Council, meaning that its five permanent members could veto any prosecutions. A large group of 'like-minded countries', led by Canada and Germany, wanted a court that was independent of the Security Council, with a powerful prosecutor endowed with universal jurisdiction who could charge suspects anywhere in the world. This was the model backed by human rights NGOs, and the decision by Tony Blair's new Labour Government to support it was probably the deciding factor that led to its adoption. This caused one of the few early splits in Blair's cabinet meetings, when Robin Cook resisted Blair's pressure to accommodate to the US Government's demands.

An independent court with universal jurisdiction was undoubtedly the right choice in principle, but efforts to win US approval led to the adoption of a deeply-flawed compromise. The ICC's statute gives it jurisdiction over a case brought by either a Chapter VII resolution by the Security Council, empowering it to take extraordinary measures to prevent a threat to peace and security, or with the consent of the state in which the accused is either a national or where the offence was committed. The ICC prosecutor can also initiate preliminary investigations into allegations of crimes on his own initiative or as a result of requests and individual complaints. It is theoretically possible that he could bring a case against a national of a state that has not ratified the statute for offences committed on the territory of a state that has. If US forces, for example, were to commit war crimes or crimes against humanity in a country that has ratified the statute, they could potentially be prosecuted even though their own state has not.

However, the prosecutor can only recommend 'the commencement of an investigation' to a pretrial hearing of the Court rather than bring the case directly. The hearing then examines the initial evidence and decides whether or not there is a reasonable basis to proceed.[12] For this initial analysis the prosecutor may 'seek additional information from States, organs of the United Nations, intergovernmental or non-governmental organizations, or other reliable sources'. Once indictments have been issued the prosecution cannot withdraw the case. However, the Security Council can use its Chapter VII powers to order an indefinitely renewable twelve-month suspension, and a pretrial hearing of the Court can also decide to end a case 'in the interests of justice taking into account all the circumstances'.[13]

This cumbersome procedure means that the prosecutor is unlikely to start an investigation unless he is fairly confident he will be able to gather enough evidence at a very early stage to justify the opening of formal proceedings at a pretrial hearing. The Court has very few resources for investigations, making it difficult to work without the co-operation of the state in which the crimes have been committed. Once it decides to charge someone, the ICC can only issue a warrant for his or her arrest and ask the state concerned to hand the person over. As the example of Sudan has shown, there is no way in practice to force a state to do so, but a co-operative state may well be grateful for material assistance in dealing with particularly difficult cases. For these reasons the ICC initially prioritized investigations where it had been asked to intervene by the state concerned.

Obviously, governments that have carried out the kind of crimes listed in the ICC statute are unlikely to request the Court to conduct investigations into their own activities, hence such requests are only likely to come from Security Council referrals. Darfur may set a trend for future investigations in this respect. The ICC statute specifies that the Court 'shall be complementary to national criminal jurisdictions' and will only prosecute where the national courts have shown themselves 'unable or unwilling' to do so.[14] In response to a number of individual complaints about US actions in Iraq, the prosecutor has stated that he will not pursue cases where the national courts and military tribunals take effective action against those alleged to have committed abuses. Nor will he investigate individual complaints unless they are part of a pattern that has reached a level of sufficient seriousness to justify such an intervention.[15] Neither Iraq nor the US has ratified the ICC statute, and the rather detailed reasoning the prosecutor issued is probably to reassure Americans that even if they had done so he would not be pursuing such cases.[16]

The heavy-handed pressure the US brought to bear on other countries – threatening to withdraw US forces unless they sign bilateral immunity agreements shielding them from the Court's jurisdiction, and the ludicrous 'invade the Hague' clause – have certainly helped alienate the US Government from the rest of the world. The ham-fisted nature of US diplomacy could prove even more counter-productive when negotiations reopen on how to define the crime of aggression. The three crimes over which the Court currently has jurisdiction are genocide, war crimes and crimes against humanity. A fourth crime, which the statute identifies as that of 'aggression', is widely understood to mean illegal attacks or threats of attack on other countries. However, the Rome conference could not agree on a precise definition for this, and so the statute states that:

> The Court shall exercise jurisdiction over the crime of aggression once a provision is adopted in accordance with articles 121 and 123 defining the crime and setting out the conditions under which the Court shall exercise jurisdiction with respect to this crime. Such a provision shall be consistent with the relevant provisions of the Charter of the United Nations.[17]

The Court agreed not to amend the statute until a formal review seven years after it came into operation, meaning that the issue of 'aggression' will be considered again in 2009.

Significantly, only states that have signed or ratified the statute can participate in these discussions, which means that the US will not be able to take part. It is entirely possible that the participants will agree on a definition, which could in turn clarify the circumstances in which states may legitimately use force against other countries on humanitarian grounds. One defence to the charge of 'aggression' could be the 'humanitarian exception', when a state or group of states uses military force without UN Security Council approval as the only means to prevent genocide or mass killing. The leaders of the states concerned would need to be sufficiently confident of their case that they would be prepared to answer for their actions in a court of law, which would bring some much needed clarity to the debate about such interventions.

Such an initiative could have far-reaching implications for the future of international relations and help create a legal framework capable of holding everyone to account for the world's worst crimes. However, the practical obstacles to enforcing this kind of global accountability show how elusive the goal of universal justice remains. The prosecutor cannot take a case retroactively, hence there is no chance that Bush or Blair will be prosecuted by it for the invasion of Iraq, but how would it deal with such a case in the future?

The record of the *ad hoc* tribunals for Yugoslavia and Rwanda provides some clues to this. It is now widely acknowledged that both bodies were mainly created as a substitute for effective military action by the UN at the time. The International Criminal Tribunal for the former Yugoslavia (ICTY) did not begin its first trial until May 1996, after the Dayton Peace Agreement, and it was not until 1999 that the more serious war criminals were taken into its custody. Likewise, the International Criminal Tribunal for Rwanda (ICTR) was not established until six months after the genocide. Although Geoffrey Robertson claims there is 'some tantalizingly intercept evidence' to suggest that the initial establishment of ICTY in 1993 may have given 'pause' to the Bosnian Serb military commanders, it certainly did not prevent the crimes they subsequently committed.[18]

The other rationale for the tribunals' establishment was that such a mechanism for bringing the perpetrators to justice could help facilitate the process of peace and reconciliation in the countries concerned. It was therefore crucial that the tribunals should conform to international standards of fairness, be free from all appearance of bias and win the trust and confidence of affected communities. Most independent observers agree that the trials conducted by both bodies were fairer than an equivalent process conducted by a national court. However, concern was expressed that decisions on whether, when and who to prosecute were taken on political grounds.

Following the Bosnian conflict, ICTY managed to arrest almost all of the 161 men it indicted; of these, it has convicted and sentenced fifty-nine. Although it has so far failed to apprehend the Bosnian Serb General Ratko Mladic, in July 2008 it arrested the political leader Radovan Karadzic. Slobodan Milošević was put on highly publicized trial, but died of natural causes before it concluded. President Franjo Tudjman, who also died of natural causes, was never charged but a number of Croatian political and military leaders have been indicted. Some Belgrade-based Serbian leaders suspected of carrying out atrocities in Kosovo have also been charged, but few of the Belgrade leaders suspected of crimes committed in Croatia and Bosnia-Herzegovina have been indicted.

Marko Attila Hoare, a researcher for ICTY on the Milošević case, claims that the tribunal's investigators originally intended to indict a larger group of his aides and allies but were overruled by the chief prosecutor Carla Del Ponte. He believes that the decision to create separate investigating teams to deal with crimes committed by different ethnic groups led to a structural pressure for each team to produce a certain number of significant prosecutions. While this gave an appearance of even-handedness, it was not necessarily justified on legal grounds since it was the

Bosnian Serb forces, with the tacit support of the Serbian Government, who committed most of the crimes.[19]

Following the Rwandan genocide, Rwanda opposed the creation of ICTR at the Security Council, of which it was a member at the time, and has repeatedly called for it to be wound up since it wants to prosecute the suspects itself. Many senior *genocidaires* were grateful for the chance to surrender into ICTR's custody instead, and some observers have complained of the supposedly luxurious treatment they now enjoy. Samantha Power, for example, has alleged that HIV-positive defendants were provided with expensive anti-retroviral treatment while it was withheld from prosecution witnesses who became infected when they were raped by *genocidaires*.[20] By October 2007, ICTR had arrested seventy-six of its ninety indicted suspects, convicted twenty-four and acquitted three. Those in custody included former prime minister Jean Kambanda and seven of his ministers.

Both tribunals were extremely slow to establish themselves and have been very expensive to run. ICTR has cost over a billion dollars and Rwanda argues this is a scandalous waste of money that could have been used to rebuild its own judiciary and dispute-resolution mechanisms. The government rounded up more than 100,000 people who it accused of participating in the genocide, a sweep that unsurprisingly overwhelmed its court and prison system. Many people have been awaiting trial in Rwandan prisons for over ten years. Human rights organizations have repeatedly criticized the conditions in which they are being held and expressed concern that some have been tortured. In an effort to speed up the process the government has introduced a 'Gacaca' court system, which draws on traditional communal law-enforcement procedures.

ICTY and ICTR are due to be wound up by the UN in 2010, but both Human Rights Watch and Amnesty International have opposed extraditions to Rwanda on the basis that it cannot guarantee suspects the right to a fair trial.[21] Rwanda has abolished the death penalty, improved conditions in some prisons and implemented other judicial reforms, but human rights organizations have also warned against the creation of a 'two-tier system of detention' in which special facilities are created in a handful of places to satisfy the international community while the rest of the prison population continues to suffer appalling conditions.

The argument over 'special privileges' highlights a major dilemma about the impact of international tribunals in many parts of the world where the ordinary criminal justice system routinely violates the rights of defendants. Clearly the treatment and trials of such bodies should conform to international standards, but what happens when a defendant ends up better off than his or her victims? When I was in Uganda I was repeatedly asked to explain the justice in giving the leaders of the LRA prison cells in The Hague where they could watch television and study for a university degree, while their victims remained in the misery of displacement camps where a thousand people a week are estimated to die due to the conditions they face. It was a very difficult question to answer.

Much of my work since leaving Afghanistan has involved looking at the way international human rights law can provide practical standards to help people in conflict and post-conflict situations. Travelling between war zones in Africa, Asia, Latin America and Europe, it was difficult not to reflect on the hollowness of some of the claims regarding the supposed universality of such mechanisms. In many meetings with African or Afghan civil servants or UN and World Bank officials, for example, we would discuss whether newly-enacted laws conformed to international standards, the need for specific legislative amendments or how to go about conducting more 'participatory research' to obtain the views of refugees and displaced people. Yet once I stepped outside their offices, I knew that the state did not really exist in any meaningful sense in many of the places most affected by conflict. The laws might specify the need for various boards, committees and tribunals, and lay down procedures for how they would conduct their business, but in many places they only existed on paper. Outside the big cities many people rely on customary legal systems rather than official laws.

In Afghanistan I saw the effectiveness of customary law as a mechanism of dispute resolution. Afghan customary law emphasizes the importance of 'restorative justice' and notions of 'shame' and 'honour'. It tries to find common ground to bring the two sides together and its judgments are aimed at providing compensation to the wronged party and requiring the 'guilty party' to demonstrate remorse. Judgments might include the ritual slaughter of a sheep as a symbolic plea for forgiveness, or require someone who has killed another person to carry the victim's coffin or lie for a moment in the grave before the burial. At many of the *Jirgas* and *Shuras* I attended I was initially shocked by how little attention was paid to the evidence presented and how much weight was given to subjective factors, such as the 'character' of the respective parties. Although I never witnessed it personally, I was told that awarding a woman from one family to another in marriage was a common way of binding the two sides together after a dispute. Many of the procedures clearly did not conform to international legal standards and sometimes violated the rights of one or other party to the dispute. Yet given the collapse of the formal court system it was difficult to see an alternative, and our legal counsellors worked with them to achieve what we could.

Many countries formally recognize customary law institutions as providing a sort of court of first instance. In Afghanistan and Aceh it is quite common for judges to suggest to parties that they use these institutions before bringing a case through the formal system. Community justice projects are growing in popularity throughout the world because they are cheaper, faster and more accessible than the formal courts. My wife is the co-ordinator of one such project in Brazil. Legal reform might not seem the most urgent task in a country emerging from conflict, but until the rule of law is re-established, most other humanitarian assistance can be only a short-term palliative. Rebuilding the capacity of judicial institutions while providing people with immediate assistance through whatever mechanisms exist has therefore become an established part of the international response to a humanitarian crisis. In Indonesia, for example, the World Bank is funding community justice projects partly to stop corrupt local officials from stealing the assistance it gives to help poor communities.

At their best, such projects help give communities a sense of ownership over projects that can ease the transition from humanitarian relief to longer-term sustainable development. The idea that 'justice' must be an essential component of a peace process is, however, a more questionable proposition than its international supporters are often prepared to admit. In northern Uganda, for instance, everyone I spoke to told me they thought the ICC indictments should be withdrawn and the LRA leaders should instead submit themselves to 'traditional justice mechanisms' by asking the community for forgiveness. A number of aid organizations have helped organize such ceremonies, which are also a way of welcoming former LRA fighters back into their families.[22]

In his book Trial Justice, Tim Allen has questioned the authenticity of these rituals and whether or not northern Uganda's community leaders really speak for the majority in favouring 'forgiveness' over 'justice'.[23] However, the recurring criticisms of the ICC I encountered were less to do with the supposed capacity of the people of northern Uganda to forgive the LRA for its crimes than with their concern that the prosecutions would damage the peace process. This process was led by civil society groups who had succeeded in overcoming President Museveni's opposition to the enactment of an Amnesty law. By the start of 2004, several thousand former LRA fighters were reintegrated into society, sometimes using traditional rituals. The timing of the ICC announcement cut across this, and part of the initial concern was that the new threat of prosecutions would deter mid-level commanders from leaving the bush. Although only five LRA leaders were eventually charged, Kony has made it clear that dropping these indictments is a prerequisite for a peace deal.

Many Ugandans, sick of twenty years of conflict and attempts to defeat the LRA militarily, consider this a small price to pay. Resentment at the ICC's failure to address the violations committed by the Ugandan armed forces, whose scorched-earth campaign against the LRA included forcible displacement, the recruitment of child soldiers and arbitrary executions and torture, also means that many think the prosecutions will be one-sided. While the army's abuses are on a lesser scale than those committed by the LRA, the ICC has damaged its local credibility by its failure to address them.

After this initial blunder, the ICC attempted to engage with northern Ugandan communities. Charles Jjuuko organized dozens of workshops and small group meetings with civil society organizations and traditional leaders to hear their concerns and combat misconceptions about the Court. The dilemma, however, is that part of the ICC's raison d'être is to remove discussions of justice from the political arena. The ICC prosecutor cannot withdraw his own case and must go back to the pretrial chamber to ask it to do so. The judges are formally permitted to close a case 'in the interests of justice taking into account all the circumstances'.[24] The UN Security Council can also order an indefinitely renewable twelve-month suspension of the prosecution.

In February 2008, it was announced that the Ugandan Government and the LRA leadership had agreed in principle to a peace deal by which alleged war criminals would be prosecuted in Uganda rather than handed over to the ICC. Amnesty International denounced the proposal saying that: 'It is not acceptable for the Ugandan government and the LRA to make a deal that circumvents international law.'[25] Human Rights Watch, by contrast, said that the agreement 'could be a major step toward peace and justice' but warned that 'provisions on war crimes trials must be effectively put into practice.'[26]

Both agreed that Uganda's courts are not currently equipped to deal with such cases and expressed the fear that any proceedings would be a sham. Given the choice between peace and justice, the majority of people living in northern Uganda appear to prefer the former. The Ugandan Government has indicated that a UN suspension of the indictments might be considered the first step of a peace process that could lead to LRA demobilization followed by either trial or exile for its leadership. Peace talks came close to reaching a deal in April 2008, although Kony failed to show up to sign the final agreement, demanding further assurances of his safety and financial security. As one northern Ugandan put it to me, 'the ICC's problem was that it simply did not understand the situation here. First we need peace and then we can worry about justice. And if someone puts a bullet in Kony's head after that, none of us will be sorry.'

This scenario will obviously set a precedent for future cases and will be watched carefully by the Sudanese Government, which is in a strong position to demand a suspension of the prosecutions in exchange for a deal over Darfur. The charging of President al-Bashir in July 2008 followed a series of warnings from the prosecutor about his failure to cooperate with the prosecution of the first two indictments and growing international frustration about his inability to stop the violence in Darfur. The threat of criminal charges being issued if peace talks fail, and the reward of suspension if they succeed, could become a feature of future UN-brokered negotiations. In other words, the ICC may soon find itself transformed from an instrument of justice to one of diplomacy.

Arguably, this has already happened with ICTY and ICTR where political rather than legal considerations are widely believed to have set the pace of prosecutions. Despite the deployment of 60,000 international peacekeeping soldiers to Bosnia-Herzegovina in 1995, very few attempts were initially made to arrest the senior commanders indicted for war crimes for fear of provoking a hostile reaction. A NATO spokesman candidly admitted in June 1996 that he did not consider the arrests to be 'worth the blood of one NATO soldier'.[27] The pace of arrests only began to increase in late 1998 as NATO headed for a showdown with Serbia over Kosovo. This culminated in the issuing of an indictment against Milošević in May 1999, when the conflict was actually taking place.

ICTY's mandate allowed it to investigate all violations of international humanitarian law committed within the former Yugoslavia, giving it jurisdiction to investigate NATO's actions during the Kosovo war. However, it rejected allegations that NATO had violated the rules of war, despite a widespread view that their choice of targets directly led to civilian casualties. Conducting its own investigation, Human Rights Watch concluded that there was no evidence of NATO war crimes but that it had violated international humanitarian law in failing to take sufficient care to distinguish between military and civilians, and in attacking non-military targets such as the Serbian television station.[28] However, in 2001, the European Court of Human Rights refused to consider a case brought by the relatives of the victims who died in this bombing, leaving them with no effective remedy for the violation they suffered.[29]

While ICTY went out of its way to arrest and prosecute people from all the local ethnic groups involved in the Bosnia conflict, ICTR decided to prosecute only Hutus, as the dominant Rwandan ethnic group that carried out the genocide. At the end of 2001, Carla Del Ponte announced that she would be addressing 'allegations of crimes committed during 1994 by members of the Tutsi-dominated Rwandan Patriotic Front forces',[30] however, no prosecutions have resulted. Shortly after this announcement, which led to a vigorous protest by Rwanda's government, the Security Council created a new prosecutor's office for ICTR, thereby removing Del Ponte from this position. A public row ensued when she stepped down from office at the end of 2007, following which the UN chose a new ICTY prosecutor against her wishes and in spite of unprecedented public objections by her team.[31]

ICTR's mandate allows it to address only crimes committed inside Rwanda in 1994, which results in a very partial perspective of events. While the genocide was undoubtedly a crime of horrific scale, it was preceded by an invasion of Rwanda by the RPF, led by Paul Kagame (now Rwanda's president) and armed and trained by President Museveni of Uganda; it was also followed by an incursion into the DRC (then Zaire) by Rwanda and Uganda, sparking a war claiming over four million lives to date. In 1999, the DRC took a case against Uganda to the International Court of Justice (ICJ),[32] which ruled, in 2005, that Uganda had 'by engaging in military activities against the Democratic Republic of the Congo (DRC) on the latter's territory . . . violated the principle of non-use of force in international relations and the principle of non-intervention'. It went on to state that

> the Republic of Uganda, by the conduct of its armed forces, which committed acts of killing, torture and other forms of inhumane treatment of the Congolese civilian population, destroyed villages and civilian buildings, failed to distinguish between civilian and military targets and to protect the civilian population in fighting with other combatants, trained child soldiers, incited ethnic conflict and failed to take measures to put an end to such conflict; as well as by its failure, as an occupying Power, to take measures to respect and ensure respect for human rights and international humanitarian law in Ituri district, violated its obligations under international human rights law and international humanitarian law . . . by acts of looting, plundering and exploitation of Congolese natural resources . . . violated obligations owed to the Democratic Republic of the Congo under international law.[33]

Unlike the ICC, which can prosecute individuals, the ICJ is a body for settling inter-state disputes and can only order parties to pay reparations. Ironically, the first person taken into the ICC's custody, Thomas Lubanga, was closely allied to the Ugandan army, which trained and equipped his militia. His forces captured the DRC town of Bunia in 2002, with Ugandan assistance, and the two forces are alleged to have carried out a massacre of civilians. He was subsequently implicated in the large-scale murder, torture and rape of civilians, the forced conscription of child soldiers and extortion in areas under his control. He was arrested by the Congolese authorities following the murder of nine UN peacekeeping soldiers in March 2005 and handed over to the ICC the following year. He is to be put on trial for recruiting child soldiers, which could help establish useful legal precedence, but again, it is difficult to see how the cause of universal justice is served by prosecuting him while ignoring his more powerful Ugandan sponsors.

The most successful international criminal tribunal established to date is the Special Court for Sierra Leone (SCSL), whose first president was Geoffrey Robertson. This court was created by UN Security Council Resolution 1315 in August 2000 and began its work two years later in the capital Freetown. The majority of its indictments were made in March 2003 and hearings began in June 2004. The initial hope that it would conclude its work within three years has not been realized, but the SCSL has made reasonable progress with its caseload while respecting the rights of defendants, victims and witnesses. A Human Rights Watch report, in late 2005, concluded that 'the court has made tremendous achievements on scarce and insecure resources.'[34]

The SCSL was established to try 'those who bear the greatest responsibility' for the atrocities that marked Sierra Leone's ten-year civil war, started in March 1991 when a group of 100 rebels and mercenaries invaded from neighbouring Liberia. They called themselves the Revolutionary United Front (RUF), and were led by a former corporal in Sierra Leone's army, Foday Sankoh. The RUF murdered village chiefs and government employees in the areas it captured and concentrated its efforts on securing the diamond-producing areas in the east of the country. It forcibly recruited child soldiers, some of whom were required to kill members of their own families, but it also found many willing recruits among the thousands of unemployed 'rarray boys' (dispossessed youths) left with few alternatives by the almost complete breakdown of Sierra Leonean society.

Sierra Leone suffered from decades of misrule, first by a clique of oligarchs and then by a succession of military dictators who plundered natural resources while making little attempt to maintain basic administrative structures. Civil servants went unpaid and education systems collapsed. The country's rulers deposited hundreds of millions of dollars in offshore bank accounts and continued to receive large sums of international aid while suppressing all internal dissent with extraordinary brutality.

The RUF was sponsored by Liberia's president, Charles Taylor, who seized power in his own country by similar means. Like Sierra Leone, Liberia had been misgoverned by a corrupt elite and then suffered a brutal military coup. In December 1989, Taylor led 100 insurgents into the country from neighbouring Côte d'Ivoire, recruiting more soldiers as they advanced. They reached the capital, Monrovia, by June 1990, while a second rebel group, led by Prince Johnson, also placed it under siege, eventually capturing and murdering the former dictator Samuel Doe.

In August 1990, a group of West African states led by Nigeria announced they were sending a peacekeeping mission to Liberia under the aegis of the Economic Community of West African States Monitoring Group (ECOMOG). Although it had no UN mandate, ECOMOG's mission was described in humanitarian terms. Its main aim, however, was to prevent Taylor seizing power since a number of countries, again led by Nigeria, regarded him as a dangerous radical with close ties to Colonel Muammar Gaddafi's regime in Libya. When ECOMOG announced the formation of a new 'government of national unity' after Doe's murder, Taylor responded by attacking its 'peacekeeping' force, who themselves became active participants in the ongoing war. ECOMOG soon gained notoriety for its corruption, earning the nickname 'Every Car Or Moving Object Gone' for its perpetual looting.

Taylor was forced to retreat from Monrovia but retaliated by sponsoring an invasion of Sierra Leone, which had been ECOMOG's rear base. He used Foday Sankoh, who he had met in a Libyan training camp, to head his proxy force. Both countries were devastated in the fighting that followed, with civilians bearing the brunt of atrocities that included cannibalism, slave labour and the common practice of hacking off limbs. Up to half the combatants were child soldiers, often high on drugs and convinced they were protected by magic spirits. The UN attempted to broker several ceasefires during the 1990s, and the different factions repeatedly made and broke agreements as nominal control of the two countries shifted from group to group. Elections took place in Sierra Leone in 1996 and were won by Ahmed Tajan Kabbah, a veteran politician with ties to the previous corrupt regime. Taylor won an election in Liberia the following year with the campaign slogan: 'He killed my ma, he killed my pa, but I will vote for him.'

Nigeria provided the bulk of the troops in the ECOMOG mission, which extended its operations to Sierra Leone as the fighting spread. Kofi Annan lobbied for a credible UN peacekeeping force during the mid-1990s, but it was blocked by the US which was still suffering the effects of 'Somalia syndrome'. The US by then owed the UN around $1 billion in late contributions and had become increasingly critical of the cost of such missions.[35] A UN peacekeeping force finally arrived in Sierra Leone in early 2000, but 500 of its ill-equipped soldiers were seized by the RUF in May. The British Government responded by sending an expeditionary force of paratroopers with air support. A spontaneous demonstration was organized outside the RUF's headquarters and Sankoh was arrested after his troops fired on the unarmed crowd.

It is commonly believed it was the British military intervention that led to the RUF deciding to sue for peace but, as Adekeye Adebajo and David Keen have noted in *United Nations Interventionism*, the British troops largely remained in Freetown and were reluctant to engage the RUF directly. They had one significant confrontation with a rogue faction of the Sierra Leone army, the 'West Side Boys', that resulted in an impressive show of strength, but the more decisive assaults on the RUF were mounted by the Guinean army and groups of self-defence forces of Sierra Leonean civilians known as the Kamajors. Britain also helped arm and train the notoriously ineffective Sierra Leonean army, many of whose soldiers had actively collaborated with the RUF in the past, and worked diplomatically to help block the export of Sierra Leone's 'blood diamonds'.[36]

The UN eventually increased the size of its peacekeeping force to 20,000 soldiers, and by January 2002 the Sierra Leone conflict was officially declared over. The UN increased its diplomatic pressure on Liberia to end its support for the RUF, whose defeat significantly weakened Taylor's position. He faced more revolts against his rule, culminating in another assault on Monrovia by rebel groups in 2003. Another West African peacekeeping force was dispatched to Liberia and Taylor eventually agreed to go into exile in Nigeria that August. A UN-sponsored agreement led to yet another 'national unity government' which proved as corrupt as many of its predecessors. However, the arrival of another large UN peacekeeping force allowed free elections to be held in October 2005, which were won by Ellen Johnson-Sirleaf, a former UN and World Bank official, who was inaugurated as president in January 2006.

One of Johnson-Sirleaf's first acts was to request that Nigeria hand over Taylor to the custody of the SCSL, which issued a warrant for his arrest in 2003. The court also indicted Sankoh, who died in custody before his trial could commence, and the leader of another rebel faction, Hinga Norman, a member of

Sierra Leone's government who was on his way to a cabinet meeting when he was arrested.

The last of these arrests proved unpopular in Freetown since Norman had helped organize the Kamajors who did much of the fighting against the RUF, including beating back an assault on the capital, known as the expressively titled 'Operation No Living Thing'. However, the prosecution was a visible demonstration of the Court's independence and its determination to pursue cases on legal rather than political grounds. The SCSL is outside the direct control of both Sierra Leone's government and the UN Security Council and was established by a bilateral agreement between the UN and Sierra Leone's government, rather than through a Chapter VII resolution. It is funded by voluntary state contributions and is a 'hybrid court' with a majority of its judges appointed by the UN and a minority by the government of Sierra Leone. It applies international rather than domestic law and these safeguards insulate it from some of the pressures other courts have come under.

The SCSL is a significant improvement on two other 'hybrid courts' established for Cambodia and Iraq where the majority of court officials are local appointees. It is independent, but has tried to involve local people in its work. It sits in public in Freetown and conducts an effective outreach programme. Ordinary people can watch its trials, which are also covered by the local media. It is helping to train members of Sierra Leone's legal profession and to rebuild respect for the rule of law. The SCSL also worked alongside a Truth and Reconciliation Commission for Sierra Leone and dealt with the obvious tensions between 'justice', 'forgiveness' and 'reconciliation' in a reasonable fashion.

While it offers a potential model for the future work of the ICC, the specific circumstances in which the SCSL is operating are comparatively rare. Two of the largest UN peacekeeping forces in the world are currently located in Sierra Leone and Liberia. Both depend on the international community not only for financial assistance but for detailed oversight on how the money is spent. Like Bosnia-Herzegovina, Kosovo and East Timor, they are effectively under international administration and donors are rebuilding their governance and judicial structures from scratch. It would be no exaggeration to describe this process as recolonization and it is resented by many people in both countries.

The ICC, by contrast, usually works with sovereign states, and the problems it faces in doing so are largely structural. The limitations of it obtaining jurisdiction and its lack of resources make it difficult to operate independently. At the same time, the focus of its investigations often seems too narrow. There is an opportunity to address some of these weaknesses when the Court's statute opens for amendment in 2009, but this also poses the question of what kind of court it really wants to be.

A court prepared to prosecute the crime of aggression would quickly come up against powerful vested interests. There are strong legal grounds for thinking that Uganda's Museveni and Rwanda's Kagame, for example, could be prosecuted for the invasion of the DRC, while Bush and Blair might be held culpable for aggression against Iraq. Would an international legal body be sufficiently robust to pursue such cases? Even if the court restricted itself to investigating 'war crimes' rather than 'the crime of war', it is not difficult to see how controversial its work would soon become.

When I was in Afghanistan I once asked a representative of the Coalition for the International Criminal Court, an NGO that closely supports its work, why the prosecutor did not investigate crimes committed there that fell within its statute but with which the local courts were unable or unwilling to deal. Although Afghanistan has ratified the statute, I was told that the precedent of conducting an investigation in a country where US forces were also operating was too controversial. Even if the investigation was confined to activities of the Taliban and warlords it could arouse the hostility of the US Government and cut across its attempts to stabilize the country. One of the early acts of

Afghanistan's parliament, which is heavily dominated by the country's warlords, was to pass an act giving themselves an amnesty for crimes committed during the country's civil war. While this is clearly repugnant on moral grounds, President Karzai's beleaguered national government was in no position to oppose it; he has personally made a similar offer to the Taliban's leadership in the hope of obtaining a peace deal.

If the ICC will not investigate Afghanistan, where will it work and how? The alternative is a body that does the bidding of the Security Council's permanent members. Although granting them a political veto on prosecutions is objectionable, it might at least help it gain the support and funding of the world's main powers and could turn out to be a compromise worth making. The ICC could become a useful mechanism for dealing with mid-level thugs and warlords, or retired dictators, where in-country prosecutions are considered too contentious. But it will not be the instrument of impartial, universal justice that its supporters claim. And for aid workers, this could make it as much of a problem as a solution in humanitarian crises.

Chapter Eight

Humanitarian Accountability

THE LONG DRIVE through central Mozambique along the Zambezi River reveals why it is one of Africa's most disaster-ridden countries. The Zambezi is the continent's fourth largest river basin and drains water from the rivers of most of Mozambique's neighbours. As the last stop before the sea it is significantly affected by what happens upstream. Towards the end of the wet season the river often swells to more than twice its average size, while by the end of the dry season it can shrink to as little as a fifth. The countryside was dry and brown when I visited in May 2007 and the rivers we crossed were reduced to trickles. Yet a few months earlier the whole area had been hit by a flood that destroyed the homes and crops of almost 300,000 people. Ten days later, tropical cyclone Favio struck Mozambique's southern coast, affecting almost 150,000 more.

More than 75 per cent of Mozambique's population are small-scale farmers, but there has been little investment in agriculture or irrigation in recent years. The most fertile land is located close to rivers and other natural water sources, which has encouraged many people to move into the lowland areas. Two dams, built while the country was still under Portuguese colonial rule, control the flooding in normal years but they do not have the capacity to cope with the far more severe floods that occur every five to ten years. At best they slow the spillage of water for a few days, giving the people living downstream a little more time to evacuate their homes. Early warning systems and 'community-preparedness' are therefore crucial in determining to what extent the flooding results in loss of life.[1]

Mozambique is one of the poorest countries in the world and has been battered by a brutal combination of colonial rule, civil war and natural disasters. Throughout its recent history it has had to cope with a succession of floods, droughts and cyclones that had a devastating impact. There is little the country can do to stop these natural calamities, all of which are exacerbated by climate change. It has a long coastline and rising sea levels threaten coastal towns and many low-lying inland areas. Warmer seas will no doubt bring more – and more extreme – tropical cyclones, while rising inland temperatures increase the probability of droughts. In April 2007, the head of the UN Office for the Co-ordination of Humanitarian Affairs (OCHA) in Southern Africa warned that global warming had already brought noticeably heavier rains and more cyclones, which displaced up to a million people from their homes in recent months.[2]

Yet at the start of 2007 Mozambique achieved the rare distinction of turning its response to a disaster into a non-news event. Nine people died in the cyclone and seventy were injured, but the early warning system helped prevent a far greater death toll.[3] One of the iconic images of a previous flood was that of South African army helicopters plucking victims from the trees. This time the evacuation was largely carried out by local people using their own canoes. The flood victims were moved to temporary accommodation centres without a single death. International agencies were unanimous in praising the government's response as a model for the rest of the world. I went to Mozambique that May for the Overseas Development Institute (ODI), to research what had gone right.

The answers were quite simple, but have important implications on the future of humanitarianism. In October 2006, Mozambique's government adopted a master plan for disaster-preparedness containing a comprehensive strategy for dealing with the country's vulnerability to natural disasters. It covered issues ranging from reforestation and the development of a national irrigation system to the cultivation of crops that will survive prolonged droughts. It said that Mozambique needs to reduce its dependence on agriculture – through, for example, the development of its tourist industry – while setting out a clear strategy for emergency response management. The plan also argued that the 're-establishment of self-esteem, self-confidence and dignity' are basic preconditions for 'combating extreme poverty and reducing the country's vulnerability to natural disasters'. It stated that Mozambique needed to break from its 'dependency culture' since most of its people had grown up in conditions of war and famine where 'begging has become almost a way of life'. The government announced its determination to avoid 'running to international donors without first exhausting national capacities'.[4]

In previous disasters the body responsible for co-ordinating responses was based in the Ministry for Foreign Affairs and mostly acted as a distributing agency for external aid from the UN. In 2006, it became part of the Ministry for State Administration, signalling that Mozambique's government intended to take responsibility for dealing with its own problems in the future. One senior UN official told me its director, Paulo Zucula, was the most effective person in this position he had ever come across in his professional life.

I spent a couple of weeks in Mozambique talking to national and international staff involved in the disaster response and travelling round the country speaking to people in the areas affected. I sat in on one government inter-departmental meeting that Zucula chaired, seeing at first hand why he impresses people with his ability to listen and take tough decisions. One particular point that struck me was how simple it can be to get things right. Of course, it makes sense to preposition emergency stocks in the places most likely to be affected, run simulation exercises involving all the agencies who will be involved in the response, and concentrate resources on preparing the communities themselves so that they know what to do. None of this came as a surprise since these are precisely the things that did not happen before the Indian Ocean tsunami and the south Asian earthquake. My colleagues and I often experience the sensation of helplessness in a complex emergency because such preplanning was not put in place.

The most technically impressive of Mozambique's innovations was a series of 'operation rooms' the government opened in the disaster zones. During the emergency these rooms were occupied by all participating agencies, significantly improving communications and co-ordination. One co-ordinator told me, 'We had national heads of government departments who rarely get out of the capital exposed to the reality of what was going on. It also meant that the international organizations had to work with us and not just come and do their own thing.' The idea for these centres was taken from Guatemala, which was badly damaged by hurricanes Stan and Mitch in 1998 and 2005. In developing its own model, Mozambique has also drawn heavily on the experiences of other Latin American countries such as Brazil, Nicaragua and Cuba. As Zucula said, 'We picked these countries because they face similar problems to us, not just in terms of floods and cyclones, but also poverty, government bureaucracy and lack of capacity. There is no point in bringing people all the way from Europe to try and train us because what works there is not necessarily going to work here. We need to adapt to local conditions. You cannot develop a model in Scandinavia and just impose it on Africa.'

Mozambique is heavily dependent on international assistance, which finances almost half its government expenditure. In recent years, donors have moved towards providing it with increasing direct budget support, rather than implementing projects through international agencies.[5] This gives the government more responsibility to decide its own spending priorities, which in turn reduces dependency and makes it more accountable to its own people. By increasing national capacity and self-reliance, the hope is that a virtuous circle can be created between good governance and economic development.[6] According to the

World Bank, Mozambique has raised a sixth of its population out of poverty over the last few years, reduced infant mortality by 35 per cent and increased the number of children attending primary school by 65 per cent. Inequality is relatively low by regional standards, and progress has been made towards the key Millennium Development Goals the UN has set itself.[7]

Mozambique bucked the trend of most post-conflict states after its civil war by dramatically cutting its military expenditure budget. Its former prime minister, Joaquim Chissano, won the first Mo Ibrahim Prize for governing honestly and then stepping down at the end of his term of office, a comparatively rare occurence in an African country. The country has held a series of elections that were reasonably free and fair and is rated among the top five African countries in terms of freedom of speech and political expression.[8]

Institutions such as the World Bank and the International Monetary Fund (IMF) have long attempted to use their lending power to promote an agenda of economic reform. However, new forms of conditionality are now being developed to promote the rule of law and good governance, and provide benchmarks against which the delivery of goods and services can be judged. Donors, including a growing number of corporate philanthropists, argue that previous failures were partly due to the bad management of aid, and that governments should be made more accountable for their behaviour. Attempts to tackle corruption, increase efficiency and share good practice between participants are all aimed at ensuring that aid gets where it is needed and benefits those it is designed to help.

The concept of accountability here is a top-down one in which those receiving the aid have to answer to donors. Accountability has long been a part of the development discourse, and many aid projects have attempted to create structures for community consultation and governance. Some argue that this concept should be extended to the humanitarian sphere and that agencies should be held accountable by those on whose behalf they claim to be acting.[9]

Proponents of humanitarian accountability have proposed three basic approaches. The first is an emphasis on technical standards, greater transparency, reporting and evaluations. Humanitarians should be more open about what they are trying to do and what they actually achieve, share good practice and encourage debate and scrutiny. The second is an emphasis on agencies drawing up their own codes of conduct, often based on international human rights and humanitarian law, such as the Humanitarian Charter discussed in chapter six of this book. The third, linked to the same concept of a 'right to protection and assistance', is for an increased focus on obtaining the 'informed consent' of potential beneficiaries to particular programme activity. By relating the delivery of assistance to objectively defined rights-based standards, agencies seek to hold themselves to account against such norms and, through their advocacy efforts, demand that governments do the same.

The case for humanitarian accountability is similar to the arguments put forward by the World Bank; badly targeted aid, which undermines local capacity, can do more harm than good to poor countries. In his critique of what he terms 'the disaster relief industry', Alex de Waal argues that 'humanitarian internationalism' weakens local political accountability and the contract between a recipient country's rulers and its ruled. He concludes, rather starkly, that 'the intrusion of the humanitarian institutions represents, in an insidious but profound way, a disempowerment of the people directly engaged in the crisis which drains their capacity to find a solution . . . most current humanitarian activity in Africa is useless or damaging and should be abandoned.'[10] Austen Davis, the former head of MSF Belgium, similarly noted that:

> Humanitarian action has been accused of prolonging wars and undermining governments' accountability to their own people, destroying markets and creating dependency, failing to address the causes of crises and so acting as a substitute for 'real' action, failing to reach the neediest, being inequitable,

corroding human dignity and providing poor quality assistance in insufficient quantities to people in desperate need.[11]

Most humanitarian aid workers would accept that there is some basis in truth to these accusations. Abuses such as the scandal in a number of West African refugee camps where it emerged that aid workers were demanding 'sex for food'[12] are still comparatively rare, but a report published by Save the Children in 2008 shows that there are very few mechanisms in place to stop such practices.[13] There are also numerous examples where badly conceived or poorly implemented aid programmes have damaged the interests of their intended beneficiaries.[14] However, the logic of de Waal's argument, that the presence of aid organizations is inhibiting poor countries from developing their own coping mechanisms and that these would develop if the agencies withdrew, begs the obvious question: but what happens if they do not?

One response to the 'sex for food' scandal was the establishment of two legal aid clinics by the American Refuge Committee in Guinea in 2002, which provide women and children with legal advice and assistance, including potential legal challenges against the perpetrators of the abuse. The project is supported by UNHCR's Protection Unit and is similar to the kind of legal projects the Norwegian Refugee Council has established elsewhere. Legal aid provides a potentially genuine accountability mechanism since, assuming there is a functioning rule of law, it can help people take action against organizations that have failed to fulfil contractual obligations.

Professor Mary Anderson has developed a broader analysis of how aid can be delivered in ways that 'do no harm' through her Local Capacities for Peace (LCP) principles, which have been influential in shaping the practices of a number of US-based aid agencies. A 2001 study by the InterAction Transition Working Group, which links together the major US-based humanitarian NGOs, outlined examples of good practice following the adoption of this framework:

In both Angola and Burundi, CRS [Catholic Relief Services] has worked to strengthen institutional capacities for justice and peace commissions. At the international level, CRS advocates with the US Government to change those policies that negatively impact on the war in Sierra Leone . . . [in Sudan] CARE modified its approach and now also dedicates significant time and funds to advocate with the Government of Sudan and with rebel groups for a just peace. World Vision has employed LCP [Local Capacities for Peace] assessment techniques to identify tensions between the community and local authorities in Yambio, Sudan . . . as one of the largest employers in the region, World Vision's recruitment and hiring policies . . . were unwittingly contributing to the conflict.[15]

The debate regarding the effectiveness of this approach continues, and critics, such as Mark Duffield, have noted that it involves a significant shift to move beyond helping people and towards supporting processes. It also implies that assistance should be withheld in certain circumstances since it is considered legitimate only if it fits into the 'transformational aims' of liberal peace activists.[16] This type of approach clearly involves considerable interference in the domestic politics of the country where the organization is implementing a programme. Who should decide what might constitute a 'just peace' in Sudan, and what gives a foreign aid organization the mandate to advocate for it? How did a particular aid organization decide that the US Government's policies were having a 'negative impact' on the war in Sierra Leone, and how can it be sure that its alternative would improve things? Should an aid organization base its hiring policies on anything other than the principles of equal opportunities and non-discrimination, and what gives it the right to engage in social engineering in another country? No doubt the aid organizations in question were making such judgments for the most noble of motives, but who are they accountable to for these decisions, and how will they be held responsible if they get them wrong?

In his preface to the official tsunami evaluation report, Bill Clinton argued that international aid agencies must stop 'descending into crises situations with nothing but good intentions', and that they needed to improve how they worked alongside local institutions in ways that strengthened the capacity of affected communities to help themselves.[17] But these are problems of delegation and research rather than accountability. An aid organization that simply consults a community about the design of a programme can hardly be said to be accountable to it since the power relationship between the two parties remains fundamentally unchanged.

Humanitarian accountability is a difficult concept because the aid is, by its very nature, almost always short-term and reactive. True accountability requires some kind of structure to reward or punish the agency in relation to agreed outcomes. It also assumes that there is sufficient information available to judge the actions undertaken and their consequences. Local communities will never have sufficient information to hold an international aid agency to account, nor are they in a position to determine how much of its resources it should allocate to a particular crisis. As Austen Davis has noted:

> Agencies have responsibilities towards the people living in the places where they choose to intervene, but they also have responsibilities towards those that they are not helping. For each humanitarian programme that is implemented there is another programme that is not . . . Humanitarian agencies are responsible for deciding when to close a programme and leave an area, and when to go to another area where they can perhaps help people in greater need. Who should have the power to hold the agency to account for its decision: the community being left, or the potential new recipients?[18]

The basic problem with the concept of humanitarian accountability is that it fails to address the huge difference in power between the different parties. Giles Bolton, a former UK Department for International Development (DFID) official, gives an inadvertent illustration of this in his book *Poor Story*, when he describes a trip to Kitgum in northern Uganda in 1998 to evaluate the effectiveness of an emergency feeding programme for children in displacement camps. He had to recommend whether or not to grant an extension for DFID's funding for the project: 'Our decision proved fairly simple. Recent months had seen an improvement in the security situation, reasonable rains and, with them, improved nutritional rates. The bottom line was that fewer babies were being brought to the clinic and nursed back to health. From our point of view, money from our limited aid budget was now saving fewer lives than before; money which, on balance, could probably be used more effectively elsewhere. We recommended against the extension. Somewhat to my surprise, I didn't lose any sleep over the decision.'[19]

Perhaps he should have. Predictions that northern Uganda's civil war is about to end have proved persistently premature. There were still an estimated two million internally displaced persons (IDPs) in northern Uganda when I was there in 2006–7. The total number of lives lost over the course of the war is unknown, but a survey by the Ugandan Ministry of Health and the World Health Organization stated that between January and July 2005, a total of 35,000 people died in the IDP camps of Gulu, Kitgum and Pader. Around 4,000 of these deaths were the direct result of violence, while others were due to diseases such as malaria, AIDS and diarrhoea and largely attributable to the living conditions in the camps.[20] Another report, published in March 2006, stated that 3,500 Ugandans were dying every month in the camps from war-related causes.[21] This was nearly double the mortality rate of Darfur, the conflict generally considered the worst humanitarian crisis in Africa. Of course, it is not fair to blame a young and inexperienced DFID official for failing to predict this, but the harsh reality is that this is how decisions get made. Even the best agencies frequently make similar mistakes and these decisions can cost the lives of hundreds and thousands of people. How many aid agency officials have ever really been held accountable for such mistakes?

Bolton also described the dilemma facing donors trying to work with governments that do not respect democratic norms. After spending a couple of years in Rwanda, he concluded that: 'It didn't take a genius to realise that there was no way that this group of people [its post-genocide government] was going to relinquish power for a long time – certainly not until they were confident that doing so didn't risk a return to the conflict and exile of the past.'[22] Even before the genocide the Tutsis were a minority in the country yet they dominated the new government, most of whose members had been in exile all their lives yet were now ruling over people they suspected of complicity in slaughtering their families and relatives. 'There were promising signs that many in the regime were trying to change and open up society,' Bolton said, but there were also 'vengeful hardliners . . . determined to keep power at any cost'. He saw the choice confronting donors in terms that are familiar to most humanitarian aid workers; you could work with the government in agreed areas for the benefit of the people, but if you made aid conditional on issues such as a full return to democracy, the government would simply refuse it. Propping up corrupt dictatorships with foreign aid may be unpalatable, but so is cutting it off from those in need to punish the sins of their rulers.

There is a broad consensus that international aid has so far failed Africa. In *The State of Africa*, Martin Meredith estimates that donors have sunk an estimated $500 billion into the continent with no discernable result on poverty reduction.[23] William Easterly in *The White Man's Burden* suggests the total could be even higher.[24] Yet Africa has seen an absolute decline in most of its indicators of human development over the last thirty years. The reasons for this are varied and include the effects of bad governance, conflict and corruption. Western trade and agricultural policies have also played a significant role in this crisis.

Agriculture is one of the few economic sectors where developing countries could compete with the west on equal terms, yet rich countries currently spend about ten times more subsidizing their own farmers than they give to the poorest countries in aid; the average EU cow receives more financial support than half the world's population struggles to live on. Africa now sustains less commercial agriculture than it did fifty years ago when most of its countries achieved independence. As *The Economist* has noted, 'The trillions of dollars spent on supporting farmers in rich countries have led to higher taxes, worse food, intensively farmed monocultures, overproduction and world prices that wreck the lives of poor farmers in the emerging markets.'[25]

Mozambique's experiences show that aid can work, though aid organizations admit the fragility of what has been achieved. My research in Mozambique was for a paper on a wider study of the relationship between national governments and international agencies in responding to humanitarian crises. Although Mozambique's achievements have been impressive in recent years, some observers caution that the country's dependence on foreign aid is leading to the development of new forms of patronage in which the ruling party is strengthening its hold on power. Transparency International's worldwide Corruption Perception Index rates Mozambique as considerably more honest than most other African countries, but it is still in the bottom half of the Index.[26] Critics warn that previous 'donor darlings', such as Uganda and Ethiopia, also earned the same kind of plaudits that Mozambique receives today, but have since reverted to corrupt autocracies.[27] How, then, should humanitarian agencies respond when a government takes a decision that appears to violate the rights of its own people to protection and assistance?

One of the few contentious issues during Mozambique's disaster response concerned the government's decision not to declare a national emergency. Had it done so, it would have made it easier for the international agencies to appeal for funds from their own donors and to bring in extra resources by circumventing the usual bureaucratic restrictions on importing goods. The government wanted to show it was capable of handling the crisis on its own. This meant it was effectively refusing extra resources which could have been used to help its people. According to the logic of the Humanitarian Charter, international agencies should have insisted on the 'right to assistance' of their beneficiaries. Had they been consulted, they would undoubtedly have wanted extra supplies of aid. Yet most of the agencies I spoke to accepted the reasoning and good faith motives behind the government's decision to rely primarily on its own national capacity. Even if they disagreed with it, none campaigned against it publicly.

Another issue concerned the government's refusal to provide assistance to those who wanted to rebuild their homes in flood-affected areas. The officials I spoke to argued that these homes would only be washed away again in subsequent years and it was better to encourage people to settle elsewhere. Not all the agencies agreed, but none adopted the Humanitarian Charter's argument that people had a 'right to return home', though most of their headquarters have endorsed a recent set of principles that locate this in international law.[28] In fact, few fieldworkers seemed to take the rights-based approach to aid delivery particularly seriously.

According to an inter-agency evaluation report on the emergency response, 'when beneficiaries were asked whether all their needs were met the answer was always a resounding "No!" '; but this, it argued, should not be taken at face value. The report noted that 'many of these needs flow from their poverty rather than from the impact of the emergency,' but that after years of receiving international assistance the people had become 'aid aware' and were used to demanding more from international agencies. The evaluation report concluded that 'the real needs for emergency relief were largely met as there were no outbreaks of serious diarrhoeal disease, or indications of acute nutritional distress.'[29]

This sets a fairly low benchmark as to what constitutes 'human need', and is clearly not compatible with either a 'rights-based' approach to programming or the demand for 'humanitarian accountability', yet these findings were endorsed by all the main UN and NGO agencies in Mozambique. The general view of the staff I talked to is that the various codes and principles drawn up by agencies in their headquarters should be regarded as statements of theoretical intent rather than practical working documents.

Aid workers in the field tend to rely on improvisation, innova-tion, risk-taking, negotiation and compromise to deliver their programmes. Of course they try to avoid doing harm, but most fieldworkers are painfully aware of the limitations of what they can achieve. The problem with trying to adhere to universal standards or a legally-defined rights-based approach is that, abstracted from particular contexts, they are often at best meaningless and at worst could prevent agencies from achieving any good.

Rather than aim for the chimera of accountability to universal human rights standards, humanitarians may be better advised to concentrate on building trust. If an agency is trusted by donors and the general public it will be given more leeway to spend its money as it sees fit, which will enable it to be more proactive in its crisis responses. Organizations earn trust by telling the truth, by not exaggerating the scale of natural or man-made disasters or claiming to be able to accomplish more than they can realistically achieve. Agencies that trust their field staff will give them more autonomy to make decisions rather than impose ever more codes and charters on them. An agency that is trusted by its bene-ficiaries is also better placed to assess their needs and support them. Agencies also show that they trust their beneficiaries by the way they distribute aid.

Currently most agencies deliver the bulk of their aid in the form of food and materials, though it is generally more efficient to give people cash since it is cheaper and faster to deliver and enables the beneficiary to choose what to spend the money on. Some agencies argue, reasonably enough, that cash can be misused, but a report published by Paul Harvey at the UK's Overseas Development Institute shows that many of these fears are misplaced.[30] Of course, care needs to be taken to ensure that aid reaches its intended recipients, particularly vulnerable women and children. Cash can be stolen, and grants intended for food or medicine may end up being spent on alcohol or guns. A sudden injection of cash could also have inflationary consequences. But all these things are also true of material aid, which is often resold in local markets for less than the cost of shipping it to the disaster zone.

At its worst, food aid is a racket through which the subsidized surplus of US and European farmers is dumped on African markets, wrecking local economies by pricing native farmers out of existence. Alex de Waal has shown that this happened repeatedly in Somalia during the 1980s and 1990s, greatly weakening the country's eventual ability to respond to a drought-related famine. I was told by IDPs in Sri Lanka that the cost of some goods fell in local markets as a direct result of the influx of aid after the tsunami. When I was in Uganda, the government promised every displaced person in the north of the country a tin roof to replace their traditional thatched one. People were grateful for the metal sheets, but their mud huts were not strong enough to support them. Many sold or exchanged them for things they really needed, and deliveries were eventually suspended when children were injured after one such structure collapsed.

Clearly cash is not appropriate in all situations, and people often need material support that cannot be purchased locally; in such circumstances there is no alternative to shipping in goods. Cash distribution can be difficult in countries without banks, though in Afghanistan we were able to move around very large amounts of cash using informal money dealers through what was called the Hawala system. There is also an obvious potential problem in giving big lump sums of money to people used to living at subsistence level and then assuming they will spend it wisely; however, the evidence so far is that they usually do. According to Paul Harvey, 'the basic questions are: can people buy what they need at reasonable prices and can cash be delivered effectively and safely? The answer to these questions has tended to be yes and more frequently than is often assumed.'

Harvey warns that the system is trapped in a dilemma of its own making. 'Agencies have the skills and capacity to deliver food aid on a large scale, so food aid gets the majority of funding because donors are confident that it can be delivered. The typical aid worker is more likely to be a nutritionist than an economist and so we are less skilled at evaluating the impact of different types of aid.' Beyond this, though, is the problem of perceptions and prejudices. The aid worker, complete with logo T-shirt and white Land Rover, dispensing food to the hungry dark-skinned baby, is one of the most pervasive clichés in the disaster relief industry. It is recycled endlessly in media images and donor appeals, with different agencies competing to prove that they can get their material to 'deserving victims' faster or spend less on overheads. But these messages bear little relation to how aid is really delivered and seems aimed more at comforting those making donations than those receiving them.

Building trust with donors will require agencies to be more transparent about what is involved in the delivery of aid, and about the limits of humanitarian approaches in certain situations. Building trust with beneficiaries will require allowing them to decide how to use the aid they are given, even if some of it may be misused. Building trust with the governments of affected countries will require respecting national sovereignty and re-cognizing that the primary responsibility for the welfare of the people within their own borders belongs with the states.

Of course, this does not mean that states can always be trusted, thus agencies need to adapt their approach accordingly. The staff in the field are best placed to make this judgment and it is difficult to provide detailed guidance for this at the global level. The problem with humanitarian accountability, like the problem with trying to base programming on international legally-defined standards, is that it attempts to impose a set of universal standards that are unlikely to be sufficiently adaptable to fit every situation. The only international principles that potentially fit all the situations in which humanitarians work are those of independence, impartiality and neutrality by which the movement has traditionally defined itself. The shift away from these principles in recent years has caused more problems than it has solved.

A couple of months before my visit to Mozambique I went to Angola, to conduct another research project for ODI. The two countries are similar in many ways, but it is their differences that are most revealing. Both are former Portuguese colonies and gained independence in 1975, then promptly descended into devastating civil wars. The two former liberation movements – FRELIMO in Mozambique and the MPLA in Angola – were backed by the Soviet Union, while apartheid South Africa backed rival militias, RENAMO and UNITA. A central tenet of apartheid's racist ideology was that black people are incapable of self-government; the South Africans encouraged their proxy forces to cause maximum destruction in both countries to prove this point.

Up to a million people died during Mozambique's conflict, which finally came to an end in October 1992. Angola's war lasted until April 2002 and cost around half a million lives. Angola stands at 161 out of the 177 countries on UNDP's human development index, while Mozambique is at 168. Both countries have managed to achieve healthy economic growth since their return to peace, over 15 per cent a year in Angola's case and 8 per cent in Mozambique's. FRELIMO and the MPLA have dropped the Marxist-Leninism they previously espoused and have liberalized their economies. But these similarities mask a significant difference between the paths the two countries chose in their social and economic development.

Angola's economy is predicted to grow by more than 20 per cent in 2008, the highest of any country in the world.[31] This economic boom is almost exclusively due to its export of oil and diamonds. China is investing heavily in Angola and a number of other African states, based on what China's President Hu Jintao has declared the 'six principles' of Sino-African relations. These include: respect for Africa's sovereignty; economic assistance with limited political conditions; and the promotion of an international environment more conducive to Africa's development.[32] Such policies contrast sharply with the policy of western donors and the World Bank, who have made their assistance conditional on good governance and human rights commitments. Many African governments have enthusiastically embraced China as an alternative to the west. Although Europe remains Africa's biggest trading partner, followed by the US, China is catching up fast. Trade has increased fivefold in five years, reaching $50 billion in 2006.[33] While I was in Angola a number of western donors were quite frank about the way this was reducing their influence. As one World Bank official told me, 'We offer them a million dollars provided that they fulfil a series of pre-conditions, while the Chinese give them five billion with no strings attached.'

China's economic rise is already having an important and indirect impact on Africa. It is, for example, one of the factors in the recent worldwide increase in oil and food prices, producing both winners and losers among Africa's poor. But whatever short-term benefits Chinese investment may bring, it will not provide the basis for sustainable economic development on its own. China's objectives are quite straightforward: it is interested in Africa's commodities to fuel its own rapidly growing economy. Chinese infrastructural investment is mainly designed to help it ship out from African countries what China wants, as quickly as possible. New roads often run directly from mines to ports, completely bypassing the towns in between.

Although the revenue from Angola's oil and diamond exports could be used to fund significant social and economic projects, the industries themselves provide only a fraction of jobs in a country where unemployment is rampant. Oil production remains largely offshore and has few links with other sectors of the economy.[34] Numerous commentators have also noted the paradox that the abundance of a particular natural resource in a poor country is sometimes a hindrance to economic development. 'Dutch disease' or 'resource curse' can distort expenditure, overvalue the currency and lead to a loss of competitiveness in other sectors.[35]

An increase in natural resource revenues also gives governments an excuse to delay economic and social reform. Angola stands very low in the rankings established by Transparency International's widely referenced Corruption Perceptions Index.[36] Human Rights Watch reported that Angola's government was unable to account for approximately US$4 billion of public money between 1997 and 2002, more than it received in foreign aid in the same period.[37] Angola is now one of the world's most unequal societies. In 2003, the combined wealth of the country's fifty-nine richest people was $3.9 billion, compared with the total gross domestic product for the country as a whole of $10.2 billion. Thousands of slum-dwellers are being evicted from their homes in urban areas, where office rents often match those found in London.

The least helpful way to examine the problems facing Africa is through a left–right ideological prism. During Angola's civil war, for example, Cuban troops using Soviet weaponry were given the task of defending American-owned oil installations from attacks by American and South African-backed rebels. Oxfam's Tony Vaux recalls how many development organizations overestimated the ideological differences between the two sides, in both Angola and Mozambique, and how Oxfam's basic position of solidarity with the people led it to adopt a naively patronizing attitude towards their governments:

Mozambique was assumed by outsiders to be incapable of feeding itself. The South African-backed attackers were supposed to have destroyed everything. In a sense we wanted

Mozambique to be weak in order to caricature the nature of apartheid. We constantly published figures showing how many roads, houses, schools and hospitals had been destroyed. Because Mozambique was too weak to defend itself, it followed from our argument that it was too weak to feed itself. Time after time during the 1980s we had to defend the Mozambique government against criticism. Yet it was now apparent that it could have done much more.[38]

Vaux ruefully describes his gradual disenchantment with the corruption and inefficiency of Mozambique's socialist rulers, as well as his realization that they enjoyed far less popular support than he had assumed. In Mozambique's first free elections in 1994, RENAMO, which most agencies dismissed as a terrorist apartheid stooge, won almost half the popular vote. It also won local elections and formed the provincial government in most of the places worst affected by the 2007 flooding. The party representatives I met when I was there were every bit as competent and committed as their FRELIMO counterparts.

Some on the left still argue that aid should be given as an act of political solidarity, which simplifies the discussion of accountability by just ignoring it. The 'sandalistas' who picked coffee in Nicaragua, for example, often overlooked the growing unpopularity of its revolutionary government during the 1980s. Likewise, many leftists take an equally uncritical view of President Hugo Chávez in Venezuela today. Others seem to think that countries need to reach a certain level of development before they can guarantee civil and political rights and that imposing conditionality on poor countries is a form of neo-imperialism. When she was minister for international development in the British Government, Clare Short once told me that Amnesty International sometimes came across as quite 'carping' in its criticisms of poor countries, and said that the discourse on human rights had 'got stuck in a denunciation of abuses of civil and political rights'.[39] The Nobel Prize-winning economist Amartya Sen argues, by contrast, that defending these rights is in fact one of the most effective ways of tackling poverty.[40]

One of the problems with humanitarian accountability is that humanitarian aid is usually delivered in situations where systems of national democracy and accountability are weak. Another, as Paul Collier, former director of development research at the World Bank, warns, is that the poorest countries in the world are caught in a number of 'traps' from which democracy alone cannot provide an escape. In his book *The Bottom Billion* he shows how competition between politicians leads to the development of patronage networks, often with an ethnic or tribal base, which are sustained through corruption. This can lead to conflict between competing groups and, Collier argues, the well-known link between poverty and conflict – which he estimates knocks over 2 per cent a year off a country's economic growth – is not only because wars keep countries poor, but because there is a far greater chance of conflicts breaking out in poor countries than in rich ones. If a democratic government is unable to satisfy the most basic demands of its population then it will eventually either be overthrown by popular dissatisfaction or forced to adopt measures of greater repression to stay in power. According to this analysis revolutions, coups and civil wars may become cyclical events as rival groups fight over the state's remaining assets.

Wars also provide a good excuse for plunder, which gives added bitterness to the term 'resource curse'. Most observers agree that oil was one of the main factors in Angola's civil war lasting so long. Collier argues that the relative prices of oil and diamonds finally led to UNITA's defeat when the government's growing oil revenues enabled it to outspend the rebels, whose access to the world's diamond market was blocked by international action.[41] 'Blood diamonds' also played an important part in Sierra Leone's conflict, sustaining the rebel forces and personally enriching Liberia's president Charles Taylor. A major reason why so many African countries participated in the devastating conflict in the Democratic Republic of the Congo was the opportunity it presented to loot the country's natural resources. An Oxfam report in 2007 calculated that conflict cost Africa's economies about $284 billion between 1990 and 2005.[42] Collier argues that this is one of the reasons why the poorest countries in the world have achieved virtually zero growth in the last few decades.

The majority of what he calls the 'bottom billion' of the world's population live in Africa, yet rich Africans are well represented on the lists of the world's wealthiest people; according to the World Bank, 40 per cent of Africa's private wealth is held in offshore bank accounts. A 2005 report published by the African Union estimated that corruption costs Africa $148 billion a year, more than a quarter of its entire gross domestic product.[43] Any long-term strategy for helping the poorest people in the world must include promoting good governance, tackling corruption and supporting peace processes. The dilemma this poses for humanitarian aid workers is how to reconcile this with the principle of humanitarian neutrality. As Françoise Bouchet-Saulnier, MSF's legal advisor, notes, 'the distinction between development and humanitarian aid has become increasingly blurred. Today we seem to have entered a period of chronic crisis and conflict in which emergency humanitarian action has become the only available form of political expression.' However, she also warns that

> using humanitarian assistance to influence a given military confrontation may indeed offer levers to affect positive changes in a country. Yet while this may be politically efficient or expedient, it jeopardizes the necessary political independence of humanitarian action. The unacceptable result is that humanitarian activities are de facto subordinated to high-level and honourable concerns that are other than humanitarian. This in itself distorts the very meaning of these actions and imperils the presence of humanitarian actors in the

field by blurring their image and the respect due to their work and intentions.[44]

There are no easy answers to this dilemma. Many statements of humanitarian principle include declarations for independence and neutrality. The Red Cross has drawn up a 'code of conduct' for NGOs which states that every organization should ensure that 'aid will not be used to further a particular political or religious standpoint' and 'we shall endeavour not to act as instruments of government foreign policy.' Yet, as the qualified nature of the last pledge indicates, the reality is that humanitarian NGOs are becoming increasingly dependent on western government donors, who comprise the only constituency that can hold them accountable.

Where agencies confine their activities to service delivery it might not present such a problem, but when aid is used for overtly political purposes, or when the agencies themselves engage in political advocacy, then the question of accountability becomes more acute. Western troops are directly involved in two current conflicts, in Iraq and Afghanistan, and western governments provide the bulk of the financial support to UN operations elsewhere. At the same time, the broader policies of western governments shape the political environment in which humanitarian crises take place. Struggles for justice, democracy, economic reform, human rights and emancipation continue throughout the world. How can human rights and humanitarian organizations engage with such movements, and what challenges does this throw up for their mandates?

Conclusion: The New Imperialists?

I N A scathing article on MSF, when it was awarded the Nobel Peace Prize in 1999, Kirsten Sellars wrote: 'Heeding the impulse to take up the latter day "White Man's Burden", battalions of NGOs marched into Mogadishu, Sarajevo and Goma armed with land cruisers, satellite phones and the latest liberal imperialist orthodoxies. Local governments retreated in their path, and soon many areas in these countries became de facto zones of occupation under the control of the humanitarian armies.'[1]

The criticisms of the humanitarian movement echo those of other people on the right and left of the political spectrum. Indeed, similar sentiments are often heard within the movement itself. As Alex de Waal has noted, one of humanitarianism's defining characteristics seems to be its 'extraordinary capacity to absorb criticism, not reform itself and yet emerge strengthened . . . The legitimacy of Western relief agencies, donor institutions and even military forces seems to be enhanced by those who dispute their effectiveness.'[2]

This is slightly unfair. The emergency relief operations mounted in Biafra in the 1960s and Ethiopia in the 1980s, like the military operations in the early 1990s to protect Somali food convoys and the Kurds of northern Iraq, were motivated by genuine altruistic concern. Political humanitarianism partly grew out of the perceived limitations of the traditional Red Cross approach to protection and assistance during these and subsequent humanitarian crises. The attempts to embrace rights-based programming, international justice mechanisms and humanitarian accountability have also developed out of critiques of existing practice. Although this book has criticized these approaches, it is important to recognize not only the motivations of those involved but the real life alternatives on offer. The arguments for non-intervention also had significant moral and political implications at the time.

Humanitarian interventions became more frequent as the 1990s wore on and the perceived successes and failures of each operation did much to influence the planning and preparation for the next. It is perhaps not surprising that the humanitarian movement is still grappling with so many practical and theoretical dilemmas given the size of the problems it has confronted over such a short space of time. As Austen Davis has noted, 'For many years humanitarianism was the small and intellectually backward cousin of development assistance. It attracted low levels of funding and there was little academic interest in its concepts or methods.'[3] Although the subject is now increasingly included in courses on development studies and human rights, it has received little independent study and is a remarkably under-analyzed area of work. The few books written about it are mainly for a specialist audience and, outside the ranks of its own practitioners, its basic terms and concepts are often little understood.

Despite its recent history, humanitarianism's influence on international relations has grown rapidly. Interventions in the Balkans, East Timor, Haiti and large parts of Africa dramatically altered the debate on national sovereignty, human rights and international law. Westphalian principles of non-interference, enshrined in Article 2 of the UN Charter, have receded as the Security Council used its Chapter VII powers to override what states had previously defined as being within their own exclusive jurisdiction. UN missions moved from peacekeeping to peace enforcement, and sometimes took on governance functions over entire territories. International criminal tribunals stripped away state immunity and indicted former and serving government ministers. The integration of humanitarian assistance into military interventions also impacted on the way such assistance is often perceived. There has been a steady increase in the number of attacks on aid workers over the last decade, partly because an increasing number of armed parties no longer respect the 'humanitarian space' within which aid workers operate.[4]

The interventions in Afghanistan and Iraq clearly cannot be classified as humanitarian, though they have influenced the response to subsequent crises, such as those in Darfur and Burma. They have also reinforced the growing suspicion of one section of the left that the doctrine of humanitarian intervention is a sham. Paul de Rooij, for example, has warned that: 'Awful wars are waged for crass motives, yet they are sold on the basis that they are driven by benevolent intent. Promotion of democracy, freedoms, human rights, women's rights, and even religious tolerance are some of the purported motives for current interventions, subversion or wars.'[5] According to David Chandler, 'human rights intervention [has become] the leitmotif of a new ethical order in international affairs . . . the humanitarian bandwagon rolls on from Iraq to Somalia to Bosnia, to Kosovo, to East Timor, to Sierra Leone, to Afghanistan.'[6]

These writers maintain that humanitarianism has been used to disguise the ulterior motives of the interventionists. Oil and resources, military bases, pipelines, private contracts or the radical restructuring of developing world economies are 'the real reasons for wars or interventions' with human rights merely providing a convenient smokescreen. Chandler argues that 'the human rights discourse is deeply corrosive of the political process.' Others accuse human rights and humanitarian organizations of acting as witting or unwitting agents in the process of legitimization. In *Humanitarian Imperialism*, Jean Bricmont slams those 'useful fools of empire' who have 'bought the arguments for war on human rights grounds'.[7]

This critique does not stand up to much scrutiny. While there are strong grounds for treating the official explanations for western interventions with some scepticism, the alternatives also deserve critical examination. Michael Moore's hypothesis that part of the motivation for the invasion of Afghanistan was to build a gas pipeline across it was based on extremely shoddy research. The view that the US intervened in Kosovo to build a military base there simply confuses cause and effect. It is China, rather than the west, that currently displays the most predatory attitude towards the natural resources of the African countries which have hosted UN missions. None of the major powers had any obvious selfish or strategic reason to intervene in places such as Somalia, Bosnia-Herzegovina, Haiti or East Timor. Indeed, it is precisely because western powers usually have not had ulterior motives to intervene that so many of these missions have suffered from lack of resources, planning and political will.

A stronger criticism comes from those who accuse the west of double standards on human rights, that is, intervening in states they deem hostile, while ignoring the violations committed by friends and allies. Professor Edward Herman, for instance, contrasts western attitudes towards Iraq, Yugoslavia and Afghanistan on the one hand with Indonesia, Israel and Turkey on the other.[8] Soumaya Ghannoushi noted how western liberals have created a 'stereotype of the oppressed Muslim woman' awaiting benevolent intervention to free her from patriarchal oppression by Muslim men, while ignoring the human rights violations women suffer from pro-western governments in Turkey and the Occupied Palestinian Territories.[9]

NATO's mobilization over Kosovo and its indifference to Turkey's repression of the Kurds is indeed striking. Western governments, and western public opinion, often give the impression that they consider some groups of victims to be more deserving than others. Serbs are now the biggest group of displaced people in Europe but their plight is rarely raised at an international level. Palestinians remain the largest group of refugees in the world, yet the international community remains quiescent towards Israel's continued illegal construction of settlements and collective punishment of civilians. Nevertheless, Herman and Ghannoushi's argument is slightly circular in that it seems to condemn the international community for both action and inaction, simultaneously and in equal measure. Herman criticizes the 'very belated' nature of the international intervention in East Timor and its failure to bring the militia leaders responsible for massacres to justice, but then goes on to condemn those 'high profile human rights activists' who favoured intervention in Kosovo while 'not one of them suggested bombing Jakarta'. Ghannoushi writes moving accounts of the courage shown by women in the West Bank and Gaza in defying their Israeli oppressors, but then rejects the notion of 'pleading with the West to intervene' because, 'the burden of liberation rests on the shoulders of the Muslim woman herself.'

Both arguments fail to deal with the question regarding humanitarian interventions famously posed by Kofi Annan in 1999: 'How should we respond to another Rwanda or Srebrenica?' Would Herman oppose every specific intervention that might prevent genocide or mass murder in one place simply because the world is full of unaddressed suffering elsewhere? Does Ghannoushi really believe that nothing should have been done to help Muslim Kurdish women fleeing from the Iraqi Republican guard in 1991 – or Bosnians in 1995 or East Timorese in 1999 – in case it was used 'as a vehicle of justification and legitimization' for interventions in the future? Once the rhetoric is stripped away, it is difficult to see what either writer believes should have been done in such real life situations. Their arguments also negate the entire tradition of international solidarity on which organizations like Amnesty International are based. Western governments may well display hypocrisy and double standards towards human rights in the rest of the world, but this should not be a reason to stop documenting and denouncing violations wherever and whenever they occur.

The human rights movement has faced a far greater challenge from the opposite end of the political spectrum. In 2004, Amnesty International warned that: 'The current framework of international law and multilateral action is undergoing the most sustained attack since its establishment half a century ago. International human rights and humanitarian law is being directly challenged as ineffective in responding to the security issues of the present and future.'[10] Irene Khan, Amnesty's secretary-general, noted her shock at the killing of her friend and former colleague, Sergio Vieira de Mello, in Iraq the previous year:

> As one of the most prominent international human rights defenders lay dying in the rubble, the world had good cause to ponder how the legitimacy and credibility of the UN could have been eroded to such a fatal degree. Bypassed in the Iraq war and marginalized in its aftermath, discredited by its perceived vulnerability to pressure from powerful states, the UN seemed virtually paralysed in its efforts to hold states to account for their adherence to international law and their performance on human rights.[11]

The Bush administration, which was isolationist before 9/11, swung into an aggressive unilateralism shortly thereafter. Bush's senior advisers soon became openly contemptuous of the constraints the international legal system placed on their freedom of action. In the run-up to the invasion of Iraq, many made little secret of the fact they regarded removing Saddam Hussein from power and weakening the authority of the UN as 'an opportunity to kill two birds with one stone'.[12] The denial of constitutional rights to the Guantánamo Bay detainees, the policy of extraordinary rendition and attempts to shield CIA operatives from prosecution for war crimes all involved significant departures from accepted human rights norms, while the doctrine of 'pre-emptive military action' is clearly incompatible with an international rules-based system.[13]

The now infamous 'torture memo', produced for the Bush administration in August 2002, referred to international human rights law as 'a useful barometer of the international view of what actions amount to torture'.[14] It argued that 'physical pain amounting to torture must be equivalent in intensity to the pain which accompanied serious physical injury, such as organ failure, impairment of bodily function or even death', and distinguished this from 'cruel, inhuman, or degrading treatment or punishment', which involved lesser degrees of pain. The memo also noted that torture – unlike cruel, inhuman or degrading treatment – is a crime of universal jurisdiction, meaning that its perpetrators can be prosecuted anywhere in the world.

The memo cited the judgment of the European Court of Human Rights in support of its definition. The case it referred to was brought by the Irish Government against the British over its treatment of a group of internees in Northern Ireland during the 1970s. The Court found that the interrogation techniques they had been subjected to amounted to 'cruel, inhuman and degrading treatment' rather than torture, and the US memo describes in considerable detail both the Court's reasoning and the techniques themselves. There is a close similarity between what the memo claims falls short of the torture threshold and the reports gathered by human rights organizations detailing the ill-treatment the detainees actually suffered. Indeed, it is difficult to read the memo without getting the impression that its author felt similar practices might suit the purposes of the Bush administration.

What the memo failed to note, however, is that the European Court has subsequently revised its view of when ill-treatment amounts to torture and has called on states to raise their standards in protecting people from abuse.[15] It also failed to mention that only the European Court has tried to distinguish between the two forms of ill-treatment on the basis of specific methods of inflicting pain. The better distinction is to look at whether severe physical or mental suffering was purposefully inflicted, or whether it occurred without a specific intent.

By the definition of torture used by most international courts and UN monitoring bodies, there is a prima facie case that prominent members of the Bush administration are liable to prosecution either in the US or in other countries that have ratified the UN Convention against Torture. There have been credible and consistent reports from human rights organizations that US interrogation methods include stripping detainees naked, holding them in prolonged stress positions, depriving them of food and sleep, subjecting them to extremes of heat and cold and disorientating noise, and interrogating them for days and nights at a time during which they are beaten, threatened and occasionally undergo simulated drownings (known as water-boarding).[16] President Bush has admitted that he knew his top national security advisers discussed and approved specific details of how some interrogations would be conducted.[17] Donald Rumsfeld wrote in one memo concerning how long people could be held in stress positions: 'I stand for eight to ten hours a day – why is standing limited to four hours?'[18] Vice President Dick Cheney told a radio interviewer that 'a dunk in the water' was a 'no-brainer' if it could save lives.[19] US courts have already permitted civil torts against torture carried out in other jurisdictions[20], and there is no reason, in principle, why the legal systems of other countries could not rely on the 'Pinochet precedent' to pursue former members of the administration under laws of universal jurisdiction.

The US government's blatant disregard for international law has also created a dilemma for the section of European liberal-left opinion that backed the invasion of Iraq on 'human rights' grounds. In April 2006, Britain's defence secretary, John Reid, appeared to endorse the US Government's policy of denying the protections of the Geneva Conventions to the Guantánamo Bay detainees, as well as its doctrine of 'pre-emptive military action'.[21] He implied that the Geneva Conventions were out of date, 'created more than half a century ago, when the world was almost unrecognisable to today's citizens', and went on to 'welcome the work the UN has been doing with the Responsibility to Protect declaration', which he hoped would widen the legal grounds on which force could be used against other states. Defending his remarks, he said that the current framework on international law was inadequate in dealing with international terrorism and mass human rights violations.[22]

Two years later, in February 2008, Foreign Secretary David Miliband delivered one of his first major speeches on the theme of liberal intervention, in which he argued that 'something strange happened' in the 1990s when 'the neoconservative movement seemed more certain about spreading democracy around the world' than the left. He claimed that 'the left seemed conflicted between the desirability of the goal and its qualms about the use of military means' to achieve it. Calling for 'civilian surges' for democracy, he argued that the lesson to draw from the 'mistakes in Iraq' was that 'interventions in other countries must be more subtle, better planned, and if possible undertaken with the agreement of multilateral institutions.'[23]

The intellectual contortions of this analysis are obvious. The debate that took place in the 1990s was not about spreading democracy but on the effectiveness of the UN's humanitarian interventions. As discussed in this book, the lawful grounds for states to use military means are in self-defence or with UN Security Council approval. A case can possibly be made for 'unauthorized interventions' on exceptional humanitarian grounds, but there is no basis in international law for invading other countries in order to democratize them.

In the same month Miliband also had to admit to Parliament that previous assurances the government had given that Britain was in no way co-operating with the CIA's rendition programme were wrong since two 'special rendition' flights had landed on British soil for refueling.[24] The practice of rendition – when terrorist suspects are secretly flown for interrogation to countries where torture is often used – is clearly a serious violation of international law. For a Labour government elected on a commitment to put human rights law at the heart of its foreign policy to show complicity in such practices is nothing short of appalling. Labour has failed to condemn the US torture policy or call for the closure of the Guantánamo Bay camp. It was left to the Conservative Party's new leader, David Cameron, to point out that democracy cannot be imposed from the outside, that Britain should stop being so 'slavish' in its support for US government policies and that humanitarian interventions should be undertaken only during genuine humanitarian crises.[25]

Blair's liberal interventionism rested on a 'doctrine of international community' and a commitment to multilateralism which presupposed the existence of an international rules-based system that President Bush, his closest ally, has done so much to undermine. Blair's commitment to exporting human rights abroad also sat uncomfortably with the way he presided over their erosion at home. The British Government has faced repeated challenges over its attempts to intern people suspected of involvement in terrorism without trial, extend the periods they can be detained without charge and deport them to countries where they are at risk of being tortured. One junior government minister, Kitty Ussher, stated that anyone who objects to holding people in police custody for ninety days without charge will 'have blood on their hands' if there is another terrorist atrocity in Britain.[26] Journalist Nick Cohen, another prominent liberal interventionist, has used his column in the *Observer* to make the case for torture in certain circumstances.[27]

In his book *What's Left?*, Cohen devotes half a sentence to acknowledging that 'there were credible reports of torture' in Guantánamo Bay, but it falls in the middle of a lengthy tirade against Amnesty International and other left-liberals for supposedly 'losing their compass' in the aftermath of 9/11.[28] Chapter titles such as 'The liberals go berserk', 'Kill us we deserve it' and

'The disgrace of the anti-war movement' provide an accurate preview of the book's style and content, and it is a curious read to anyone familiar with the arguments about humanitarian intervention. In his account of the conflict in Bosnia-Herzegovina he seems genuinely unaware that European governments committed ground troops to the UN mission while the US categorically refused to risk the lives of its soldiers. 'All that you need to know' about the conflict, he claims, is that it 'followed Milošević's desire for an uncontaminated homeland' and that Europe appeased him out of a cowardly unwillingness to sacrifice blood and treasure due to its low economic growth and birth rates.[29] It is perhaps no surprise that Cohen admits to being a rather recent convert to the interventionist cause:

> My instant reaction to the 9/11 attacks was that they were a nuisance that got in the way of more pressing concerns . . . The easy option was for me to carry on as if nothing had happened. I berated Bush for failing to predict the atrocities . . . I followed up with articles calling for the Americans to suspend the invasion of Afghanistan because Oxfam and Christian Aid said the bombing campaign would stop aid reaching starving villages . . . I wanted anything associated with Tony Blair to fail because that would allow me to return to the easy life of attacking him. If propagating scare stories from Oxfam and Christian Aid allowed me to undermine him then I was more than prepared to do it.[30]

Cohen's instrumentalist attitude reflects a long-standing ambivalence by a section of the left towards human rights and humanitarianism. The idea that rights should be defended for their own sake or that interventions should be judged by the criteria of whether they help or harm people is derided as naive. The more important issue, these leftists argue, is 'whose side you are on' in a global ideological struggle. This used to be defined in cold war terms but is increasingly presented as one of 'anti-imperialism' versus 'liberal interventionism'. Traditionally, many on the left and right of the political spectrum were prepared to overlook human rights violations when committed by their allies, or refrain from denouncing them lest it provide 'propaganda' for their opponents. Cohen is continuing in the tradition of his unreconstructed former comrades. He has just defected to what he would previously have regarded as the other side of the struggle.

But the problems some political activists have with human rights interventionism are often matched by the problems humanitarians have with political advocacy. Abby Stoddard, of New York University's Center on International Cooperation, notes that while political advocacy by humanitarian organizations has sometimes been instrumental in drawing attention to a particular crisis, it has been much less effective in influencing the more detailed direction of policy.[31] After reviewing the work of a number of humanitarian agencies in Darfur, Sorcha O'Callaghan and Sara Pantuliano of the Overseas Development Institute (ODI) warned, 'There is a lack of clarity around humanitarian actors' role in advocacy' which 'can lead to aid actors overstepping humanitarian boundaries and being drawn into discussions in which they have limited competence or expertise'.[32] They suggest that agencies should consciously distance themselves from 'non-neutral campaigners' in order to safeguard their humanitarian identity. Many francophone aid agencies, such as MSF and Action Against Hunger, have also become increasingly critical of the way US and British NGOs have overstepped the line between humanitarian action and politics.

As previously discussed, the Darfur crisis highlighted this problem in a number of ways. The Save Darfur Coalition has been scrupulous in its attempts to build a broad-based non-partisan movement in the US, but it seems not to have considered how this might be perceived by the rest of the world. Its website, for example, lavishes praise on the Bush administration, stressing that: 'We are both cognizant and appreciative of the fact that the President has done more for the people of Darfur than any other world leader. In fact, it is because of his leadership thus far that we direct our pleas to President Bush now.'[33] However, members of the Bush administration, and the wider US neo-conservative movement, made little secret of the fact that they regarded the Darfur crisis as an opportunity to attack both Sudan's Islamic government and the supposed weakness and inactivity of the UN. The Coalition's use of inflated death toll figures and its calls for military enforcement of a no-fly zone have been eagerly taken up by prominent US Republicans and the influential American Israel Public Affairs Committee (AIPAC) because it fits their broader ideological world view. However, it is seen by most people as anything but neutral or benevolent.

Human rights groups, such as Amnesty International and Human Rights Watch, have been more scrupulous in their use of facts and their efforts to avoid aligning themselves with overtly political agendas. One of the noticeable differences between human rights and humanitarian organizations is that the former err on the side of caution when reporting violations, whereas the latter never knowingly understate the scale of a crisis. Advocacy reporting is not humanitarianism's core business and many organizations often use their reports for other purposes, such as fund-raising. Even with the best intentions, there may be a temptation to dramatize a particular crisis, since the general view is that no harm can come from making people care too much about suffering. This means there will always be potential issues of fact-checking, quality control and manipulation, which may affect the authority of the report itself and the reputation of the organization that published it.

Political advocacy is not incompatible with humanitarian work and some of the reports produced by organizations such as Oxfam, CARE, the International Rescue Committee, Save the Children and MSF have been invaluable in drawing attention to violations during various conflicts. However, humanitarianism as a whole has yet to develop a coherent policy on the challenges political action throws up. Human rights organizations, such as Amnesty International, sometimes appear obsessive in their attempts to maintain strict neutrality, but procedures, including the 'own country rule', have valuable functions. Forbidding national sections from campaigning on human rights violations in their own countries not only gives them the appearance of greater objectivity, it also removes a source of potential pressure on their activities. Humanitarian organizations, by contrast, will always have to weigh advocacy against access, which will affect the consistency of its reporting. It is worth asking whether an organization has stopped condemning certain violations because the situation is getting better, or because things are suddenly much worse.

Most humanitarian agencies already understand this dilemma, and there is minimal support for the proposal that NGOs should be given the task of reporting when military interventions might be justified on human rights grounds. Already some have found that the ICC is seriously complicating their work. Many humanitarian organizations continue to be involved in 'peace-building' programmes, but there is little evidence that these have had more than a marginal influence on conflict resolution.

International military interventions during humanitarian crises have brought mixed results. Some of the responsibility for the failures can be laid at the UN's door, though the record of 'unauthorized interventions' is no better. The belief that the international community can ever conjure peace out of chaos created an arrogance of expectation over what can be accomplished in such circumstances. This has gradually given way to a cynical disillusionment that little can be done to really help people. Both views are wrong and one of the challenges facing humanitarianism is to develop a much more pragmatic and realistic approach to the issue of intervention.

It is difficult to draw a single thread through what went right and wrong during the various humanitarian interventions of the last couple of decades. Specific issues such as mandates, mission goals and resources have proved far more crucial to their success or failure than sweeping statements of principle, such as the 'responsibility to protect'. Successful interventions tended to be those that supported locally-driven peace processes (based on good intelligence and with a clear strategic aim) and were properly funded and blessed by the UN's official sanction. The perceived neutrality of the intervening forces was usually a positive factor, as was good co-ordination between military and humanitarian parties in which both sides stuck to their own mandates.

International humanitarian law recognizes the right of the Red Cross and other 'impartial, neutral and independent' humanitarian agencies to take action during conflicts to help relieve human suffering. If a government is deliberately starving a civilian population as a means of waging war, then humanitarian organizations are legally and morally justified in taking the 'borderless doctors' approach in flouting its authority to deliver life-saving aid. Beyond this though, once humanitarians assume responsibility for aspects of state-building, adopt a rights-based approach to aid delivery or the use of such aid for peace-building purposes, they inevitably compromise their principles of independence and impartiality. There will probably be situations in the future when humanitarian organizations feel that only international intervention will prevent mass killing or where their programme activity can help promote peace, justice and reconciliation, but the experience of recent years strongly suggests that the principle 'first, do no harm' is best preserved by humanitarian neutrality.

Humanitarian interventions are at best a necessary evil since by their very nature they cause harm to the societies they are trying to help. Even at their most benign, relief assistance operations, such as the one following the tsunami, lead to economic and social distortion, weaken local capacity and encourage dependence. Military interventions are even more destabilizing and result in significant costs for both the occupier and occupied.

It is noticeable how few places where large-scale humanitarian interventions took place in recent years have succeeded in making the transition to stability. Virtually all these countries remain deeply fractured societies with weak national authorities. Some are effectively still governed as international protectorates, to the increasing frustration of their own populations. As Daniel Korski noted, even Bosnia-Herzegovina, site of the largest and most expensive intervention ever, remains paralyzed by ethnic tensions despite fifteen years of 'peace-building'.[34]

Many commentators have also noted striking similarities between today's debates on humanitarian interventions and those that took place towards the end of the nineteenth century during the 'scramble for Africa'.[35] The missionaries, teachers and doctors who followed the soldiers of European armies presumably believed they were helping to spread the benefits of 'civilization' to 'backward races'. Anti-slavery activists enthusiastically supported military action against the largely Arab-controlled slave trade. The British navy's decision to interdict slave ships flying foreign flags and liberate their victims was a humanitarian assault on the previously accepted international legal doctrine of respect for state sovereignty. The treaties enabling slave traders to be put on trial by any state that captured them also laid the basis for subsequent laws of universal jurisdiction.[36] John Stuart Mill could be seen as one of the earliest advocates for the establishment of international protectorates, when he argued that: 'Despotism is a legitimate form of government in dealing with barbarians, providing the end be their improvement.'[37]

Of course, the analogies can be overdone but they require western liberals to think more seriously about the supposed universal values they hope their interventions will promote. As Professor Boaventura de Sousa Santos wrote, international human rights and humanitarian law were primarily drafted by western political leaders and the supporters of both movements remain overwhelmingly middle-class, liberal and western in their social backgrounds, yet the main focus of their efforts is in places where quite different conceptions of these notions prevail:

> Throughout the world millions of people and thousands of NGOs have been struggling for human rights, often at great risk in defence of oppressed social classes and groups that in many instances have been victimized by authoritarian capitalistic states. A counter-hegemonic human rights discourse and practice have been developing, non-Western conceptions of human rights have been proposed, cross-cultural dialogues of human rights have been organized. The central task of an emancipatory politics of our time, in this domain, consists of transforming the conceptualization and practice of human rights from a globalized localism into a cosmopolitan project.[38]

This suggests the need to develop a rather different discourse on human rights interventionism, one which is more modest in recognizing its limitations, but more ambitious in recognizing what needs to be done. A useful starting point would be to acknowledge that the conception of human rights western liberals have created, refined and prepackaged for export, is not the only one in existence. A broader dialogue is needed for the ways in which respect for human dignity, personal freedom and individual autonomy can be located in discussions of how to address the injustices caused by the imbalances of wealth and power in the world today. Combating extreme poverty requires economic growth, but since poverty and inequality are two of the most important underlying causes of conflict and humanitarian crises, human rights and humanitarian organizations have an important role to play in the arguments for economic justice.

For example, the World Social Forum, initiated by supporters of the Brazilian Workers' Party, has now become an important arena for south–south debate. Despite their sometimes anarchic nature, these gatherings are noticeable for the interaction they stimulate between trade unionists, social movements and religious organizations throughout the developing world as well as for how few members of the mainstream European and North American left bother to attend. A genuine 'global justice movement' needs to engage with the forces represented in this and similar forums. To their credit, human rights, humanitarian and development organizations are becoming increasingly involved in these talks since they are among the few organizations with global reach. The focus of their work is in the south, but their headquarters, leadership and financial support tend to be located in the north. Some have tried to build national sections in countries such as India, Brazil and South Africa, and their advocacy work prefigures the kind of global campaigning necessary to address the causes of humanitarian crises and their roots in global poverty.

The campaign for the International Criminal Court, for instance, showed that international lobbying can help overcome the vested interests of even the world's most powerful state. Although the court which emerged contains many flaws, its statute is due to be amended in 2009 and could provide an opportunity for addressing many of its current weaknesses. A strengthened independent court which included the crime of aggression in its statute might begin to fulfil the hopes of those who believe that 'justice' could assume a leading role in the conduct of international relations. The 'Make Poverty History' initiative used a similar and more high-profile model of international campaigning, and the Live 8 concerts of 2005 made real, albeit limited, progress towards its aims of trade reform, debt relief and an increase in international aid to help the world's most impoverished countries. An end to the subsidies and agricultural protectionism of rich countries should become a rallying cry for the world's poor. Reform of the UN and the need to strengthen and democratize other institutions of global governance remain critical outstanding tasks.

There is surprisingly broad agreement on the range of policies needed to tackle the problems faced by the poorest people in the world today. What is absent is a lack of political will to put them into effect. Until this can be forced onto the domestic political agendas of the most powerful states the humanitarian crises these countries suffer will continue. Occasionally it will lead to calls for international intervention. However, emergency responses can never be more than palliatives until the underlying roots of the problems are addressed. Human rights and humanitarian organizations can make a contribution to this broader political movement but they cannot be a substitute for it.

In the final days before the bombing of the UN's headquarters in Baghdad in August 2003, Sergio Vieira de Mello is reported to have become increasingly depressed over the failure of his efforts. He was a career diplomat and some of his colleagues accused him of compromising his principles too readily in order to 'side with power', but by July 2003, he had become openly critical of the high-handed arrogance of the US administration in Iraq and the behaviour of its occupation forces. He visited Abu Ghraib prison in early August and warned that there were not enough safeguards in place to protect detainees against abuse. He also spoke out against the killing of journalists and civilians by US soldiers. In his last recorded interview he told a Brazilian journalist that the US was trampling on Iraq's dignity and wounding its national pride. 'Who would like to see his country occupied?' he asked. 'I would not like to see foreign tanks in Copacabana.'[39] Yet for all these reservations, Vieira de Mello believed that once the invasion had happened, the UN needed to work with the US administration to achieve the best possible outcome it could for the Iraqi people. He was prepared to 'wrap the blue flag' around the occupation because he could not see any alternative. The decision was ultimately to cost him his life for a cause that he probably by then knew was not worthwhile.

Tens of thousands of humanitarian aid workers are confronted with the same moral dilemma every day. They might help individual people in a crisis zone, but they can never be absolutely certain that the overall impact of their presence does more good than harm. While their presence pricks the world's conscience that 'something must be done' it simultaneously reinforces the delusion that humanitarian action can ever be enough. In reality they are just another part of the problem.

Acknowledgements

The ideas contained in this book developed during my time in a variety of human rights and humanitarian organizations. I have erred on the side of caution when naming friends and colleagues – and, for obvious reasons, not identified any national staff or programme beneficiaries – but my biggest intellectual debt is to the people whom I have worked alongside in over a dozen crisis zones.

Some of the material in the book was directly drawn from a series of letters home sent to friends and family which eventually developed into a series of articles for the *Guardian*'s Comment page and its Comment is Free website. I am particularly grateful to Georgina Henry and Seumas Milne, the CiF editorial team and the thousands of, mainly anonymous, contributors who have debated these themes.

Thanks are also due to the following, in their individual capacities, for helping to inform the content of this book: Dara Katz and Caroline Howard of OHCHR Afghanistan; Iesha Singh, Kate Mackintosh and Harriet Cochrane of MSF; Aisling Reidy and Clive Baldwin of Human Rights Watch; Paul Harvey of the Overseas Development Institute; Dan Lewis of UN-Habitat; Kevin Boyle, Nigel Rodley and Françoise Hampson of the University of Essex; my former colleagues at Amnesty, UNHCR, the Norwegian Refugee Council and the International Rescue Committee; Marko Attila Hoare of Kingston

University and Oliver Kamm of *The Times*. As the last two names should indicate, none of the above is in any way responsible for my conclusions and any errors or omissions are my sole responsibility

Abigail Fielding Smith suggested the idea of a book. Andrew Lownie and Linda Grant provided me with useful advice at a critical juncture in getting it published. Tom Penn, Anna Swann, Charles Peyton, Clara Heyworth, Tania Palmieri and the rest of the Verso team were a pleasure to work with. Thanks, again, to you all.

Notes

Introduction

1 Samantha Power, *Chasing the Flame: Sergio Vieira de Mello and the Fight to Save the World*, Allen Lane, 2007, pp.451–95. Larriera recalls begging the soldiers who were escorting her away to start digging to save him. She also implored the cameramen to help her. 'Don't film – help,' she cried.

2 Message from Secretary-General Kofi Annan for the special issue of *Secretariat News* honouring victims of the bombing of the United Nations mission in Iraq.

3 Text of speech delivered by the prime minister, Sedgefield, 5 March 2004.

4 UN Charter, Article 2 (7).

5 Geoffrey Robertson QC, *Crimes Against Humanity*, Penguin, 2006.

6 *Independent*, 'Iraq is a tragedy, but Blair's global goal will live on – and he will be vindicated', 6 May 2007.

7 Clare Short, *An Honourable Deception*, Free Press, 2005, pp.93–6.

8 Mike Jackson, *Soldier: The Autobiography*, Bantam, 2007.

9 *Report of the International Commission of Inquiry on Darfur to the United Nations Secretary-General, Pursuant to Security Council Resolution 1564 of 18 September 2004*, United Nations, 25 January 2005.

10 Save Darfur Coalition, *New Analysis Claims Darfur Deaths Near 400,000*, 21 April 2005.

11 *New York Times*, 'Advocacy group's publicity campaign on Darfur angers relief organizations', 2 June 2007.

12 *Ibid.*

13 ASA Adjudication, 8 August 2007.

14 Reuters AlertNet, 'Watch your facts, UK ad watchdog warns campaigners', 14 August 2007.

15 Action Against Hunger press statement, 'A Political Solution Is Essential to Achieving Security in Darfur, Says Action Against Hunger', 18 May 2007.

16 Save Darfur Coalition statement, 8 August 2007.

17 *Observer*, 'A life-saver emerges from the Left Bank', 27 May 2007.

18 *Guardian*, 'Comment & Debate: Darfur wasn't genocide and Sudan is not a terrorist state', 7 October 2005.

19 *Observer*, 'Britain hails hope for peace in Darfur', 16 September 2007.

20 *Guardian*, 'Blair wants no-fly zone enforced over Darfur', 28 March 2007.

21 *Guardian*, 'Anger over Straw's dossier on Iraqi human rights', 3 December 2002.

22 *Observer*, 'How the UN lets genocidal states get away with murder', 29 October 2006.

23 Alex de Waal, *Famine Crimes*, James Currey, 2002, p.73.

24 Martin Meredith, *The State of Africa*, John Ball, 2006, p.204.

25 *Ibid.*, p.74.

26 David Reiff, *A Bed for the Night*, Vintage, 2002, p.84.

27 Maggie Black, *A Cause for Our Times*, Oxford University Press, 1992.

Chapter 1: Human Rights and Humanitarians

1 UN Genocide Convention 1948, Article 8.

2 Universal Declaration of Human Rights 1948, preamble.

3 Bouventura de Sousa Santos, 'Toward a Multicultural Conception of Human Rights', in Berta Hernandez Truyol (ed.), *Moral Imperialism: A Critical Anthology*, New York University Press, 2002.

4 See, for example, William Easterly, *The White Man's Burden*, Oxford University Press, 2007, and Paul Collier, *The Bottom Billion*, Oxford Univerity Press, 2007.

5 Kevin Watkins, *The Oxfam Poverty Report*, Oxfam, 1995.

6 See David Reiff, *A Bed for the Night*, Vintage, 2002.

7 Fiona Fox, *The Politicisation of Humanitarian Aid: A Discussion Paper for Caritas Europa*, Internal discussion paper, CAFOD, June 2000, p.5.

8 Francesca Klug, *Values for a Godless Age: The Story of the UK's Bill of Rights*, Penguin, 2000, p.147.

9 *Ireland v United Kingdom*, Series A 25 (1978) and *Selmouni v France*, 28 July 1999. Only the European Court has tried to distinguish

between the two on the basis of severity of suffering. The better distinction, used by the UN committees, is to look at the purposive element.

10 See Sir John Stevens, 'Stevens Inquiry 3', 17 April 2003.

11 *Finucane v the United Kingdom*, Application No. 29178/95.

12 Reiff, 2002, p.214.

13 *Amnesty International Annual Report 2000*, Foreword by Pierre Sané, AI secretary-general.

14 'The Chile Reconciliation Fringe Meeting', Conservative Party conference, 6 October 1999.

15 *International Herald Tribune*, 'Decision causes dilemma for Blair's government', 26 November 1998.

16 Ruling of the Nuremberg War Crimes Tribunal 1946, quoted on 24 March 1999 in the Pinochet House of Lords judgment.

17 Reiff, 2002, p.214.

18 Richard Norton-Taylor, 'From killing to cuddling', *Guardian*, 17 August 2000.

19 Reiff, 2002, p.138.

20 Reiff, 2002, p.215.

21 HRW press release, 'Human rights groups call upon the European Union and World Bank to promote compliance with the Dayton Peace Accords through effective conditionality', 10 January 1997.

22 'The Responsibility to Protect', the International Commission on Intervention and State Sovereignty (ICISS), p.34.

23 Jonathan Goodhand, Tony Vaux and Robert Walker, 'Conducting conflict assessments: guidance notes', Department for International Development, 2002, p.19.

24 *Ibid.*, p.23.

25 Mary Anderson, *Do No Harm: How Aid Can Support Peace – Or War*, the Collaborative for Development Action Inc., 1996, p.1.

26 See, for example, Judy Adoko and Ian Levine, *Land Matters in Displacement: the Importance of Land Rights in Acholiland and What Threatens Them*, CSOPNU, 2004, and Liz Alden Wiley, *Land Rights in Crisis: Restoring Land Tenure to Afghanistan*, Afghan Research and Evaluation Unit, 2003.

Chapter 2: Humanitarian Interventions

1 For details see Helena Cooke, *The Safe Haven in Northern Iraq*, Essex Human Rights Centre and Kurdish Human Rights Project, 1995.

2 Report of the Secretary-General on the Work of the Organization, UN GAOR, 46th Sess., Supp. No. 1, at 5, UN Doc. A/46/1 (1991).

3 Christine Gray, *Use of Force in International Law*, Oxford University Press, 2001, pp.108–9, and Sir Robert Jennings QC and Sir Arthur Watts, *Oppenheim's International Law*, Vol. I, 9th edn, Longmans, 1996, p.421.

4 See, for example, Danielle Coquoz, 'The Involvement of the Military in Humanitarian Activities' in *The Challenges of Complementarity, Fourth Workshop on Protection for Human Rights and Humanitarian Organizations*, ICRC, 2000, pp.14–15.

5 Simma, 'NATO, the UN and the Use of Force: Legal Aspects', *European Journal of International Law* 10, 1999, p.3; see also Gray, 2001, p.24.

6 UN Charter Article 2 (4) and (7).

7 *Barcelona Traction* case *Belgium v Spain*, ICJ Reports, 1970, Judgment of the Court, para. 39.

8 See Nigel Rodley (ed.), *To Loose the Bands of Wickedness – International Intervention in Defence of Human Rights*, Brassey's, 1992.

9 'Corfu Channel Case (Assessment of Compensation)', ICJ Reports, 1949, p.4.

10 *Case Concerning Military and Paramilitary Activities in and against Nicaragua*, ICJ Reports, 1986, para. 202.

11 *Ibid.*, para. 268.

12 Strictly speaking this can only be exercised in response to a prior armed attack across an international frontier, and provided that the state concerned has notified the Security Council and is awaiting its final judgment. However, the use of the word 'inherent' suggests that Article 51 was not intended to restrict the customary law right to self-defence that predates the Charter. This can include anticipatory self-defence and the right to protect nationals abroad, subject to tests of necessity and proportionality established by the *Caroline case 1841–42*. See D. J. Harris, *Cases and Materials in International Law*, 5th edn, Sweet and Maxwell, 1998, pp. 894–917.

13 See Helen Duffy, *The 'War on Terror' and the Framework of International Law*, Cambridge University Press, 2006, pp.144–214.

14 UN Charter, Articles 39–42. See also *Certain expenses of the United Nations (Article 17[2] of the Charter) Advisory Opinion*, 20 July 1961, ICJ Reports, 1962, p.151.

15 *Case concerning questions of interpretation and application of the Montreal Convention arising out of the aeriel incident at Lockerbie (provisional measures) Libya v UK*, ICJ Reports, 1992, p.3. See also *Legal Consequences for States of the Continued Presence of South Africa in Namibia*, dissenting opinion of Judge Fitzmaurice, ICJ Reports, 1971.

16 Peter Malanczuk, *Akehurst's Modern Introduction to International Law*, 7th edn, Routledge, 1997, p.426.

17 *An Agenda for Peace: Preventive Diplomacy, Peacemaking and Peace-keeping: Report of the General Secretary*, UN Doc. A/47/277 (1992), para. 11.

18 UNSC Resolution 54 (1948) Palestine; Resolution 161 (1961) The Congo; Resolution 232 (1966) South Rhodesia; Resolution 307 (1971) Bangladesh; Resolution 353 (1974) Cyprus; Resolution 418 (1977) South Africa; Resolution 573 (1985) Israel's attack on the PLO headquarters in Tunis.

19 Korea, the Congo and limited action on the borders of South Rhodesia.

20 UNSC Resolution 217 (1965), Resolution 221 (1966), Resolution 232 (1966) and Resolution 418 (1977) imposed sanctions on the racist regimes of Rhodesia and South Africa.

21 See Stanley Hoffmann, *The Ethics and Politics of Humanitarian Intervention*, University of Notre Dame Press, 1996; Henry Shue, 'Let whatever is smouldering erupt', in Paolini, Jarvis and Reus-Smit (eds), *Between Sovereignty and Global Governance: The United Nations, the State and Civil Society*, Palgrave Macmillan, 1998, pp.60–84; Steven Wheatley, 'Chechnya and Humanitarian Intervention', *New Law Journal*, Vol. 150, No. 6918, 14 January 2000, p.30.

22 Hugo Slim, 'Military Humanitarianism and the New Peace-Keeping: An Agenda for Peace?', *The Journal of Humanitarian Assistance*, http://www.jha.ac/articles/a003.htm, document posted: 3 June 2000.

23 Fernando Teson, 'Collective Humanitarian Intervention', *Michigan Journal of International Law* 17: 2, 1996, pp.346–65.

24 Thomas Weiss and Cindy Collins, *Humanitarian Challenges and Intervention*, Westview Press, 2000.

25 Quoted in Guy Goodwin Gill, *The Refugee in International Law*, 2nd ed., Clarendon, 1998, p.286.

26 UNGA Resolution A/RES/46/182 (1991).

27 Quoted in Francis Kofi Abiew, *The Evolution of the Doctrine and Practice of Humanitarian Intervention*, Martinus Nijholf, 1999, p.141.

28 *An Agenda for Peace*, UN Doc. A/47/277 (1992).

29 UNSC Resolution 745 (1992).

30 Kofi Annan, 'Peacekeeping and National Sovereignty', in Moore (ed.), *Hard Choices: Moral Dilemmas in Humanitarian Intervention*, Rowman & Littlefield, 1998, p.60.

31 UNSC Resolution 794 (1992).

32 *Ibid.*

33 UNSC Resolution 814, 26 March 1993 and Resolution 837, 6 June 1993, adopted unanimously.

34 Alex de Waal, *Famine Crimes*, 1997, p.162.

35 Mohamed Sahnoun, 'Mixed Intervention in Somalia and the Great Lakes', in Moore (ed.), 1999, p.98.

36 Tony Vaux, *The Selfish Altruist: Relief Work in Famine and War*, Earthscan, 2001, p.150.

37 Thomas Weiss and Cindy Collins, *Humanitarian Challenges and Interventions*, Westview Press, 2000, p.82.

38 Ioan Lewis and James Mayall, 'Somalia', in Mats Berdal and Spyros Economides (eds), *United Nations Interventionism 1991–2004*, Cambridge University Press, 2007.

39 M. Sahnoun, 1998, p.96.

40 MSF, 'Communication on the violations of humanitarian law in Somalia during UNSOM operations', 23 July 1993, cited in Slim, 2001, p.13.

41 African Rights, *Somalia: Human Rights Abuses by the United Nations Forces*, 1993; Amnesty International, *Peacekeeping and human rights*, AI Index IOR 40/01/94.

42 Roméo Dallaire, *Shake Hands with the Devil*, Knopf Canada, 2003, and Roméo Dallaire, 'End of innocence: Rwanda 1994', in Moore (ed.), 1998, p.73.

43 Bruce Jones, 'Rwanda', in Mats Berdal and Spyros Economides (eds), 2007.

44 *Guardian*, 'UN troops stand by and watch carnage', 12 April 1994.

45 Jones, 2007, p.155.

46 Martin Meredith, *The State of Africa*, Jonathan Ball, 2006, pp.485–523.

47 Dallaire, 2003, p.515.

48 *Ibid.*

49 MSF, *Appel Rwanda, On n'arrete pas un genocide avec des medecins!*, 1994.

50 Ian Martin, 'Hard Choices After Genocide: Human Rights and Political Failures in Rwanda' in Moore (ed.), 1998, pp.157–75.

51 See Philip Gourevitch, *We Wish to Inform You That Tomorrow We Will Be Killed With Our Families: Stories from Rwanda*, Picador, 1998.

52 For example, Rageh Omaar, 'A bitter harvest', *Guardian*, 30 April 1997.

53 Mark Duffield, *Global Governance and the New Wars*, Zed Books, 2001, pp.81–2.

54 Martin, in Moore (ed.), 1998, pp.163–66.

55 Fox, 2002, p.23.

56 Weiss and Collins, 2000, pp.104–07, and Jones, 2007, p.158.

57 Amnesty International, *Rwanda: Human Rights Overlooked in Mass Repatriation*, January 1997, AI Index: AFR 47/002/1997.

58 Martin, in Moore (ed.), 1998, p.167. Non-refoulement is one of

the most important principles of refugee law. It prescribes that no refugee should be returned to any country where he or she is likely to face persecution or torture.

59 For contrasting personal accounts and views see Kenneth Cain, Heidi Postlewait and Andrew Thomson, *Emergency Sex and Other Desperate Measures*, Miramax Books 2004, and Aidan Hartley, *The Zanzibar Chest*, Harper Perennial, 2003.

60 Hartley, 2003, p.322.

61 John Hirsch, *Sierra Leone: Diamonds and the Struggle for Democracy*, Lynne Reinner, 2001, p.63.

62 Spyros Economides and Paul Taylor, 'Former Yugoslavia', in Mats Berdal and Spyros Economides (eds), *United Nations Interventionism 1991–2004*, Cambridge University Press, 2007.

63 Human Rights Watch, 'Somalia Faces the Future: Human Rights in a Fragmented Society', April 1995, Vol. 7, No. 2.

64 Susan George, *How the Other Half Dies*, Penguin, 1976.

65 Quoted in Vaux, 2001, p.157.

66 De Waal, 1997, p.174, and Weiss and Collins, 2000, p.84.

67 Lewis and Mayall, 2007, p.136.

68 Sahnoun, 1998, p.96.

Chapter 3: Kosovo

1 Tim Judah, *Kosovo, War and Revenge*, Yale University Press, 2000.

2 Amnesty International, *Kosovo: The Evidence*, AI-UK, September 1998.

3 Misha Glenny, *The Balkans*, Granta, 1999.

4 Thomas Weiss and Cindy Collins, *Humanitarian Challenges and Intervention*, Westview Press, 2000, p.105.

5 See 'Report of the Secretary-General on the fall of Srebrenica', UN doc. A/54/549, 15 November 1999.

6 Misha Glenny, *The Balkans 1804–1999: Nationalism, War and the Great Powers*, Granta, 2000, pp.641–42.

7 *New York Times*, 'UN Bosnia commander wants more troops, fewer resolutions', 31 December 1993.

8 Adam LeBor, *Complicity with Evil*, Yale University Press, 2006.

9 Karin Landgren, 'Safety zones and international protection: a dark grey area', *International Journal of Refugee Law*, Vol. 7, No. 3, Oxford University Press, 1995, pp.437–58.

10 Marco Attila Hoare, *How Bosnia Armed*, Saqi Books, 2004, p.118.

11 *Washington Post*, 'Coalition calls for action in Bosnia: groups want more allied military force to stop genocide', 1 August 1995.

12 UN Security Council Resolution 1199 of 23 September 1998.

13 David Reiff, *A Bed for the Night*, Vintage, 2002, p.221.

14 Noam Chomsky, *The New Military Humanitarianism*, Pluto, 1999.

15 Quoted in *Kosovo: Contending Voices on Balkans Interventions*, William Joseph Buckley (ed.), William Eerdmans Publishing Company, 2000, p.253.

16 International Court of Justice, *Legality of Use of Force (Serbia and Montenegro v United Kingdom), Preliminary Objections, the Court Finds That It Has No Jurisdiction to Entertain the Claims Made by Serbia and Montenegro*, press release 2004/46, 15 December 2004.

17 Amnesty International, *Kosovo: The Evidence*, AI-UK, 1998.

18 Samantha Power, *Chasing the Flame*, Allen Lane, 2007, p.366.

19 Ivo H. Daalder, Brookings Institute, senior fellow, Foreign Policy, 'US Diplomacy before the Kosovo War', Testimony to the Senate Committee on Foreign Relations, Subcommittee on European Affairs, 29 September 1999.

20 *CNN News*, 'Transcript: Clinton addresses nation on Yugoslavia strike', 24 March 1999.

21 *Washington Post*, 'Nato continues attacks on Kosovo',17 May 1999.

22 Power, 2007, p.243.

23 Resolution 1244 adopted by the Security Council at its 4011th meeting, on 10 June 1999.

24 Two US pilots also died in a training accident.

25 Alistair Campbell, *The Blair Years*, Hutchinson, 2007, p.362.

26 *Ibid.*, p.372.

27 Text of speech by Tony Blair, 'Doctrine of the International Community', 24 April 1999.

28 Tony Blair, 'This is a battle with only one outcome: victory', *Guardian*, 3 October 2001.

Chapter 4: Afghanistan

1 Afghanistan National Development Strategy, *An Interim Strategy for Security, Governance, Economic Growth and Poverty Reduction*, summary report, (I-ANDS), 13 February 2006.

2 UNSC Resolutions 1373 (2001), 28 September 2001 and 1368 (2001), 12 September 2001.

3 See Bob Woodward, *Bush at War*, Simon and Schuster, 2003, p.314.

4 See *Afghanistan: The Problem of Pashtun Alienation*, International Crisis Group, August 2003.

5 See Crisis Group Asia Briefing No.13, *Securing Afghanistan: The Need for More International Action*, 15 March 2002.

6 International Crisis Group, *Afghanistan: The Need for International Resolve*, 8 February 2008.

7 *Ibid.*

8 Briefing by Lakhdar Brahimi, special representative of the UN secretary-general to the Security Council S/PV.4469, 6 February 2002.

9 UN Security Council Resolution 1401, paragraphs 3 and 4.

10 Crisis Group Asia Report no. 116, *Afghanistan's New Legislature: Making Democracy Work*, 15 May 2006, p.4. In the end, thirty-four candidates were excluded for links to armed groups, but none for illegal funding or human rights abuses.

11 Asia Development Bank, press release, 6 June 2003.

12 Foreign and Common Office website, Afghanistan, 20 January 2005.

13 *Afghanistan: Provincial Reconstruction Teams*, project memorandum, DFID Western Asia Department, June 2003.

14 *http://www.theirc.org/news/colleagues_friends_mourn_loss_and_pay_tribute_to_two_irc_staff_members.html*

15 Liz Alden Wiley, *Land Rights in Crisis: Restoring Land Tenure to Afghanistan*, Afghan Research and Evaluation Unit, March 2003.

16 Presidential Address to the Nation, Washington DC, 7 October 2001.

17 BBC News, 'The cluster bomb controversy', 3 April 2003.

18 Text of speech by Secretary of State Colin Powell, Washington, DC, 26 October, 2001.

19 Jane Barry and Anna Jefferys, *A Bridge Too Far*, ODI, 2002.

20 John Reid, 'British task force has a vital job to do in southern Afghanistan', Ministry of Defence news, 26 January 2006.

21 *Daily Telegraph*, 'A year in Helmand: 4m bullets fired by British forces', 12 January 2008, and 'British troops face decades in Afghanistan', 19 April 2008.

22 BBC News, 'MoD criticized for soldier deaths', 15 February 2008.

23 *Economist*, 'Policing a whirlwind; Afghanistan', 15 December 2007.

24 *Falling Short: Aid Effectiveness in Afghanistan*, Agency Co-ordinating Body for Afghan Relief (ACBAR), 25 March 2008.

25 Oxfam, *Afghanistan: Development and Humanitarian Priorities*, January 2008.

Chapter 5: Sri Lanka and Indonesia

1 John Telford and John Cosgrave, *Joint Evaluation of the International Response to the Indian Ocean Tsunami: Synthesis Report*, Tsunami Evaluation Coalition, July 2006.

2 Caroline Nursey, Humanitarian Exchange, December 2005.

3 *Ibid.*

4 *Rebuilding a better Aceh and Nias*, The World Bank and the Aceh Reconstruction and Rehabilitation Authority (BRR), October 2005.

5 John Telford and John Cosgrave, July 2006.

6 Naomi Klein, *The Shock Doctrine*, Penguin, 2007, p.477.

7 Narayan Swamy, *Inside an Elusive Mind*, Vijitha Yapa Publications, 2003, and *Tigers of Lanka*, Vijitha Yapa Publications, 1995.

8 BBC News, 'Sri Lanka accused over massacre', 1 April 2008.

9 Klein, 2007, p.485.

10 *Access to Justice: A Review of the Justice System in Aceh, Indonesia*, UNDP, August 2003.

11 *Aceh: A New Chance for Peace*, International Crisis Group, August 2005.

12 Adam Burke and Afnan, *Aceh: Reconstruction in a Conflict Environment*, Department for International Development, August 2005.

13 Simon Chesterman, 'East Timor', in Mats Berdal and Spyros Economides (eds), *United Nations Interventions 1991–2004*, Cambridge University Press, 2007.

14 UN Security Council Resolution 1246, 11 June 1999.

15 UN Security Council Resolution 1264, 15 September 1999.

16 Samantha Power, *Chasing the Flame*, Allen Lane, 2007, p.290.

17 *Ibid.*

18 Robertson, 2006, p.498.

19 *Ibid.*, p.499.

20 Quoted in Power, 2007, pp.300–1.

21 UN Security Council Resolution 1272 on East Timor, 25 October 1999.

22 See Rory Stewart, *Occupational Hazards*, Picador, 2006, for an excellent account.

23 *Ibid.*

24 Chesterman, 2007.

25 *Ibid.*

26 Power, 2007.

27 See *Timor-Leste's Displacement Crisis*, International Crisis Group, March 2008, and *Resolving Timor-Leste's Crisis*, International Crisis Group, October 2006.

28 Graham Hancock, *Lords of Poverty*, Camerapix Publishers, 2006.

29 Text of speech by Donald Rumsfeld, 'Beyond nation-building', 14 February 2003.

Chapter 6: A Responsibility to Protect

1 Hansard, House of Lords, Written Answer, col. 646, 17 March 2003.
2 Clare Short, 2004, p.190.
3 *Observer*, 'War chief reveals Iraq legal crisis', 7 March 2004.
4 Opinion of the attorney general, 'Iraq', 7 March 2003.
5 Quoted in Philippe Sands, *Lawless World: Making and Breaking Global Rules*, Allen Lane, 2005, p.185.
6 Quoted in Power, 2007, p.360.
7 Henry Kissinger, *Does America Need a Foreign Policy? Toward a Diplomacy for the Twenty-first Century*, Simon & Schuster, 2002.
8 *The Iraq Study Group Report*, Institute for Peace, December 2006.
9 Tony Blair speech on the UN, Labour Party spring conference, Glasgow, 15 February 2003.
10 Text of Tony Blair's speech to the US Congress, 18 July 2003.
11 Text of speech delivered by the prime minister, Sedgefield, 5 March 2004.
12 Gareth Evans, *Hypocrisy, Democracy, War and Peace*, 16 June 2007.
13 *Observer*, 'Why the West should not fear to intervene', 18 November 2007.
14 See Kouchner and Bettati (eds), *Le Devoir d'ingerence*, Denoël, 1987.
15 *The Responsibility to Protect*, report of the International Commission on Intervention and State Sovereignty, Canadian Ministry of Foreign Affairs, December 2001.
16 For discussion see David Forsythe, *Human Rights in International Relations*, Cambridge University Press, 2000; Thomas Biersteker and Cynthia Weber (eds), *State Sovereignty as a Social Construct*, Cambridge University Press, 1996; Thomas Weiss, *Collective Security in a Changing World*, Lynne Reinner, 1993; Oliver Ramsbotham and Tom Woodhouse, *Humanitarian Intervention in Contemporary Conflict*, Polity Press, 1996.
17 Marc Weller, 'Armed Samaritans', in *Counsel*, August 1999, p.21.
18 David Forsythe, 2000, p.23.
19 Quoted in Thomas Weiss, 'UN Responses in the Former Yugoslavia: Moral and Operational Choices', *Ethics and International Affairs* 8, 1994, p.6.
20 India's invasion of Bangladesh in 1971, Tanzania's invasion of Uganda in 1978 and the Vietnamese invasion of Cambodia in 1979 are frequently cited, but none passes the 'humanitarian tests' set out in the R2P doctrine below.
21 Shue, in Paolini, Jarvis and Reus-Smit (eds), *Between Sovereignty and*

Global Governance: the United Nations, the State and Civil Society, 1998, p.73.

22 *Ibid.*, p.65.

23 Geoffrey Robertson, *Crimes Against Humanity: The Struggle for Global Justice*, Allen Lane, 2006, p.72.

24 *Ibid.*, pp.200–01.

25 Independent International Commission on Kosovo, *The Kosovo Report*, Oxford University Press, 2000.

26 *Ibid.*, para. 6.9.

27 Holzgrefe and Keohane, *Humanitarian Interventions*, Cambridge University Press, 2003.

28 The belief that certain behaviour conforms to a legal obligation.

29 Allen Buchanan, 'Reforming the law of humanitarian intervention', in Holzgrefe and Keohane, 2003, p.139.

30 Fernando Teson, 'The liberal case for humanitarian intervention', in Holzgrefe and Keohane, 2003, p.122.

31 Cassese, 'A Follow-Up: Forcible Humanitarian Countermeasures and Opinio Necessitatis', *European Journal of International Law* 10, 1999, p.791–99; see also Cassese, 'Ex iniuria ius oritur: Are We Moving Towards International Legitimation of Forcible Humanitarian Countermeasures in the World Community?', *European Journal of International Law* 10, 1999, pp.23–30; Cassese, International Law, p.321.

32 Interview with the author, London, June 2002.

33 Ian Brownlie, *Principles of Public International Law*, Oxford University Press, 2003; and Michael Byers, *War Law: International and Armed Conflict*, Atlantic Books, 2005.

34 *House of Commons Select Committee on Foreign Affairs*, Fourth Report, 1999, Appendix 2, para. 102.

35 Helen Duffy, *The 'War on Terror' and the Framework of International Law*, Cambridge University Press, 2005, p.181.

36 Tony Aust, Foreign and Commonwealth Office Legal Counsellor, in response to questions about northern Iraq by the Foreign Affairs Committee in 1992. Quoted in Harris, *Cases and Materials in International Law*, 5th edn, Sweet and Maxwell, 1998, p.921.

37 Statement by the UK representative to the Security Council, S/PV 3988 (1998). Quoted in Duffy, 2005, p.181.

38 *UK Foreign Office Policy Document*, No. 148. Quoted in Harris, 1998, p.918.

39 UNSC Resolution 1674 (2006), 28 April 2006.

40 ICISS report, 2001, para. 2.15.

41 *Ibid.*

42 *Question of the Violation of Human Rights and Fundamental Freedoms in*

all Countries, Sub-Commission Resolution 1999/2, UN Doc. E/CN.4/SUB.2/RES/1999/2.

43 *An Agenda for Peace*, UN Doc. A/47/277 (1992).

44 Boutros Boutros-Ghali, in Gordenker and Weiss, 1996, p.10.

45 Thomas Weiss and Cindy Collins, *Humanitarian Challenges and Intervention*, 2nd edn, Westview Press, 2000, p.67. See also Colin Granderson, 'Military ambiguities in Haiti', in Moore (ed.), 1998, pp.99–118.

46 *Washington Post*, 'Coalition calls for action in Bosnia: groups want more allied military force to stop genocide',1 August 1995.

47 *Statement on the crisis in Eastern Zaire*, Oxfam UK and Ireland, 5 November 1996.

48 Letter to Robin Cook, British foreign secretary, Oxfam, 9 May 2000.

49 Vaux, 2001, p.21.

50 *Ibid.*

51 Robertson, 2006 p.585.

52 *Ibid.*, p.x.

53 *Ibid.*, p.626.

54 Associated Press, 'McCain favors a "League of Democracies" ', 30 April 2008.

55 *Financial Times*, 'The case for a league of democracies', 13 May 2008.

56 *Humanitarian Charter and Minimum Standards in Disaster Response*, The Sphere Project, 2000.

57 *Ibid.*

58 Protocol I, Article 54, Protocol II, Article 14.

59 Geneva Convention IV, Articles, 59, 61 and 142. Protocol I, Articles 70 and 71.

60 Common Article 3 of the four Geneva Conventions, Geneva Convention III, Article 9, Geneva Convention IV, Article 10, Protocol I, Article 70i Protocol II, Article 18.

61 Protocol I, Article 81. See also the Statute of the Movement of the Red Cross and the Red Crescent.

62 Geneva Convention IV, Articles 30 and 143.

63 Common Article 3 of the four Geneva Conventions, Protocol II, Article 14.

64 Common Article 3 of the four Geneva Conventions, Protocol II, Article 18.

65 Protocol II, Article 8.

66 Protocol II, Article 18 (2).

67 Theodor Meron 'The Geneva Conventions as Customary Law,' *The American Journal of International Law* 81, 1987, p.361.

68 *International Review of Red Cross and Red Crescent*, 'The Federation promotes the development of International Disaster Response Law', June 2001, ICRC Publication No. 842, pp.546–8.
69 *Case Concerning Military and Paramilitary Activities in and against Nicaragua*, ICJ Reports, 1986, para. 242.
70 *Ibid.*, para. 243.
71 Daniel Warner, 'The politics of the political/humanitarian divide', *International Review of the Red Cross and Red Crescent*, 83, 1999, pp.109–118.
72 Françoise Hampson, 'The ICTY and Reluctant Witnesses', *International Comparative Law Quarterly*, Vol. 47, January 1998, pp.5–74, and Stephane Jeannet, 'Non-Disclosure of Evidence Before InterNational Criminal Tribunals: Recent Developments Regarding the International Committee of the Red Cross', *International Comparative Law Quarterly*, Vol. 50, July 2001, pp.643–56.
73 *Prosecutor v Blagoje Simic, Milan Simic, Miroslav Tadic, Stevan Todorovic and Simo Zaric*, Decision on the Prosecution Motion Under Rule 73 Concerning the Testimony of a Witness, No. IT-95-9-PT (27 July 1999). Press release issued by ICTY 8 October 1999.
74 Jeannet, 2001.
75 Adam Roberts and Richard Guelff, *Documents on the Laws of War*, 3rd edn, Oxford University Press, 2000, p.624.
76 Robertson, 2006, p.211.
77 Denise Plattner, 'ICRC Neutrality and Neutrality in Humanitarian Assistance', *International Review of the Red Cross and Red Crescent* 311, 30 April 1996, pp.161–79.
78 William DeMars, 'Contending Neutralities, Humanitarian Organizations and War in the Horn of Africa', in *Transnational Social Movements and Global Politics*, Jackie Smith, Charles Chatfield and Ron Pagnucco (eds), Syracuse University Press, 1997, p.112.
79 Rony Brauman, 'Refugee Camps, Population Transfers and NGOs', in Moore, 1998, pp.179–89.
80 *Ibid.*
81 Brauman, in Moore, 1998, p.188.
82 DeMars, in Smith *et al.*, 1997, p.112.
83 James Firebrace and Gail Smith, *The Hidden Revolution: An Analysis of Social Change in Tigray (Northern Ethiopia) Based on Eyewitness Accounts*, War on Want, 1982; James Firebrace and Stuart Holland MP, *Never Kneel Down: Drought Development and Liberation in Eritrea*, Red Sea Press, 1985.

Chapter 7: Justice and Peace

1 IRIN Humanitarian News, 17 October 2005.
2 Tim Allen, *Trial Justice*, Zed Books, 2006.
3 Amnesty International press statement, January 2004.
4 *Herald Sun*, 'Two Ugandan aid workers killed', 27 October 2005.
5 Kate Mackintosh, *Humanitarian Exchange*, December 2005.
6 Alex De Waal, *Famine Crimes*, James Currey, 1997, p.215.
7 Jeannet, 2001.
8 Genocide Convention, Article 6.
9 Human Rights Watch press release, 'US: 'Hague Invasion Act Becomes Law', 3 August 2002.
10 Kate Mackintosh, December 2005.
11 Robertson, 2006, pp.419–67.
12 Rome Statute 1998, articles 15–20.
13 *Ibid.*, Article 53.
14 *Ibid.*, articles 1 and 17.
15 Letter from the office of the ICC prosecutor, 9 February 2006.
16 *Economist*, 'Let the child live; International Criminal Court', 27 January 2007.
17 Rome Statute 1998, Article 5 (2).
18 Robertson, 2006, p.377.
19 Marko Attila Hoare, *The Capitulation of the Hague Tribunal*, Henry Jackson Society, 16 June 2005.
20 Samantha Power, 'Rwanda: the two faces of justice', *New York Review of Books*, 16 January 2003.
21 Amnesty International, Rwanda: *Suspects Must Not Be Transferred to Rwandan Courts for Trial Until It Is Demonstrated that Trials Will Comply with International Standards of Justice*, AI Index: AFR 47/013/2007, 2 November 2007, and Human Rights Watch, *UK: Put Genocide Suspects on Trial in Britain*, 1 November 2007.
22 Dennis Paine, 'The Bending of the Spears', International Alert, 1997.
23 Tim Allen, *Trial Justice*, Zed Books, 2006.
24 Rome Statute 1998, Article 53.
25 Amnesty International, *Uganda: Government Cannot Negotiate Away International Criminal Court Arrest Warrants for LRA*, 20 February 2008.
26 Human Rights Watch, *Uganda: New Accord Provides for War Crimes Trials*, 20 February 2008.
27 *Independant*, 'War in Europe: the Milošević indictment', 30 May 1999.

28 Human Rights Watch, *New Figures on Civilian Deaths in Kosovo War*, 7 February 2000.

29 *Bankovic and Others v Belgium and 16 Other Contracting States*, Application No. 52207/99.

30 Address by the prosecutor to the UN Security Council, The Hague, 27 November 2001.

31 Impunity Watch, 'Brammertz to succeed Del Ponte as chief prosecutor', 14 November 2007.

32 Rwanda does not accept the ICJ's compulsory jurisdiction.

33 International Court of Justice, *Armed Activities on the Territory of the Congo (Democratic Republic of the Congo v Uganda)*, press release 2005/26, 19 December 2005.

34 Human Rights Watch, 'Justice in motion: the trial phase of the Special Court for Sierra Leone', November 2005.

35 Adekeye Adebajo and David Keen, 'Sierra Leone', in Mats Berdal and Spyros Economides (eds), *United Nations Interventionism 1991–2004*, Cambridge University Press, 2007.

36 *Ibid.*

Chapter 8: Humanitarian Accountability

1 *Mozambique: Gestao de Risco de Calamidades ao longo do Rio Buzi, Estudo de Caso sobre os Antecedents, o conceito e a Implementacao da Gestao de Risco de Calamidades no Ambito do Programa de Desenvolvimento Rural (PRODER) da GTZ*, German Federal Ministry for Economic Co-operation and Development, December 2005.

2 IRIN News, 'Southern Africa: extreme weather threatens over a million people', 5 April 2007, *http://www.irinnews.org/Report.aspx?-ReportId=71204*

3 World Food Program Mozambique, *2007 Post-Emergency Report*, 28 May 2007.

4 *Master Plan: Director Plan for Prevention and Mitigation of Natural Disasters*, approved by the fifth session of the Council of Ministers, Government of Mozambique, 14 March 2006.

5 *Republic of Mozambique Action Plan for the Reduction of Absolute Poverty, 2006–2009, Final Version Approved by the Council of Ministers on 2 May 2006*, Government of Mozambique (PARPA II) (2006).

6 World Bank, Country Brief, Mozambique, 15 June 2007.

7 *Ibid.*

8 *Worldwide Press Freedom Index*, Reporters Without Borders, 2006, *http://en.wikipedia.org/wiki/Reporters_Without_Borders*

9 John Mitchell, *Humanitarian Exchange*, June 2007.

10 Alex de Waal, *Famine Crimes*, James Currey, 2002, p.16.

11 Austen Davis, *Concerning Accountability in Humanitarian Action*, Overseas Development Institute, Humanitarian Practice Network Paper, March 2007.

12 BBC News, 'Sex for aid widespread', 8 May 2006.

13 *Guardian*, 'Field notes', 30 May 2008.

14 See, for example, Nicholas Stockton, Humanitarian Accountability Partnership, *Accountability for Protection Delivery*, Third UNHCR-NGO Global Retreat on International Protection, 7–8 March 2008.

15 Mancino, Malley and Cornejo, June 2001, p.11.

16 Duffield, 2001, p.18.

17 John Telford and John Cosgrave, *Joint Evaluation of the International Response to the Indian Ocean Tsunami: Synthesis Report*, Tsunami Evaluation Coalition, July 2006.

18 Austen Davis, *Concerning Accountability in Humanitarian Action*, Overseas Development Institute, Humanitarian Practice Network Paper, March 2007.

19 Giles Bolton, *Poor Story*, Ebury Press, 2007, pp.288–9.

20 Ministry of Health, Republic of Uganda/World Health Organization, *Health and Mortality Survey Among Internally Displaced Persons in Gulu, Kitgum and Pader Districts, Northern Uganda*, July 2005.

21 Civil Society Organizations for Peace in Northern Uganda, *Counting the Cost: Twenty Years of War in Northern Uganda*, 30 March 2006.

22 Giles Bolton, *Poor Story*, Ebury Press, 2007, pp.123–24.

23 Martin Meredith, *The State of Africa*, John Ball, 2006, pp.676–88.

24 William Easterly, *The White Man's Burden*, Oxford University Press, 2006.

25 *Economist*, 'The end of cheap food', 8 December 2007.

26 Transparency International, *2006 corruption Perceptions Index*, http://www.transparency.org/policy_research/surveys_indices/cpi/2007

27 *Economist*, 'Not quite as stellar as it looks', 29 November 2007.

28 *Housing and Property Restitution in the Context of the Return of Refugees and Internally Displaced Persons: Final Report of the Special Rapporteur, Paulo Sérgio Pinheiro: principles on Housing and Property Restitution for Refugees and Displaced Persons*, E/CN.4/Sub.2/2005/17, 28 June 2005.

29 John Cosgrave, Celia Goncalves, Daryl Martyris, Riccardo Polastro and Muchimba Sikumba-Dils, *Inter-agency Real Time Evaluation of the Response to the February 2007 Floods and Cyclone in Mozambique*, Inter-Agency Humanitarian Standing Committee, Humanitarian Country Team, Mozambique, April 2007.

30 Paul Harvey, *Cash-based Responses in Emergencies*, Humanitarian Policy Group Report, Overseas Development Institute, 24 February 2007.

31 *Economist*, 'Economic and financial indicators', 22 December 2007.

32 *China's Interest and Activity in Africa's Construction and Infra-Structure Sectors*, Department for International Development and the Centre for Chinese Studies, Stellenboch University, no date.

33 *Economist*, 'A desperate suitor', 8 December 2007.

34 Jenny Clover, 'Land Reform in Angola: Establishing the Ground Rules', in Chris Huggins and Jenny Clover, *From the Ground Up: Land Rights, Conflict and Peace in Sub-Saharan Africa*, African Centre for Technology Studies and the African Security Analysis Programme of the Institute for Security Studies, June 2005.

35 Frederic Deve, *Lessons Learning in Policy Assistance, Case Study Angola, Support to a Decentralised Land Management Programme*, FAO, February 2007.

36 Transparency International, *2006 Corruption Perceptions Index*. http//www.transparency.org/policy_research/surveys_indices/cpi/2007

37 Human Rights Watch, *Some Transparency, No Accountability: The Use of Oil Revenue in Angola and Its Impact on Human Rights*, January 2004.

38 Tony Vaux, *The Selfish Altruist*, 2001, p.107.

39 *Guardian*, 'Short attacks Amnesty view', 24 May 1998.

40 Armartya Sen, *Poverty and Famines*, Clarendon Press, 1981.

41 Paul Collier, *The Bottom Billion*, Oxford University Press, 2007, p.26.

42 Oxfam, *Africa's Missing Billions*, October 2005.

43 Mustafa Hussein, 'Combating Corruption in Malawi', *African Security Review* 14: 4, 2005.

44 Françoise Bouchet-Saulnier, *The Practical Guide to Humanitarian Law*, MSF and Rowman & Littlefield, 2002, pp.6–7.

Conclusion: The New Imperialists?

1 Kirstin Sellars, 'The New Imperialists', *Spectator*, 23 October 1999.

2 Alex De Waal, *Famine Crimes*, James Currey, 1997, p.16.

3 Austen Davis, *Concerning Accountability in Humanitarian Action*, Overseas Development Institute, Humanitarian Practice Network Paper, March 2007.

4 Stoddard, Harmer and Haver, *Providing Aid in Insecure Environments: Trends in Policy and Operations*, Overseas Development Institute, September 2006.

5 Paul de Rooij, 'Humanitarian Wars and Associated Delusions', *Counterpunch*, 14 August 2007.

6 David Chandler, *From Kosovo to Kabul*, Pluto Press, 2002, pp.1 and 227.

7 Jean Bricmont, *Humanitarian Imperialism: Using Human Rights to Market Great Power Wars*, Monthly Review Press, March 2007.

8 *Ibid.*, p.xiii.

9 *Guardian*, 'The banished voices of Mustim women', 10 November 2006.

10 Amnesty International, *Annual Report*, 2004.

11 *Ibid.*

12 Strobe Talbott, *The Great Experiment: From Tribes to Global Nation*, Simon & Schuster, 2008, p.364.

13 Helen Duffy, *The 'War on Terror' and the Framework of International Law*, Cambridge University Press, 2006.

14 *Memorandum for Alberto R. Gonzalez, Counsel to the President, re.- Standards of Conduct for Interrogation Under 18 USC 2340–2340A*, US Department of Justice Office of Legal Counsel, 1 August 2002.

15 *Ireland v United Kingdom*, Series A 25 (1978), and *Selmouni v France*, 28 July 1999.

16 Human Rights Watch, 'Getting away with Torture? Command Responsibility for the US Abuse of Detainees', April 2005; Human Rights Watch, 'Leadership Failure: Firsthand Accounts of Torture of Iraqi Detainees by the US Army's 82nd Airborne Division', September 2005.

17 ABC News, 'Bush aware of advisers' interrogation talks', 11 April 2008.

18 *Washington Post*, 'The logic of torture', 27 June 2004.

19 *Interview of the Vice-President by Scott Hennen, WDAY at Radio Day at the White House, The Vice-President's Office*, Office of the Vice-President, 24 October 2006.

20 *Filartiga v Pena-Irala* 630F 2d 876 (2nd cir.1980).

21 John Reid, text of a speech delivered to the Royal United Services Insitute, 3 April 2006.

22 *Guardian*, 'Response: I do not reject the Geneva conventions', 5 April 2006.

23 Foreign secretary speech on the democratic imperative, 12 February 2008.

24 *Washington Post*, 'US fueled "rendition" flights on British soil', 22 February 2008.

25 David Cameron, text of a speech delivered as the annual J.P. Morgan lecture at the British American Project, 11 September 2006.

26 *Guardian*, 'Blood on their hands', 14 November 2005.

27 *Observer*, 'We have to deport terrorist suspects – whatever their fate', 5 November 2006.

28 Nick Cohen, *What's Left?*, Fourth Estate, 2007, pp.322–25.

29 *Ibid.*, pp.127 and 137.

30 *Ibid.*, p.277.

31 Abby Stoddard, *Humanitarian Alert: NGO Information and Its Impact on Foreign Policy*, Kumarian Press, 2006.

32 Sorcha O'Callaghan and Sara Pantuliano, *Protective Action: Incorporating Civilian Protection into Humanitarian Response*, Overseas Development Institute HPG Report 26, December 2007; *The 'Protection crisis': A Review of Field-Based Strategies for Humanitarian Protection in Darfur*, Overseas Development Institute HPG Report 26, December 2006; and *Humanitarian Advocacy in Darfur: The Challenge of Neutrality*, HPG Policy Brief 28, October 2007.

33 Frequently Asked Questions, *http://www.savedarfur.org*

34 *Guardian*, 'The Boston blueprint', 18 April 2008.

35 David Reiff, *A Bed for the Night*, Vintage, 2002, pp.57–89.

36 Robertson, 2006, p.241.

37 Quoted in Reiff, 2002, p.60.

38 Boaventura de Sousa Santos, 'Toward a Multicultural Conception of Human Rights', in Berta Hernandez Truyol (ed.), *Moral Imperialism: A Critical Anthology*, New York University Press, 2002.

39 Power, 2007, pp.421–55.

Index